**Hallie Rubenhold** is an award-winning and bestselling historian and an authority on women's lives in the eighteenth and nineteenth centuries. She has worked as a curator for the National Portrait Gallery, a broadcaster and as a university lecturer. She is the author of two novels, *Mistress of My Fate* and *The French Lesson*, and her biography, *Lady Worsley's Whim*, was made into the hit BBC drama *The Scandalous Lady W.* Her book *The Five: The Untold Lives of the Women Killed by Jack the Ripper* was a number one *Sunday Times* bestseller and won the 201 Baillie Gifford Prize for Non-fiction.

She lives in London with her husband.

Chat with her on Twitter @HallieRubenhold

www.penguin.co.uk

*Also by Hallie Rubenhold*

FICTION
Mistress of My Fate
The French Lesson

NON-FICTION
Harris's List of Covent Garden Ladies
Lady Worsley's Whim
(*reissued as* The Scandalous Lady W)
The Five: the Untold Lives of the
Women Killed by Jack the Ripper

# The Covent Garden Ladies

## HALLIE RUBENHOLD

**BLACK SWAN**

TRANSWORLD PUBLISHERS
Penguin Random House, One Embassy Gardens,
8 Viaduct Gardens, London SW11 7BW
www.penguin.co.uk

Transworld is part of the Penguin Random House group of companies
whose addresses can be found at global.penguinrandomhouse.com

Penguin
Random House
UK

First published in Great Britain in 2005 by Tempus Publishing Ltd.
Published in ebook by Transworld Publishers in 2012.
This revised edition published in Black Swan paperback in 2020.

A CIP catalogue record for this book is available from the British Library.

ISBN
9781784165956

Typeset in 10.75/15pt Caslon540 BT by Jouve (UK), Milton Keynes.
Printed and bound in Great Britain by Clays Ltd, Elcograf S.p.A.

future for                                                                 le from

# CONTENTS

# NEW FOREWORD BY THE AUTHOR

Fifteen years have passed since *The Covent Garden Ladies* 'first appeared upon the town' and so much has changed since then. Until 2005, *Harris's List* was mainly the preserve of scholars and specialists, written about in journals and referenced in history books. Beyond those with an interest in the Georgian underworld and obscure eighteenth-century literature, few would have recognized the names Jack Harris, Samuel Derrick and Charlotte Hayes. However, in the intervening decade and a half, they and *Harris's List* have crept into popular culture. The women who inhabited the houses in Covent Garden and around the West End have inspired novels – not only my own, *Mistress of My Fate*, but numerous others, including Imogen Hermes Gowar's *The Mermaid and Mrs Hancock* and Maria McCann's *Ace, King, Knave*. *Harris's List*, and the lives of those it chronicles, have also made frequent appearances on our television screens in the form of documentaries and dramas, most recently the hit series *Harlots*. Far from being of interest only to a niche audience, a quick online search for '*Harris's List*' now turns up hundreds of mentions in newspapers, magazines and blogs. Over the years, I've been quietly delighted when people tell me about the works of art, lines of jewellery, exhibitions, Ph.D. theses and student films that these Covent Garden ladies have inspired. It is gratifying to know that, in so many ways, these previously forgotten individuals have reached down through the centuries and touched us.

However much they have contributed to our conversation, the conversation itself has also moved on. Advances in research mean that *Harris's List* can now tell us even more about the eighteenth-century sex trade and the lives of ordinary London women. When I began my work on *Harris's List* in 2002, the digitization of rare books was still relatively new. Since then, vast collections from across the globe have made their way online, and this, along with improved search facilities, has allowed for greater access to this material. The result has been the discovery of even more copies of *Harris's List* than I found originally. When I submitted the manuscript for publication in 2004, I had located volumes from the years 1761, 1764, 1773, 1774, 1779, 1788, 1789, 1790 and 1791. Work conducted by Janet Ing Freeman in 2012 has uncovered additional copies from 1765, 1766, 1771, 1777, 1783, 1786, 1787, 1790 and 1794.[*] Some of these, like the 1787 and 1788 editions acquired by the Wellcome Library in 2015, have emerged from private collections and made their way into the public domain. In my work on the first nine volumes, I amassed data on over a thousand names, some of whom I was able to trace through various editions of the *List* and locate in additional sources, such as memoirs, letters, court records, birth and

---

[*] 'Jack Harris and the "Honest Ranger": The Publication and Prosecution of Harris's List of Covent Garden Ladies, 1760–95', J. I. Freeman, *The Library*, Dec 2012, 13 (4), pp. 423–56.

death records, or other eighteenth-century documents and literature. Now, that collection of names would be roughly double in size, and bursting with further insights into the lives of people who had once been perfectly anonymous to us.

Needless to say, were I to have written *The Covent Garden Ladies* in 2020, it would be a very different book. Not only would I have included extensive footnotes (I had initially been asked to keep my book clear of distracting references), but I would have drilled even more deeply into the lives of the women featured on the *List*'s pages. I would have asked more questions of my sources and, most importantly, I would have paid closer attention to the language employed, both by myself and by others.

The world is a different place now from what it was in the late eighteenth century and, equally, from what it was in 2005. A heightened awareness of women's experiences, especially vis-à-vis sex and the sexualization of female bodies, has altered how we look at their lives, both in the present and the past. This is not revisionism, but rather a sharpening of focus on important details, such as turns of phrase and circumstances that might have been otherwise overlooked. For example, in the eighteenth century there was no more than a fine line between 'seduction' and rape. A great number of the women who appear on *Harris's List* found their way into the sex trade on account of what would today be considered rape. If the picture presented by the *List* is to be believed, many also ended up in prostitution on account of child sexual abuse. The authors of *Harris's List* and those who made use of it took a very different view of these matters from our own and frequently expressed beliefs that today would be considered abhorrent. To these men, many of whom possessed titles and wealth, women and girls from the lower ranks of society existed to be used by their social superiors. When I wrote *The Covent Garden Ladies*, I was not so attuned to the flippant tone taken by those telling these women's stories: I am much more so now. In *Harris's List*, we are not hearing the women's voices, but the voices of men who spoke on their behalf, sometimes sympathetically and sometimes not. Today, I would not permit such a perspective to pass unchallenged into my own writing.

Views on appropriate nomenclature for those in the sex trade, and the debate surrounding the use of the word 'prostitute' (versus 'sex worker'), have also changed a great deal in the past fifteen years. As this edition is essentially a reprint of the original text, space did not allow for anything other than small amendments. A more substantial rewrite was never the objective. This is a debate worthy of discussion, but it is best left for another publication where it can be explored in depth.

The stories of those who feature in this book have haunted me since I first started researching *Harris's List*. I often find myself musing on their experiences in Georgian London, their mundane daily routines or their moments of joy. I remember all the entries I combed through and compiled, sifting through small snippets of human lives, come and gone; the bittersweet stories of those determined to make a better life for themselves, and others who sank under the weight of their circumstances.

To this day, I walk through the streets of Fitzrovia,

Holborn, Soho, St James and Mayfair, looking for their addresses. On a warm summer's night I can imagine a house with its windows open, close enough to the Euston Road to hear the lowing of cattle being driven to Smithfield market. I can see the house's three slightly bored female inhabitants sitting in the front room in damp, creased muslin dresses, smelling of Hungary water and sweat, drinking ratafia liqueur and waiting for a knock at the door. I wonder where they went. I wonder where these women ended their days, and who is descended from them today, carrying their legacy in their eyes or their gait or bearing any of the unique physical characteristics described in *Harris's List*. After recovering so many of these lost lives, it feels strangely comforting to believe that these women did not just disappear with the final *List* in 1795. Rather, I like to believe that some trace of them remains in the present day, walking among us still, ever a part of this ancient city.

Hallie Rubenhold
London, 2020

# ABOUT THE BOOK

In 1757, a down-and-out Irish poet, the head waiter at Shakespear's Head Tavern in Covent Garden, and a celebrated London courtesan became bound together by the publication of a little book: *Harris's List of Covent Garden Ladies*. This salacious publication detailing the names and 'specialities' of the capital's prostitutes eventually became one of the eighteenth century's most successful and scandalous literary works, selling an estimated 250,000 copies. During its heyday (1757–95) *Harris's List* was the essential accessory for any serious gentleman of pleasure. Yet beyond its titillating passages lay a glimpse into the sex lives of those who lived and died by the *List*'s profits during the Georgian era.

*The Covent Garden Ladies* tells the story of three unusual characters: Samuel Derrick, John Harrison (aka Jack Harris) and Charlotte Hayes, whose complicated and vibrant lives were brought together by this publication. The true history of the book is a tragicomic opera motivated by poverty, passionate love, aspiration and shame. Its story plunges the reader down the dark alleys of eighteenth-century London's underworld, a realm populated by tavern owners, pimps, punters, card sharps and, of course, a colourful range of sex workers and brothel-keepers.

# 1

# THE CURTAIN RISES

ALTHOUGH YOU MAY NOT recognize it, you are standing in Covent Garden. It may look strange to you without its glass-and-steel market arches and its swirl of tourists. The buskers are gone, as are the rickshaw bicycles and shops peddling plastic gadgetry. What is left behind is the piazza in *puris naturalibus*, in its mid-eighteenth-century state, complete with cobblestones, dust and open drains.

It's a colourful place, even by the first thrust of morning light. At this early hour, the market square is alive with London life. Fruit and vegetable sellers, carters, ballad singers, knife grinders and milkmaids circle one another in their daily dance of work. Under wide-brimmed straw bonnets, women with red elbows balance baskets of produce on their hips. Men in wool frock coats or leather aprons toil, their tricornered hats pulled over their sleepy eyes. There are children running barefoot, chasing dogs. There are old men hobbling on makeshift walking sticks as crooked as their backs. There are toothless, wrinkled women, who are much younger than they look. Many of those who have come to haggle, wrapped up against the dawn's chill, belong to the

1

metropolis's army of domestic servants. They will scurry back to their employers' homes with heavy baskets before their masters and mistresses have stirred from their beds.

This visual carnival is not without its scents and sounds. The market, stacked high with fresh and rotting produce, emits a sweet stench of cabbage and apple. The wet pungency of horse droppings is unavoidable, as is the fug of yellowy coal smoke and the incense of burning wood. It is, however, the murky puddles that give off some of the more unexpected odours. In the absence of an operational sewage system, London droops under its own stink. The wealthy have become adept at fending off the sudden olfactory assaults of decomposition and human waste, shielding their noses with perfumed handkerchiefs and nosegays. The poor have just learned to live with the unpleasantness. Those of the labouring classes discovered long ago that many of their hardships could be smothered through song, and it is their melodies that take to the piazza's air. Many of the tunes whistled or hummed come from those heard at the two local theatres. Music is one of the mainstays of an evening's entertainment at the Covent Garden Theatre, sitting at the eastern edge of the piazza, and its rival, the Theatre Royal on Drury Lane. This part of town has always been a spot for instruments and voices, day or night. When the stage lights are extinguished, the market provides a chorus of sound instead. Higglers cry their wares, their tones floating together discordantly. Between melodic solicitations to buy quinces and oranges, they flirt and banter, challenging one another boisterously. Above their declarations can be heard yet another type of music, the urban clatter of horses' hooves, the squeak and bounce of wooden wheels, doors slamming, the roll of barrels, the cries of babies, the squeals and brays of animals. There are no silently ticking engines, no electricity or automation to do their work for them, only the grunts and sweat of men and beasts.

Despite the pulsing activity of the marketplace, there is much more to Covent Garden than this hustle of morning commerce. Not everyone comes here to purchase fruit for their pies and puddings. As morning matures into afternoon and the vendors have sold the last of their wares, the piazza's more lucrative trade begins to stir from its slumber. The centre of the action shifts from the ring-fenced vegetable exchange at the square's heart to the stone-faced buildings at its periphery.

From our vantage point looking northwards, a number of the more infamous haunts are visible. In the most north-easterly corner, slightly obscured behind the arcaded walk, lies one of the set pieces of our story. Beneath a magnificent swinging signboard featuring the face of England's best-loved bard, is the entrance to a tavern known as the Shakespear's Head. The sordid details of what transpired in its dim rooms I will leave for later. Next door, to the south of the Shake-spear's Head, is the Bedford Coffee House, a slightly more respectable establishment, although only just. Its distin-guished dramatic and literary clientele bestow on it a certain fashionable cachet, which barely saves it from sharing its neighbour's dubious stigma. On the opposite side of the Shakespear, to the north, are the elegant premises of the bawd Mrs Jane Douglas. As the tavern drunks ensure that Mother Douglas's girls never go patronless, business thrives well into the early 1760s. After that time, any woman of Jane

Douglas's profession will be turning her sights towards the more fashionable parts of town, first Soho, then St James's, Mayfair and Piccadilly. For the moment, however, Jane Douglas and her sister Covent Garden procuresses are doing quite well, nestled in this nook of sin. The keepers of Haddock's Bagnio, on the piazza just south of the corner of Russell Street, are also doing a booming trade. The aristocratic set finds the novelty of indulging in a Turkish bath, a meal and the company of a prostitute all under one roof quite pleasing. On any given night they can be seen bumbling between Haddock's and the adjoining Bedford Arms Tavern (not to be confused with the Bedford Coffee House, or the Bedford Head Tavern on Maiden Lane). In fact, there is so much here in the way of carnal diversion you might be forgiven for omitting to notice the parish church, St Paul's Covent Garden, in all of its austere beauty, occupying the west side of the square. It has sat there, silently observing, for over a hundred years.

Even under the censorious gaze of St Paul's, the piazza seems quite at home with abandonment. There are many more wanton establishments that hug the perimeter of the square. All of the neighbouring streets are filled with brothels, rowdy taverns, noisy coffee houses and warrens of cheap accommodation for 'working girls'. Bow Street, Drury Lane and Brydges Street, to the east of the square, are the most notorious. The Shakespear's Head's rival tavern, the Rose, is situated on the corner of Brydges Street (Catherine Street, as you know it) and Russell Street. This is a 'lewd and low place', where 'posture girls' writhe around naked on the tables. Here, glasses and tankards fly through the air, people lose eyes and have their noses broken. But neither are the streets safe at

4

night. Thoroughfare and alleyway alike are the haunts of foot-pads and muggers. Even the cherubic-faced link-boys who offer to light you home with their lanterns frequently work with robbers. People in this part of London try to get what they can by any means. Gentlemen wise to the ways of Covent Garden are certain to keep an eye on their watch and a hand on their purse when enjoying the services of one of its 'ladies'.

As baffling as it might seem, right at the heart of this village of sin, on Bow Street, sandwiched between a brothel and a tavern, is the headquarters of the area's law enforcement. Justice John Fielding, ably assisted by his brother Henry before his death, is the magistrate here. A police force as we know it does not exist. The night watch is virtually useless and easily bribed. Nevertheless, Justice Fielding is committed to tackling crime and has employed a team of eight men to apprehend law-breakers. At the moment, they haven't made much of a difference. It's a villains' paradise.

Of course, those who first lived in Covent Garden would never have envisioned such a future for it. In the 1630s, the 4th Earl of Bedford commissioned the architect Inigo Jones to lay out a genteel, Italian-style square. Initially, this was a place where the nobility had their London homes, but the neighbourhood took a turn for the worse when the Theatre Royal opened in 1663. The ever-immoral theatre and its companies of actors brought the rabble, and the rabble liked drinking and whoring, or so the story goes. However, it takes no more than a brief glance around the piazza to confirm that the aristocracy are as much devotees of debauchery as anyone else. Certainly, it was their money that helped fan the flames of the area's prosperity. By the time the produce market had pitched its stands in 1670, the purveyors of flesh had already set up shop.

In the evening, when the lamps are lit and the bowed tavern and coffee-house windows glow dimly orange, the piazza shows its painted face. There is laughter and shouting, pranks are played and punches thrown. Walls and floorboards shake to the motion of urgent coupling. Children are conceived, and fortunes lost at cards. Both men and women succumb to the enticements of gin, wine, beer and brandy. Some slide under tables, some are sick on their own clothes. The pursuit of pleasure is this society's greatest leveller. It brings together the sons of dukes to drink with the daughters of tailors and penniless poets. Wealthy city merchants and military officers, lawyers, painters and common criminals interact freely. In a Britain wholly governed by the divisions of class, what transpires here in Covent Garden is quite remarkable. Even those who witness it agree, as one anonymous scribe observed:

> *Here buskin'd Beaus in rich lac'd Cloathes*
> *Like Lords and Squires do bluster;*
> *Bards, Quacks and Cits, Knaves, Fools and Wits*
> *An Odd surprising Cluster.*

This 'Odd surprising Cluster' is made more luminous by a sprinkling of eighteenth-century celebrities. At the Bedford Coffee House or at Charles Macklin's Piazza Coffee House, David Garrick, the A-list actor of his day, along with Dr Samuel Johnson, the acclaimed lexicographer, might have been spotted deep in conversation. The actor Samuel Foote would also have been seen, accompanied by a crowd of aspiring actresses and playwrights. Undoubtedly, the author Samuel Derrick would have been among them. (There is more of his story to come.) When Derrick finished with Foote, he would most likely have moved on to the actor Ned Shuter, arm in arm with the dancer Nancy Dawson. With no long-lensed paparazzi angling for perfect shots, what an easy life such superstars must have enjoyed.

On an evening in the piazza, it might also occur to you that the men outnumber the women quite considerably. There are no 'genuine ladies' to be found here late at night. The ones who appear respectable, in their elegant hats and glimmering jewels, are merely the more successful members of 'the fallen sisterhood'. Society has many names for these tainted women who have sacrificed their prized virtue and the sanctity of their bodies in order to service men: women of the town, Cyprians or members of the Cyprian Corps, impures, strumpets, light girls, thaises, wantons, demi-reps, demi-mondaines, jades, hussies, tarts, votaries of Venus, nymphs, jezebels, doxies, molls, fallen women, trollops, whores and harlots. They come from a variety of locations and backgrounds. Some, like Charlotte Hayes, a 'devotee of Venus' who features prominently in this tale, were born into the sex trade. Others are its recruits: orphans, seduced servants, poor seamstresses, trained milliners, hopeful actresses and rape victims. They come from London and all points beyond it, from the outlying counties and from Scotland and Ireland. Some have washed up on these shores from as far afield as the American colonies and the West Indies, as well as from France, Italy, the Netherlands and Germany. In this city of immigrants, they represent a cross section of races and ethnicities.

Contrary to popular belief, not all the 'ladies' who work in Covent Garden started their lives nuzzled at the breast of poverty. In the eighteenth century, one's standard of living is a mutable thing. There are no guarantees for anyone. There are no state benefits or workers' pensions, no unemployment or disability pay. If you lose your job, you don't eat. If you want to eat, you work until you die. The concept of nationalized health care isn't even a twinkle in a moral reformer's eye. This is an awkward age to be a Londoner: change is afoot in all respects, economically, socially and politically. Britain stands on the cusp of losing an old empire in America and gaining a new one in India. Raw materials are pouring into the country; useful and interesting goods decorate shopfronts. New buildings, streets and squares seem to appear with each passing season. It feels as if opportunities to make money are everywhere, but do not be fooled. The newspapers, with their shameful lists of the bankrupt, tell another story. London is populated by speculators and debtors. A number of middle-class families buckle under the weight of loan repayments. The pressure to own the latest household items is inescapable. Everyone wants to appear in the finest clothing and to have a home furnished with status symbols, but meeting the cost of the rent can be difficult and levels of personal debt are spiralling out of control. (Sound familiar?)

Being middle class is a fairly new phenomenon, and these people are still a strangely amorphous group. Those at the top are often as wealthy as the aristocracy; those towards the middle and at the bottom – the small shopkeepers, the master craftsmen, the apothecaries, publishers, schoolmasters and petty clergy – are more often than not struggling to hang on. It is this 'precarious middle class', and those families that bounce up and down the lower end of the social ladder, that have donated a number of their daughters to the metropolis's more exclusive brothels. A bad year of trade, a fire, a legal battle or an imprudent night at the gaming tables could bring ruin. As the debtors' prison – the Fleet – beckons, the china, table linens, fine silks and furniture may have to go to the pawn shop. The family that has enjoyed the luxury of owning a house may now live in two rented rooms. From this plateau, the dip into criminality is only a wrong foot away. The following year, the unfortunate individuals may recover their fortunes, retrieve their goods and move back into their terraced house. Alternatively, they may slip further into the ranks of the poor.

In the eighteenth century, there is nothing worse than being poor. True poverty means constantly fending off disease as it feeds on the malnourishment of your body. It means continuous hunger and physical discomfort; horrific living conditions, sharing your bed not only with other unwashed humans but with rats, mice, lice, fleas and bedbugs. It means feeling the cold acutely through ragged clothing and not owning even a change of undergarments. In eighteenth-century London it means having no voice, no vote and virtually no legal protection or access to true justice. More than anything, it means being feared and reviled by those above you. You are disrespected, regarded as subhuman by some and ignored by others. You are likely to be a victim of violence and to numb your soul with large quantities of cheap gin. It is a degrading and miserable existence to which not everyone is willing to submit. Hard work may help raise you out of this sink, but most available jobs are not well paid. A life of crime is always a viable possibility. Prostitution helps quite a few women; some even scale the social heights by means of the profits it brings. Pickpocketing, robbery, housebreaking, dealing in stolen goods, procuring women for lascivious men, and forgery can also be quite profitable, as can cheating at cards. These may be your only hopes of survival in brutal London if you have the misfortune of falling upon hard times.

The story of the *Harris's List of Covent Garden Ladies* is the tale of these people. They are the ones who linger at the fringes of eighteenth-century society. Their footing on the social ladder is perpetually unsure and their acceptance into the 'normal' circles of the respectable population will never be sanctioned. John Harrison (aka Jack Harris), Samuel Derrick and Charlotte Hayes are our representatives of this realm. In this parable, fate has provided us with an interesting cross section of history's minor players – or outcasts, if you like: the hardened criminal, the determined but impoverished poet, and the daughter of a bawd. In the telling of it we must remember that these personalities are as much the products of their era as are we. Their judgements and biases belong to a time less forgiving than our own. Do not make the mistake that moralists of their own age might have been inclined to – that it is their badness that motivates them. This reeks of the simple-mindedness that sent petty pickpockets to the nooses at Tyburn. You have been provided with a glimpse into their world, the extreme difficulties, the cruelties, abuses and inequalities. In the heart of each one beats an indomitable desire not to suffer the miseries of the poor, even if it means bringing about the suffering of others. This is not a tale where wrongdoers are punished and the exploited are vindicated. This has nothing to do with the gilded, safe and privileged Georgian era of Jane Austen. She and others like her are on the inside of society looking out, and their sight does not extend as far as these dark corners. There is no comfortable moral to be found within the lurid biographies of *Harris's List*, or between the covers of this book. But history rarely provides a comfortable moral to a good yarn.

## 2

# THE LEGEND OF JACK HARRIS

J ACK HARRIS WAS BORN in the very cradle of illusion, in the
space that existed between two theatres. Nothing was as
it seemed in Covent Garden, where actors assumed the
identities of imaginary characters and masked men and
women moved anonymously through the pleasure-seeking
swarms. Against such a backdrop it was easy to vanish or
become someone else. Until he grew proud and foolish, Jack
Harris had never stepped into the direct glare of the lime-
light; he had never allowed anyone to truly know him or his
story. He had hidden well – and what little he had revealed
to the world about himself was complete fabrication.

After his sensational arrest in 1758, however, he engaged
a hack journalist to help him offer an explanation for his
wickedness and tell his tale.

Long before his parents brought him into being, destiny
had marked out Jack's family for suffering. His father, he
claimed, came from 'a good Somersetshire family', but had
the misfortune of being born a younger son with no inheritance and few prospects. The marriage he contracted with
Harris's mother had been formed out of love and consequently

12

had fallen foul of his upstanding relations. Cast adrift with no money and no position, the young couple set out for London, where Harris senior had been given 'many promises from great men of places, sinecures and pensions'. As a member of the landed class, he believed that he had no shortage of allies within the government willing to assist him in his ambitions. Unfortunately, upon his arrival in the capital he found that doors were shut to him, that men who had at one time guaranteed him their favour could only shrug their shoulders and wish him the best of luck elsewhere. With the birth of Jack in the mid-1720s, the young family found their resources rapidly expiring. In order to keep the wolf from the door, his father turned to his pen. Fuelled by his sense of anger and betrayal at those who had lured him to London on false hopes, Harris senior lashed out in a series of invectives and 'failed not to abuse those who had so abused him'. A Whig by birth, he began to rethink his political affiliations. If his traditional associates among the aristocracy would not have him, he would cross the floor and wound them as a member of the opposition. He 'soon made himself very remarkable among the anti-ministerial writers of those days; and the Country Party enlisted him under their banner'.

In spite of stringent libel laws, Harris senior flaunted the dangers inherent in being so vicious an antagonist of the parliamentary leader, Sir Robert Walpole. Once he had whetted his sharp pen, he found it difficult to put down, especially as his hostile epistles were at last bringing in money and winning him the support of several wealthy backers. It seemed that the Harrises' situation had begun to brighten, and they were now contemplating an appropriate education for their eldest son. Then, quite unexpectedly, when his father 'was upon the point of sending [him] to Westminster School', events took a turn for the worse; Harris senior was arrested.

He had made the fatal error of attaching himself to Nathaniel Mist, a notorious thorn in the side of the establishment. *Mist's Weekly Journal*, a scurrilous publication renowned for spouting unabashed Jacobitism, rolled off a secret printing press until the authorities sniffed it out and smashed it to bits in 1728. Despite stints in prison and in the stocks, however, Mist and his numerous colleagues continued to publish their libel, this time in the form of *Fog's Weekly Journal*. A series of raids soon put an end to this enterprise as well. Among the handful of anti-ministerial writers rooted out during the course of the arrests was Harris senior.

Once again, but this time locked away in the local compter, he looked to his friends and political associates to assist him in his time of need, but no one came. 'He was there for some weeks in want of bail, all his party deserting him, as soon as they had notice of his misfortune,' Jack recounted. His father soon sank into an irretrievable depression, and matters would only grow worse. The authorities looked upon his crime with gravity and he was transferred to the King's Bench Prison, where 'he was sentenced to be imprisoned for three years'. Additionally, he was 'fined the penalty of five hundred pounds', a crippling amount for a family in the Harrises' position. During this time, in the mid-1730s, Jack made regular visits to his father, 'although his keeper pretended that he had strict orders to let nobody see him'. In later years, Jack admitted that observing his father in such a despondent and

14

weathered state had profoundly affected him. Harris senior had been broken:

> His misfortunes had so sowered his natural temper that he had become a perfect misanthrope. The ill treatment he had received from both parties had given him an utter detestation of all; and he seemed now to languish at his confinement, only because he had not an opportunity of imposing upon the world, as much as they had imposed upon him.

Betrayed, exhausted and ill, Harris's father bid his son to learn from the mistakes he had made and not to waste himself in pursuit of an honest life. In a final paternal gesture, he reached for his pen and committed his instructions to paper. In his 'Wholesome Advice to His Son for His Conduct in Life', he summarized those thoughts he had expressed to his child as they sat together in his cell. He reminded his boy that as he had no fortune, a conventional education would be of no use to him. At any rate, it was his experience that there was 'nothing so great an obstacle to getting money as learning'. 'No, no, my son,' he continued, 'I have taken care to prepare you for quite another employment':

> Would you get money, my son – study men's passions; ply them. Is a man ambitious of fame – go through thick and thin, to make him the greatest patriot that ever existed; but be sure of your reward before you give the finishing stroke to his reputation. Does he love wenching – pimping is a thriving calling, it must be orthodox, or some who do would not possess it. Does he want a seat in the House – vote for him, bribe for him,

swear for him; there is no harm in all this. A scrupulous man indeed may object to an oath because it is false, but it may be true; read it not, and then you can not tell which it is, and they administer it so fast that you can not understand it, even if you would. If your patron loves Play, learn dexterity of Hand and cheat as much as you can; take care, do not be detected, if you are, swear and bluster, challenge, fight and kill, and then your honour is retrieved. This is done every day with success; there is nothing washes off the slur of infamy, but the man's blood you have offended! Let no scruple of your conscience preponderate with you; to thrive in this world, a man must not have a grain of that commodity.

Although shocked at first by his father's recommendations, Jack Harris eventually came to understand the logic in it. It was a message touched with poignancy, one that had been placed in his hand upon his father's death.

In death, Harris senior had left his family nothing but the prospect of starvation. He had also laid the seeds of vice in his eldest son. Armed with his father's advice, which he 'looked upon as my only personal estate', Jack plunged himself headlong into a career of criminality. In order to gain the confidence of society, his first act was to appear convincing. With the appropriate attire and gait, Harris assumed the respectable persona of a gentleman, 'without any other pretensions to that rank, but impudence and ignorance; which indeed make so great of the modern man's accomplishments'. Unfortunately, he admitted, it required some trial and error before he alighted upon his true calling. In the first instance, he looked into becoming a political bully, one who lived by the extraction of bribes. For this purpose, he states that he 'took a house in Westminster in hopes of making my fortune by elections; but no general one soon ensuing, I was obliged to lay aside, with my house, all my hopes upon that score'. Harris then tried his luck as a card sharp, teaching himself how to 'cheat at play', but sighed that, 'having no head for calculations and no knowledge of figures, it was of little avail to me'. It was sometime shortly thereafter that he realized where his true talents lay. With a flattering, obsequious bent to his personality, his destined path unfurled before him. 'Nature,' he announced quite frankly, 'designed me for a pimp.'

This was Harris's sad tale. Those who read it when it featured as part of *The Memoirs of the Celebrated Miss Fanny Murray* would have been quite taken in by the narrator's earnestness. It was a history that suited his identity well; it added flesh to the bones of his legend. But as Jack Harris generally preferred to lead his life unobtrusively, lingering behind the dim yellow light of the tavern candles rather than in the full blaze of public view, these few snippets were all that most of his clients ever learned of him. Only a select handful knew the truth. In 1779, twenty years after Jack Harris's story appeared in print, one ripe old member of the debauched Hell-Fire Club decided to dispel the ambiguity once and for all. In his chronicle of London's sexual underworld, *Nocturnal Revels*, he decried, 'No such man as Harris (as he is called) a Pimp, now or probably ever did exist.' He was right, of course. Harris's real name was John Harrison, and his story was very different from the one he had invented to fit his alias.

Unlike Harris's early years, Harrison's were distinctly unremarkable. He had been born the son of George Harrison, keeper of the Bedford Head Tavern in Maiden Lane, a street that just trimmed the outskirts of Covent Garden piazza. While John Harrison could hardly boast of a landowning lineage, there were a few, very loose, parallels to his tale of John Harris. As with Harris, it seems that the Harrison family at the time of John's birth were not local to the parish of St Paul's Covent Garden. John would have been a child when the Bedford Head (one drinking establishment of several going by that name in the area) threw open its doors to business in 1740. When John's father, George, assumed the role of proprietor, the tavern, with its freshly cut wooden interiors, was a new venue, unsoiled by the stench of coal smoke, the sourness of alcohol and the odour of bodies. For a publican, there were few other locations as ideal as Covent Garden for setting up shop. Here he could draw from the circulating pool of carelessly spent wages and inherited wealth and make a tidy income for himself. As taverns were regularly managed as family businesses in the eighteenth century, it is possible that the Harrisons may have been in the tankard-serving trade for generations and had moved their enterprise from somewhere not so very distant from the piazza. Irrespective of its location, however, London taverns on the whole were not ideal nurseries for rearing scrupulous, law-abiding children. In the dinginess of the taproom, young John Harrison would have learned through observation about the libidinous and violent sphere into which he had been brought.

As the child of a tavern-keeper, he would have been put to work from an early age. His first defined role within the

Bedford Head would have been as a pot-boy, or general assistant, helping to ferry drinks to customers and carry away their empties. As reading, writing and figuring would have been considered skills necessary for the management of a public house, he would have received some formal education, most likely provided through a local charity school. Most of his truly useful learning, however, would have been acquired by shadowing his father, or any other elder male family member, as they performed their tasks. When not assisting at the tap or counting the profits of his labour, George Harrison would have overseen the work of the waiters who tottered from table to table with their containers of ale and kept a narrowed eye on suspicious characters. As he approached an appropriate age, John would have joined his father in these duties and then the ranks of the Bedford Head's devoted male waiting staff, assuming the role of a compliant servant to his father's clientele and hoping for tips. While respectfully laying plates of meat and glasses of port before gentlemen may have earned him a few pennies, he would have learned that gratifying their less legitimate requests might supply him with far more handsome sums.

Although the Bedford Head Tavern was a family-run business, that did not make it an honest one. There is nothing to suggest that its reputation was any better than those of its sister establishments, the notorious watering holes that blighted Maiden Lane. Only a few doors down from the Bedford Head throbbed a stinking sore of a public house, Bob Derry's Cider Cellar. Bob Derry, with his wife, daughter and son-in-law, just about managed the alcohol-fuelled traffic that pushed in and out of his rancid den. 'As its name implied,' wrote John Timbs, a chronicler of tavern history, the interior and fittings of the Cider Cellar 'were rude and rough'. Bob Derry's was open all night and accepted into its fold the dregs of an evening out: those already too intoxicated to walk or talk straight. There, under Derry's blind eye, pickpockets and streetwalkers riddled with 'the pox' did a roaring trade. As Samuel Derrick wrote in 1761, the establishment was noted for its regular hiccups of violence – spectacles of brutality where men bludgeoned their rivals, and ladies of the night tore at each other's faces. Patrons of Derry's were not known for interceding in a good fight, but rather for placing bets on its outcome. On one occasion, the outcome was the double murder of two drinkers, who, after a fierce argument, were mercilessly stabbed to death.

Although the annals of Covent Garden never placed the Bedford Head's name on a par with that of its vice-ridden neighbour, in its day it would hardly have been considered a paragon of lawfulness. The majority of the area's establishments would have involved themselves in some form of criminal trade, whether this entailed permitting sex workers to solicit openly (a generally accepted practice), receiving stolen goods or harbouring known criminals from the watch. Frequently, far worse activities committed by proprietors or their staff, such as coin-clipping, counterfeiting, theft, extortion, violent assault and incidents of rape, were allowed to transpire in upstairs rooms and cellars. In an environment where the orderly and the unlawful were woven inextricably into a single fabric, John Harrison would have been initiated into the realm of the law-breaker before he could have even differentiated between the two. As tavern-waiting and pimping were virtually inseparable practices, it is unlikely that George Harrison would have discouraged his son from earning money by 'making introductions'. Not unlike his alter ego, it would have been circumstance as well as a father's encouragement that made him a pimp.

In the eighteenth century, the urban tavern and its cousin, the coffee house, were primarily male domains. They could at times be quite similar, serving as social meeting houses and as a forum where business and news could be discussed between gentlemen. Although certain professions might hold preferences for specific locations, generally a range of occupations and social strata brushed elbows under their roofs. While the coffee houses' main attraction was the caffeinated novelty tipple they peddled, they also, like the cafés of continental Europe, provided alcohol. The better venues of both variety offered food in addition to liquid refreshment, which could be taken either in the communal taproom or in a private above-stairs space, if the patron was wealthy enough. Over the course of the century, the activities that took place in these upstairs rooms took on a history of their own. They were ideal areas for the members of gentlemen's societies to host their monthly or yearly gatherings. These events, which frequently began in the evening hours with discussions of politics, science or art over a formal meal, had a habit of degenerating into a night of wholesale debauchery. Respectable society dictated that men could not be considered either dignified or safe when soused with liquor, and therefore any woman who had pretensions of calling herself a lady would not venture near the door of such an establishment. Nevertheless, women abounded in taverns and coffee houses, especially those around Covent Garden. These were the women that writers of the age might argue were designated by virtue of their class to entertain men. For centuries, where men drank, women sold their bodies. Once satiated with alcohol and a full belly of food, the only urge left to be fulfilled was the venereal one, making the prostitute's job of searching for punters as straightforward as fishing in a barrel. The man who just happened to be standing between the inebriated customer and his much-desired sexual release was the waiter.

'Passing an evening a few weeks ago at a certain tavern near Covent Garden, the wine operated so strongly upon the blood of some of my companions, that they rang for the gentleman porter and actually asked him if he could get them some girls,' wrote a young journalist inexperienced in the customs of contemporary procuring. Although a number of means existed whereby lustful men could satisfy their needs, seeking a sexual partner through the intermediary of a procurer might offer fractionally more protection against disease than an encounter with a random streetwalker. This, at least, was the theory. A waiter-pimp's job in the most basic sense might only amount to ushering over the appropriate women currently within the tavern, or those local girls nearby with whom the waiter was familiar. As Jack Harris himself clarifies, 'By pimp, nothing more was signified than to run about the neighbourhood and bring the first bunter to the gentlemen then come a table at the tavern I belonged to.' This gesture fell within the remit of keeping customers content while they sojourned in the tavern-keeper's rooms. As long as patrons were willing to continue spending their money at his establishment, a taverner would have little cause for complaint.

Unfortunately, the epithet of pimp, one which conjured (and still conjures) some of the nastiest, most remorseless images of men, was applied even-handedly to any man who 'introduced women into company'. While the author E. J. Burford's assessment of pimps throughout history as being 'evil, heartless, vile creatures, without any redeeming features – wretched men living off wretched women' is not incorrect, the position of the eighteenth-century waiter-pimp differs somewhat from this commonly held perception. Just as there existed a range of different statuses within the profession of prostitute, so the same held true for procurers. Not every pimp was a brutish bully lurking in a dark, filthy alley. The practice of pimping, or what the era occasionally called 'pandering', beneath the veneer of table-waiting sought to remove at least a whiff of ugliness from this pursuit. In any case, Harrison had come to believe that there was no harm in simply bringing two willing parties together. In later years, this was all that he as Jack Harris had claimed to have done as a pimp. It was in itself, he reasoned, something that he 'need not be ashamed of'.

Rather than actively seeking to become a procurer, purveying sex was a vocation that found John Harrison once he assumed the responsibilities of a waiter. Fortunately for him, it was a calling that suited his circumstances. Many of the young women who haunted the Bedford Head would have been those he had known since childhood as neighbours and playmates. The daughters of needy families within the parish, those who lived in nearby houses or who worked as servants or marketers in the piazza, were the girls who would one day turn to prostitution in order to earn their bread. Stories of their entrée into the life would have been common public-house banter; Harrison may even have heard about their circumstances from their own mouths. In many cases he would have been intimate with their parents or siblings. It is equally likely that he would have known their debauchers and, eventually, their keepers. Harrison's ears would have hummed with the gossip of the neighbourhood – whose daughter's belly was looking unusually round, and who had been caught with his hands up his kitchen maid's skirts. He would have had a better idea of who carried 'the pox' (or syphilis) than most punters, a valuable insight for a pimp to possess. Irrespective of when he began 'making introductions', Harrison did not come to recognize himself as a pimp until around 1751, shortly before the creation of his alias, Jack Harris.

As easy as it may have been to prosper in his role at his father's tavern, John Harrison did not earn his infamous name at the Bedford Head. Fate had another venue in mind for him. In 1753, something occurred in Harrison's life that catapulted him from his familiar Maiden Lane surroundings into an altogether different sphere. Whether through death or financial mismanagement, by 1754 George Harrison was no longer the proprietor of the establishment where John had passed his youth. What became of the members of the Harrison family, where they lived or how they continued to win their bread, is a mystery. Only John chose to remain in Covent Garden, a place that he, perhaps more than the others, chose to recognize as his home. Now released from the ties of his family's enterprise, his future lay elsewhere. Fortunately, he did not have to travel far in order to find it. In the eastern corner of the piazza, under a colourfully embellished sign, sat the Shakespear's Head Tavern.

# 3

# THE IRISH POET

JUST AS THE ROUGH taverns and back streets of Covent Garden had already pressed their indelible ink on to John Harrison's character, so the theatres and bookstalls of Dublin were in the process of leaving their mark upon another young man. At about the time that the youthful Harrison was ferrying pots of ale to the patrons of the Bedford Head, a privileged Irish schoolboy was frantically scribbling rhyming couplets. Already by the age of thirteen Samuel Derrick had determined that he would be a poet. Not a second-rate poet or an author of menial, insignificant works, but rather one whose name would be recorded alongside that of Jonathan Swift and William Congreve in the pantheon of Anglo-Irish literature. His tutors, as well as 'some ingenious men in the world of letters', had seen promise in his early works. One of them, Swift's publisher, George Faulkner, and perhaps even the celebrated author himself, had offered praise. Little were these 'ingenious men' to know that their early 'approbation' would set into motion a chain of events that would take Samuel Derrick far off his prescribed path.

Verse-writing would not be a skill required in the life

that others intended for Sam. His aunt and guardian, the formidable widow Mrs Elizabeth Creagh, had resolved to make a linen merchant (or draper) of her nephew. As his fourteenth birthday approached, the period when his formal schooling would come to an end, Sam began to grow anxious. In a few months his beloved Latin grammars and Greek texts, the history books and works of French literature over which he had bent his head so studiously would be packed away. In exchange Sam would be handed fat ledgers filled with mind-numbing accounts. The fingering of linen and the measuring of its nap would take the place of his passions. His apprentice-master would lecture him about the wonders of bleaching and the costs of transportation; he would be taught all of the nuances of the linen trading hall, the posturing, the bartering, who to fleece and who to pay fairly. For seven years Sam would be bound to a draper before he emerged as a fully-fledged one himself. For seven years he would live under the roof of a stranger who would examine his every movement, impose a curfew, forbid excessive drink and venal association with members of the opposite sex. There would be no time and no need for works of literature, be they the hide-bound tomes of Addison and Pope or his own inventions.

As he felt his last months of schoolboy freedom slip away, Sam launched into a fury of writing in the hope that he might create something worthy of publication. He began producing poetic paraphrases of the Psalms but was most inspired by the work of the Tudor poet John Skelton upon whose 'Truth in a Mask' he composed his own verses.

Sam's youthful pen, still too inexperienced to wax lyrical about the joys of love or the mysteries of women, produced a moralizing allegory: 'The Caterpillars; a Fable'. But between his preachy lines advising patience to an impetuous caterpillar unwilling to wait for his butterfly's wings lurked an alarming taste of Sam's private sentiments:

*Teach fools such fancies to believe,*
*Me with such flams you'll ne'er deceive;*
*Content with smaller joys, I chuse*
*To live, nor real pleasures lose*
*For doubtful hopes, nor shall abstain,*
*But quick the leaf alluring gain;*
*And wherefore should I thus delay,*
*When instinct kindly points the way?*
*Farewel, fond dupe to fortune's pow'r –*
*'Tis mine t'improve the present hour.*

Had those closest to the boy scrutinized the work, they might have caught a glimpse of what his future life would hold.

Beyond the most basic facts of his birth, very little is known about this Dublin boy who came into the world in 1724. Even the identities of Sam Derrick's parents have been lost to us, possibly through his own contrivance. In later years, ever reaching for greatness, Sam presented the world with a version of his lineage that was romantically suited to a poet. He was, he said, descended from the Derrick family of County Carlow in the south-east of Ireland, who were said to have come over from Denmark 'at an early period'. The Derricks rose to become Protestant landowners and, until the uprising of 1641, maintained holdings in Carlow and Meath, in addition to a manor house known as 'Old Derrick' near

Carlow Town. In 1641, however, when the country was plunged into religious unrest, the family was divested of their land. The bloody struggle, as the author claimed, resulted in the 'massacre . . . of several of my kindred', who had been hunted down '. . . and murdered upon the seacoasts'. Only a few survivors managed to escape to England. The war brought the ruin of his father's family, although his mother's side, the Drakes of Devonshire, prospered under the rule of Oliver Cromwell. Sam's grandfather, he proudly boasted, had been a Parliamentarian general.

Cromwellian generals and landed gentry aside, what Sam neglected to relay about his circumstances was that his immediate family were tradespeople. There is nothing among the remnants of his correspondence, or within any of his writings, to suggest that while Sam lived he had either parents or siblings. The reality of their situation may not have fitted the legend he sought to construct for himself. Only a rumour that his mother 'moved in the humble sphere of a petty linen draper' presents an enticingly possible glimpse of the truth. As for his other relations, irrespective of any loss they may have suffered during the previous century, their fortunes had taken a more positive turn by the 1720s. Having recaptured something of their lost stature through an involvement in Dublin's prospering linen industry, by the period of Sam's birth they were able to include themselves among the city's quietly comfortable and diversifying middle classes. Success smiled broadly on those who bought and sold the cloth that supplied the English with their undergarments and adorned their tidy tables. While cottage workers wove and embroidered in gloomy sod houses, the wealthy merchant-drapers lived off their labour, selling their wares at Dublin's cavernous linen hall. For centuries, Irish linen would be the country's pride, and off its profits the drapers would grow into the town burghers.

It was linen money, in part, that fuelled the expansion of Dublin during what would become its Georgian golden age. The sturdy terraced houses with their delicate fanlights soon became the homes of the city's successful tradesmen. Street upon street and square upon square appeared in the thriving quarter around Temple Bar, and across the River Liffey near Oxmanstown Green. These houses were occupied by Protestant families, who, by contrast with their Catholic counterparts, could afford to indulge in Dublin's luxuries. Their houses would have been well appointed, not only with the finest linen but with the objects that indicated wealth during the eighteenth century: fine dark wood furnishings, imported carpets and china, silver tea services and stern-faced portraits. This was the comfortable existence that Sam Derrick would have known, at least for part of his youth.

When and under what circumstances Mrs Creagh's nephew entered her household, Sam never discloses. Whatever the story may have been, whether one of illegitimacy, hardship or untimely death, Sam had been chosen to become the heir of his aunt's substantial fortune, a hoard that had been spun from the trade of linen. Her husband's toils as a draper had yielded a comfortable profit, and although the precise amount of what she intended to pass on to her nephew is never mentioned in Sam's correspondence, he certainly remained under the impression that it was a considerable sum. While she lived, Derrick also stood to benefit from her generosity. The expenses of his maintenance and his education were absorbed into her accounts, as were the costs of his prestigious linen-draping apprenticeship. In spite of standing to inherit, Sam, like most boys of the successful class of merchants and the younger sons of the gentry, was expected to turn his mind to some form of worthy profession. Generally, the future careers of such boys were non-negotiable. The highly esteemed avenues of the law, the clergy or the military, along with the top end of trade for those of the middle classes, were the only acceptable options. In eighteenth-century Ireland, a linen-draping apprenticeship was one of the more expensive training schemes available to young men. A tradesman or a master craftsman would expect some financial compensation from a young man's family for taking a boy into his home, for feeding him, watering him, putting up with his adolescent antics and teaching him a craft. During the early part of the century, Daniel Defoe wrote of the extortionate size of indentures demanded by London apprentice-masters, and that it was 'very ordinary to give a thousand pounds with an apprentice to a Turkey merchant, £400 to £600 to other merchants; from £200 to £300 to shopkeepers and wholesale dealers, linnen drapers especially; and so in proportion to other trades'. In Dublin, however, an apprenticeship with a linen draper or merchant would have required one of the more sizeable deposits. By the standards of the day, these were enormous sums, more than most middle-class family's yearly income, but they were passports to a guaranteed living and the position of prestige that would one day accompany it.

Mrs Creagh had also seen to it that her nephew received schooling suitable for the heir to a merchant's fortune. In the eighteenth century, the calling card of any man who considered himself to be a gentleman was a classical education. Those who could quote from Virgil and Pliny, who could debate the worth of Socrates and hurl insults in Latin, would more easily acquire access to the drawing rooms of their superiors. As a boy, Sam would have been sent to a respectable grammar school and placed under the tutelage of a clergyman, as was the practice among middle-class Dubliners. It is possible that he, alongside his lifelong friends, the future actors Francis Gentleman and Henry Mossop, attended Butler's School on Digges Street, where he would have been immersed in Latin declensions and Greek philosophy. French also played a large role in his education. As the language of diplomacy and the refined man, a grasp of it was necessary for success in the world at large. Instruction in these subjects, along with the study of mathematics, geography, religion and history, with a cursory nod to the sciences and perhaps some of the more significant works of literature, would have formed the essence of his educational endeavours. However, irrespective of how much he may have enjoyed his hours with Shakespeare and Milton, Latin poets and French philosophers, his future was not designed for leisured contemplation, a privilege reserved for the titled and exceptionally wealthy.

Even in his early years, as he yearned to write poetry, Sam must have recognized that his soul was not that of a cloth merchant. His position, however, was not one he could argue. What Mrs Creagh expected of him had always been clearly expressed, but no matter how diligently Samuel Derrick applied himself to his prescribed profession, an errant instinct bucked within him. Sam could not and would not shelve his aspirations alongside his schoolbooks. While he should have been labouring as an apprentice, he continued reading Rousseau and John Donne. By the light of his candle stubs came more pages of verse, scrawled out in the hours when he should have given in to sleep. Derrick accumulated these poems for years, filling enough sheets by the age of twenty to begin laying the groundwork for their publication. It is likely that his aunt never knew the extent of Sam's interest in writing. While the composition of poetry was deemed a worthy pursuit for the ennobled landowning classes, it could only slow the progress of a man of trade. Poetry, however, was to be the least of Sam's distractions.

Given what the wits would one day write about Sam Derrick's excitable temperament, it would be surprising if his aunt hadn't at some point harboured serious doubts about her nephew. Throughout his life he displayed none of the characteristics requisite in a level-headed master of business. He was reckless, impassioned and at times deeply irreverent. If a person can be judged by the company he keeps, then even at a young age Sam was gravitating towards those who, like him, would end up casting off their respectable livelihoods for morally reprehensible existences. Francis Gentleman, several years his junior and just as impassioned about literature and theatre, was to become his closest companion in his youth. Enoch Markham, another friend, bound for the clergy, was already in his teenage years displaying a tendency towards thoughtless philandering. Like Sam, these young men opted to live according to their hearts rather than their minds, choosing immediate gratification over thrift or prudence, a creed which not only coloured their behaviour but also the state of their finances. Sam, it seemed, was not interested in a conventional life, which may go some way towards explaining why many found him so crass and offensive. In the year of his death, an unnamed wag compiled a number of the more memorably profane gems to have fallen from his lips. *Derrick's Jests; or the Wit's Chronicle* remains one of the only legacies left to the world by Sam Derrick, a man who was until the end an inveterate hard-drinking, bailiff-dodging charmer who delighted or insulted society according to his whim. How much of this side he displayed while living under his aunt's protection may never be known, although it would be hard to believe that his adolescence came and went without incident. Whatever the situation, Mrs Creagh would eventually come to believe that the corruption of her nephew occurred through the influence of his vice-tainted friends. The finger of blame, however, would not be pointed at Sam's literary associates, but rather at those dwelling in a much lower sphere: that of the theatre.

It was only a matter of time before the enticement of the stage, with all its fire and fiction, was to captivate Sam Derrick's imagination. Outside of London, he could not have found a better place to experience the thrill of live performance than in Dublin. Each autumn and winter, packet ships filled with a peculiar cargo would depart from Liverpool or Holyhead bound for Ireland. Their hulls would be packed with an entire season's entertainment, from set machinery and costumes to acrobats and actors. Dublin's literati – men and women like Mary Delany and George Faulkner – were among many who eagerly awaited their arrival as a kind of cultural lifeline from artistically vibrant London. Fortunately for Irish enthusiasts of the stage, Dublin's playhouses acted as a receptacle only for London's most successful theatrical productions. While audiences remained sceptical about Italian opera, they delighted in productions of John Gay's *The Beggar's Opera*, in Congreve and Vanbrugh's plays and, most devotedly, in revivals of Shakespeare. Irish plays, much to the discouragement of home-grown talent, were not performed, forcing those with ambition to seek their fortunes in London.

During the winter season, all of Dublin society, respectable or otherwise, packed into the badly lit, poorly ventilated playhouses at Smock Alley and Rainsford Street. An evening at the theatre offered the best entertainment available in the eighteenth century, not only for what appeared on the stage but for the spectacle that unfolded all around. Night upon night, top-billed plays such as *Miss in Her Teens*, *The Recruiting Sergeant* and *Richard the Third*, featuring celebrated names such as David Garrick, Peg Woffington and Charles Macklin, drew audiences on to the benches. Stage managers employed the most technologically advanced set designs and special effects, springing actors from trapdoors, bringing storms to the stage and cries of wonder from the spectators. They offered what seemed like an endless round of performances, including comedy and tragedy, singing, dancing, acrobatics, fire-eating and magic, all of which continued throughout the evening, from half-past six until close to midnight.

The activity on stage, however, was just part of the theatre-going experience. The early-eighteenth-century playhouse was more of a circus than a seat of refined cultural activity. All night, full-scale battles raged between actors and audience members. Hooting and heckling flowed liberally from the pit, the acknowledged haven for drunken men. Female orange sellers and sex workers circulated among the crowd, offering edible and sexual refreshment. On a bad night, this volatile combination of rowdiness, alcohol and lust could erupt without warning. The consequences were sometimes devastating, as audiences degenerated into violent mobs intent on ripping apart the theatre's gilded interiors. However, the threat of such perils did not keep genteel society from its doors. Provided they stayed clear of the pit, where they were likely to be spat or urinated upon, they could enjoy the evening's events from the sanctuary of their boxes. Dublin's mercantile and trade classes were also careful to keep their distance, choosing to occupy the upper and middle galleries.

In every direction there was something to see or someone to observe, turning an evening's outing into an occasion for flirting, gossip and conversation. For many, the activity on stage was a mere sideshow to the main event of socializing. Under the dripping wax chandeliers a perpetual din rose from the house, as actors struggled to perform over shrieks of intoxicated laughter, shouts, jibes, coughs and the constant movement of bodies in and out of the playhouse. Contributing to the sense of mayhem were the obstructions of audience members, who until 1747 were even permitted to stand on stage during a performance. There was nothing sanctimonious about the theatre. Amid the noise and spectacle, it provided a carnival-like atmosphere of abandon. The colourful audience of women in paint and men unrestrained in their manners competed with the elaborate stories of love, betrayal and courage played out on the stage. As an apprentice, Samuel Derrick would have attended the theatre whenever he had the opportunity. Scraping together the necessary pennies to secure himself a seat and slipping out, perhaps against the orders of his apprentice-master, would have added to the thrill. There, both in the pit and backstage, he would have met with some of his more wanton companions and their thespian circle. The easy lifestyle of loose sexual morals and seemingly endless laughter would have been a profound enticement and would have presented the young apprentice with an opportunity to chat with those who shared his love of words and poetry.

Remarkably, given the myriad distractions and temptations, Sam successfully completed his period of apprenticeship. A fear of the consequences of his failure to do so may very well have been the only impetus he required. Presumably, Sam saw his occupation as a means by which he could achieve his greater aims. For all of the dullness entailed in a life based around the exchange and production of cloth, the profession did offer the benefit of frequent travel to London, giving him the opportunity to peddle his poetry to potential sponsors. While Dublin was home to a small publishing industry, London offered far greater prospects. All forms of creative output in the eighteenth century required patronage or sponsorship, and any meaningful financial backing was a luxury bestowed by society's most influential. Although Ireland had its share of well-endowed aristocrats and fat merchants with social-climbing ambitions, this class of person existed in a much higher concentration in England, and especially in London, a message that Sam would have heard repeatedly from his friend and mentor, George Faulkner.

As Dublin's literary society was a closed circle, it is likely that Sam's acquaintance with George Faulkner began through the introductions of school tutors while he was still a boy. Although twenty-five years his senior, Faulkner felt a great affection for Sam and took the young man under his wing in the hope of encouraging his career. As a friend not only to the estimable Swift but to Alexander Pope, Samuel Johnson and Lord Chesterfield, Faulkner's was a useful name to drop in London circles. Undoubtedly, it was his letters of introduction that opened the few significant doors to Sam's literary future in London. The rest he prised open by himself.

At around the age of twenty-two, in 1746, Samuel Derrick undertook one of his first exploratory journeys to the English city. Although he would have left port with a consignment of linen, his thoughts probably did not dwell long upon its sale. Instead, his mind was occupied with the poetry he hoped to publish and the friendships he sought to renew among the travelling actors he had met in Dublin. Those he intended to visit included Francis Gentleman, now a lieutenant in His Majesty's Army. Like Sam, Gentleman was passing frustrated days in his appointed profession, waiting for deliverance in the form of an inheritance which might allow him to pursue his ambitions on the stage. Having only recently completed his apprenticeship, Sam was elated at the prospect of his newly acquired freedom and the liberties his presence in London might allow him. En route, he composed a stream of verses addressed to 'dear Frank', his 'first among friends', which lyricized his choppy sea passage and the lameness of his hired horse. Upon his arrival, Sam promised Gentleman that they would enjoy 'the gay pleasures of the town' together, but, unwilling to wait for those particular joys, for which he already seems to have gained a taste, Sam broke his southward journey at the Falcon Tavern. There, he not only 'sup'd and drank some claret' but partook of the favours offered by Miss Kenea, a 'fair lady' whose 'hand extends to ev'ry customer', before returning to the road.

At about the time Sam's hired mount limped into London, the city was home to roughly 650,000 people. Although Dublin bustled with a population near 150,000, nothing could match the breadth or confusion of the scene that awaited him. London's streets and neighbourhoods sprawled in all directions. Its length ran to the banks of the Thames and then exceeded it, splashing into Southwark and Lambeth. It stretched backwards, pushing its expanding districts of Marylebone, Bloomsbury and Islington further north. The ferocious scent and roar of London would have met him before he so much as laid foot upon its cobbles. The traffic of those entering its limits – foot passengers, coaches, herders with flocks, carts packed with saleable goods – congested its inward-bound arteries. Once Sam had found his way into the centre of town, he would have been overwhelmed by the melee of faces and accents, the noise and the spectacle. The theatricality of the capital was something he would never cease to find inspirational. Dublin, George Faulkner had warned him, was a place unappreciative of either authors or actors; London, by contrast, was saturated with men of talent.

Like Sam, men and women who believed in their abilities

to perform or create arrived regularly through London's gateways. Although he possessed the advantage of Faulkner's letters of introduction, whatever assistance they were able to provide was likely to have been superseded by several evenings spent in lively Covent Garden conversation. While Fleet Street, the hub of London's publishing enterprise, had its own share of convivial taverns and coffee houses, some of the more intellectual haunts were based in the nearby piazza. Here, at the Bedford Coffee House and the Shakespear's Head, gathered a complete cross section of noted authors, old hacks, affluent publishers and small-time booksellers. As the piazza was also, by proximity, the principal turf of actors, theatrical managers and a variety of professions linked to the playhouses from set painters to musicians, the resulting social scene was one of the most stimulating in all of London. It was also prime hunting ground for patrons. After a night at the theatre, wealthy landowning gentleman could be found in abundance, attracted by the Garden's bacchanalian delights and the lure of the gaming tables. The area's watering holes played host to a range of smaller but equally desirable catches. The ears of moneyed City bankers, merchants, important visitors, as well as established personalities such as David Garrick, Dr Johnson and Samuel Foote, were available for the cost of a mere tankard of ale or a glass of claret. Covent Garden was a networker's dream, a honeypot of promise for those hoping to earn distinction through their art. Not surprisingly, it was on the itinerary of every literary visitor to town; it was the first stop of the dramatist or the poet who had leapt off the London-bound wagon.

When not tending to the business of linen trading, Sam

Derrick was passing most of his time in the piazza. Increasingly, over the course of his visits, the time devoted to spending his living began to outweigh the hours dedicated to earning it. A good deal of Sam's days and nights were passed at the Bedford Coffee House, brushing shoulders with the literati and the leading lights of the London stage. At the Bedford, according to *Connoisseur* magazine, 'Almost everyone you meet is a polite scholar and a wit. Jokes and *bon mots* are echoed from box to box; every branch of literature is critically examined, and the merits of every production of the press or performance of the theatres weighed and determined.' Even more so than at the Shakespear's Head, those who filled the rooms at the Bedford represented a type of London 'in-crowd', by whose glamour Sam was entirely seduced. With its lively characters, spirited discussion and easy morals, Covent Garden was his ideal spiritual home, and the longer he remained there, the less likely his return to Dublin became.

It has been suggested that Sam's ultimate decision to abandon his trade was taken when he was offered a role in a play. While succeeding as a poet had always been his primary objective, an interest in treading the boards had grown from his fascination with the theatre, and had been a stepping stone for many playwrights. It did, however, present a number of obstacles.

Until this period in his life, his aunt had believed Sam to be devoted to the linen trade. While she may have tolerated his interest in poetry, provided it did not detract from his abilities to earn an honest living, she would have never countenanced Sam's desire to act. In spite of many revelling in theatrical entertainment and even following the lives and loves of the players when offstage, in the eyes of reputable society the playhouse was a seat of moral degradation. No self-respecting gentleman or lady would be seen exhibiting themselves so brazenly in public. Actors and actresses compromised their virtue; the very fact that they were willing to assume the roles of vulgar characters, reciting lewd lines and spewing curses, was unconscionable. Theirs was a profession where every concept of decency was flaunted, particularly by actresses, who, it was felt, displayed a complete disregard for modesty, being willing to appear in men's clothing on the stage and partially clothed off it. In addition to being noted for their violent tempers, actors were renowned for their marital infidelity and their sexual rapacity. One moralist wrote in 1757:

> Play-actors are the most profligate wretches, and the
> vilest vermine, that hell ever vomited out; . . . they are
> the filth and garbage of the earth, the scum and stain of
> human nature, the excrements and refuse of all man-
> kind, the pests and plagues of human society, the de-
> bauchees of men's minds and morals.

Under such a hail of condemnation, an appearance on stage would have marked one's official exit from an acceptable life.

While Sam lived in London, he must have felt safely removed from the gossip that dominated Dublin's drawing rooms, enough so to believe that news of his decision to accept the part of the Duke of Gloucester in a performance of Nicholas Rowe's *Jane Shore* would never reach his aunt's ears. As long as Mrs Creagh knew nothing of his activities in London, the inheritance upon which he staked his future happiness would be safe. This might have been a difficult charade to maintain if, through a stroke of good fortune, Sam's debut had been triumphant, but this wasn't to be the case. Sam's days of performing were to be short-lived, although his reputation as an actor would endure. Years later, when he wore the hat of the Master of the Ceremonies at Bath, he was approached by a gentleman who had experienced the misfortune of sitting in the audience when Sam had graced the stage. 'As a player,' Sam was told, 'he might justly be called an original, for any other man might labour all of his life, and at last not get into so bad a method of playing.' However, although his experiment with the theatre had proven disastrous, the playhouse continued to draw Sam back. Failure never deterred him from making further attempts as an actor, or as a playwright, critic or dramatic coach.

For some time he maintained a double life, balanced precariously between two cities. When he could escape to London, he was the author and actor he had always hoped to become. When in Dublin, he was simply Sam Derrick, merchant of linen. To George Faulkner and his other friends he would have expressed his growing dissatisfaction and his impatience. In 1751, when he could tolerate it no longer, Sam, with enough money reserved from his trade, resolved to set himself up in London on a more permanent basis. For the meantime, Elizabeth Creagh would know nothing of this scheme, but how long he could maintain the deception, how many lie-soaked letters he would have to concoct in order to placate her, would prove to be a challenge.

By the early 1750s, with the friendship of numerous London personalities to bolster his ego, Sam was more convinced than ever of his ability to become 'a poet of the first rank'. Inspired by the sight of Dublin, perhaps on the occasion of one of his final voyages between England and Ireland before settling permanently in Covent Garden, he poured out his sentimental hopes for immortality:

> *Eblana! Much lov'd city, hail!*
> *Where first I saw the light of day,*
> *Soon as declining life shall fail,*
> *To thee shall I resign my clay.*
>
> *Muses, who saw me first your care;*
> *Ye trees, that fostering shelter spred;*
> *The fate of man you shall see me share;*
> *Soon number'd with forgotten dead.*
>
> *Unless my lines protract my fame,*
> *And those who chance to read them, cry*
> *I knew him! Derrick was his name,*
> *In yonder tomb his ashes lie.*

One day, Samuel Derrick would get his wish and be remembered in death. However, it would not be on account of his poetry.

# 4

# THE BIRTH OF A VENUS

IT IS A RARE occasion when men who have gorged themselves on carnal pleasures, who have moved between the
silk-lined walls of courtesans' boudoirs and the underskirts of
streetwalkers, can single out one particular 'Impure' to hold
so universally in high regard. Even in her old age, when the
final traces of beauty had left her weathered face, gentlemen
of noble birth and influence gathered around, calling her
'inimitable' and 'respectable', words not usually bestowed
upon elderly brothel-keepers. What they saw in her – the
manifestation of a pure heart, generosity, warmth and an
unaffected honesty – had gripped all who came into her presence, from her earliest years in the trade until the last days of
her life. But this was only a part of Charlotte Hayes, and a
fanciful one at that. The truth, which they would never know,
was that she hid behind a fluttering fan of deception
bequeathed to her from the day of her birth.

That specific day, like the occasion of her death, has
slipped into the recesses of history; only the year, 1725, and
the location are known. It was in the Italian port of Genoa that
a Londoner by the name of Elizabeth Ward brought her baby

45

girl into the world. The father, a wealthy English gentleman, had through the folly of his own lust made her pregnant and his life far more complicated. How did Elizabeth Ward come to be in Genoa? Abandoned with a rapidly rounding belly, did she attempt the journey over the Alps to find her lover? Or, young and impassioned, did he defiantly bring his inamorata on a foreign posting, or in the entourage of his grand tour? However she got there, shortly after the birth the young mother and the infant she named Charlotte found themselves on a homeward-bound ship, packed off by a man eager to dispose of his mistress and the embarrassment of an illegitimate child. Before her departure, the self-styled 'Mrs Ward' was paid a handsome settlement to ensure that any connection between her and her lover was severed. It was also agreed that should the child live to adulthood she would not come in search of paternal favours. As far as Charlotte Ward was concerned, she only ever had one parent and one guide in the ways of the world.

Wherever Mrs Ward's origins lay before her Italian interlude, whether she had been plucked from a brothel or an apple seller's cart, once she had returned to the capital she had no intention of suffering any demotion in her status. Having gained worldly wisdom and contacts among the more affluent elements of society, she turned her hand, and what remained of her lover's allowance, to the opening of a brothel. Moving from prostitute to procuress once one's physical charms had begun to flicker out was a marked promotion of rank: a retreat from the immediate dangers of the front line of active sexual service and into the protection of the background. Those women who from a young age had sold their services to men could look forward to utilizing the charms of others to reap their livelihood. Whether or not she herself had at one point worked from the confines of a brothel, Elizabeth Ward had observed the trade closely enough to determine how she would conduct her own business. London's streets were lined with ramshackle examples of filthy, poorly run brothels where barely lucid girls suffering from sexually transmitted diseases received their beaus' three pennies in a draughty garret. 'Mother' Ward had no interest in operating such an enterprise. The type of client she sought was more discerning in his tastes and considerably more particular when it came to his venereal well-being. Equally, she was not interested in competing with the large emporiums of flesh based in Covent Garden; instead it was her plan to find a select niche in a burgeoning area of the West End.

Spring Garden, a location that would one day be consumed by Trafalgar Square and its surroundings, was a quiet and genteel spot, just off the lip of St James's Park. It was near enough to Pall Mall to assume an air of exclusivity but also close enough to the new Little Theatre that had sprung up in the Haymarket to attract a more indulgent and lascivious crowd. Above all, however, it was the modest nature of the area that appealed. Elizabeth Ward's business was small scale, but she had a preferred collection of patrons, quite possibly drawn from the well-travelled contacts she had made while residing in Genoa. Only those who knew of the brothel's existence were able to identify it behind its façade, that of a simple milliner's business, not unlike the one operated by Mrs Cole, the madam featured in John Cleland's novel *Fanny Hill*. At Elizabeth Ward's establishment, young ladies innocently toiled away in the front room, 'making capuchins, bonnets, &c', a useful cover for 'a traffic in more precious commodities'.

But in spite of its tidy and welcoming appearance, life under her roof would not have been pleasant. Most bawdy-house-keepers believed that the women and girls who worked for them were not to be trusted and had to be observed at all times. Money and gifts were not to be placed directly into their care; a madam's carefully tended 'flock' were not permitted to slip away on errands or enjoy the company of visiting friends. Granting liberties had a way of leading to trouble – namely, employees cheating their employer, rather than the other way around. If Mrs Ward was intent on securing her and her daughter's future, the ship she ran needed to be a tight one. An effective madam used all means available in order to keep her women on board, including various forms of punishment and coercion. In the eighteenth century, madams also made use of the law to keep that which they felt belonged to them within their rightful possession. Any girl foolish enough to bolt from her premises was likely to be hauled before a magistrate and prosecuted for the theft of her clothing. In most cases, the items with which she absconded were those given to her by her procuress as suitable apparel in which to see clients. Such was the case with Ann Smith, who in 1752 was accused by Mrs Ward of running off with 'one holland gown . . . one pair of laced ruffles . . . one pair of silk stockings . . . one satin hat and one pair of paste earrings . . .' – essentially, the clothes on her back. After only a short period, Elizabeth Ward had gained notoriety among the brothel-hopping set for the severity of her methods. What catalogue of horrors prompted Ann Smith's hasty flight from there can hardly be imagined.

As a child, Charlotte would have stood on the periphery of these dramas. For many years she would have been far too young to understand that what Mrs Ward did, every penny she prised out of her harlots' hands, she did in order to ensure Charlotte's comfort and future. A brothel must have been a strange nursery. Charlotte's earliest memories would be of her small but irregular family of females, who sat and embroidered, gossiped and, occasionally, giggled. Men would come and go like shadows, while animal grunts and gasps swept under doors and passed through walls. Sometimes great storms of emotion would buffet the home, and the faces seen previously simpering while sewing would heave into sorrowful wails and acts of violence. Charlotte may also have remembered the tempest of her mother's anger, and how their fatherless household would cower at its appearance. She would have learned much through the observation of her mother and the well-ordered routines of her strange home, but the life Mrs Ward envisioned for her daughter required a more appropriate education than this.

As evidenced in her later life, Charlotte's schooling bore the hallmarks of a slightly more privileged background. Whereas the curriculum at local charity schools would have been based entirely on comprehension of the basics – reading, writing, arithmetic, religious study and preparation for an apprenticeship – the slightly more up-scale, although not necessarily more academically rigorous, academies for young ladies would have included inculcation in female 'accomplishments'. In addition to literacy and numeracy, pupils would receive instruction in French, dancing, deportment and music. If especially fortunate, they might also be exposed to Italian, needlework, accountancy and perhaps a hint of history, geography and the works of classical antiquity. As the social reformer Francis Place mentions, Georgian London contained a number of 'respectable day schools' for girls that offered just such an academic regime, for a small fee. However, given the manifest pitfalls of her mother's profession, it would have been in Charlotte's best interest if she were to attend school as a boarder.

Mrs Ward would not have been the first procuress or courtesan to place her daughter into the care of a school's matrons. Given gentlemen's predilections for pubescent virgins, the presence of a nubile girl in the indecent surroundings of a brothel would raise too many temptations. Elizabeth Ward did not want her daughter's most precious commodity squandered in a rape or through the softly whispered persuasions of a love-struck but penniless suitor. Instead, the disposal of Charlotte's maidenhead would have been planned in meticulous detail, as one of her mother's greatest business transactions. For approximately fourteen years Mrs Ward would have cultivated her daughter's charms and funded her education in preparation for what would become the most important day of her life: her initiation into the rites of Venus.

When the time was deemed appropriate, usually upon the onset of womanhood, Charlotte, like any society daughter, would have been introduced into a public whirl of spectacle and entertainment. As a new face seen beside Mrs Ward at the theatre or in the pleasure gardens, the signals would become clear: Charlotte was the latest delight on offer.

Although her appearance would have aroused interest from a variety of curious parties, Mother Ward would have had her own shortlist of especially wealthy, high-ranking customers in mind to perform the two essential roles ahead.

No sexual experience was more coveted in the eighteenth century than intercourse with a virgin. A genuine maidenhead was a delicacy to the carnal connoisseur and commanded a hefty price. As untouched young women were not in the habit of wandering accidentally into disorderly houses, any bawd would know that the expense of procuring such treasures was considerable. The going rate for the privilege of spending the night with a chaste girl could vary from £20 to 50 guineas. Particularly skilful bawds with especially beautiful young recruits might manage to raise this sum to £100. And it was not simply the selfishly erotic pleasure of introducing an innocent to the sin of fornication that commanded these fees; it was the guarantee of what might be considered the only truly safe sexual encounter available. Whoever he was, Charlotte's deflowerer was likely to have been comfortably wealthy, and certainly not of her personal choosing. As the author of the *Nocturnal Revels* would have his readership believe, with regard to the pawning of her daughter, Mrs Ward's devious reputation was not unfounded. Charlotte, it seems, was 'passed off as a virgin' several more times to the unsuspecting, undoubtedly for similarly exorbitant prices.

Upon her entrance into the profession Charlotte was passed around like a dish to be sampled by the ranks of her mother's clients. Even one night with the brothel's novice would have brought Mrs Ward a healthy ladleful of cash, in addition to gifts of jewels and other bits of frippery. Enticing as these first proofs of her success were, her mother sought the ultimate prize for her daughter: an offer to be placed in 'high keeping'.

In the eighteenth century, all sex workers were not created equal. Some came into the profession by chance, others through a specific determination to scale the ladder of society. Those of the 'meretricious sisterhood' ranged in rank from the destitute and diseased 'bunter' or 'bulk-monger' to the high-living, silk-and-jewel-bedecked 'kept mistress' (often referred to as a courtesan) at the top end. Like a luxury item, the company of an accomplished, charming and beautiful mistress might be borrowed for an exclusive price, but it could also be owned outright, at least in theory, if her lodgings and living expenses were covered by an admirer. If the admirer was very wealthy, a young woman fortunate enough to 'enter into keeping' could have access to any extravagance money could procure. In order to demonstrate his financial prowess, fashion demanded that a gentleman of influence keep a mistress as lavish in her spending habits as he was. Kept mistresses were given free rein with shopkeepers and dressmakers, at the gambling tables, taverns and theatres, placing all expenses on their lover's generous credit accounts. Much to the dismay of the era's moralists, kept mistresses lived as well as the noble wives they mirrored, dressing in the same clothing, wearing the same jewellery and riding in the same private coaches. They lived at some of the most modish addresses, in lodgings decorated with gilded furniture, the walls lined with damask. They kept entire households of servants, often attired in their own unique livery. They threw lavish dinners and parties and offered an alternative existence to the staider world inhabited by virtuous wives and daughters. It was for this life that Mrs Ward was equipping her daughter, not for one of street-trawling, or even dependency upon a bawd. Prostitution of this sort presented the only means by which a low-born, illegitimate daughter of a 'whore' might raise herself from the chamber pot of society, as it was not entirely unknown for devoted keepers in time to become legal husbands.

While Charlotte was to be the primary beneficiary of a life in high-keeping, her mother stood to gain as well. Brothel convention dictated that in order to compensate a madam for parting with a woman who earned her house great repute, a sufficient gratuity was required. Bawds preferred these parting gestures to be paid in banknotes – the higher the amount, the better. Even after the event, this would not be the last favour Mrs Ward received from her daughter. Any devoted child was sure to provide for a parent from her lover's unbounded pocket, making expensive gifts of clothing and food as well as paying the bills. Most ladies in keeping had entire retinues of needy family members and friends who followed closely behind, living off the scraps of her endowment. A bountiful lover would have permitted such expenses in moderation, but Charlotte's uncomfortably close association with the notorious Mrs Ward would not have sat easily with her patrons. Instead, they would have watched her with a sceptical eye, wary of the tricks that mother may have instilled in daughter. The choice of a professional name, free from associations with the bawd who commanded the brothel in Spring Garden, was necessary to ensure Charlotte's success in the pleasure-seeking arena.

The shedding and altering of names was by no means an

unusual practice among women of Charlotte's profession. Without a direct association with a great lineage or a family of rank, a surname was a negligible, valueless thing. It was far better to choose a moniker which conveyed a sense of allure and alluded to an illustrious birth or one's special talents. If she was fortunate enough to be placed in keeping, a mistress might also elect to adopt her lover's surname, a practice which conferred on her the status of a de facto wife while simultaneously outraging respectable society. Why Charlotte alighted on the name of Hayes as a replacement for Ward is unknown. It may perhaps provide us with a clue as to who her first paramour might have been, although any evidence of a Mr, Lord or Captain Hayes has not been recorded in the annals of her history.

In 1740, at about the time Charlotte Hayes made her appearance, two other girls 'came upon the town from obscurity': Lucy Cooper and Nancy Jones, who, along with the courtesan Fanny Murray, would prove to be her greatest rivals. The most business-minded bawds of the day were often compared to horse trainers and were constantly in search of young, promising blood from which they might be able to mould a winner. While Mrs Ward poured her resources into preparing her daughter for entry into the stakes, other procuresses cultivated their own favourites. When Charlotte entered her profession, Fanny Murray had already established a name for herself as mistress to Beau Nash, the reigning Master of the Ceremonies at Bath, but it was Lucy Cooper who looked to be Charlotte's most serious challenger. Like Charlotte, she was the daughter of a bawd, born straight into the arms of a brothel. There were no aspirations for Lucy's future, though. If nature

hadn't blessed her with such overwhelming beauty, it is probable that she would have sunk into obscurity, along with the
others who lodged under her mother's second-rate roof. It was
only through the insight of Elizabeth Weatherby, one of Covent Garden's 'super-bawds', that Lucy was polished and
presented. She was judged to be a finished product while in
her early teens and therefore 'ripe for high whoredom'.
Although lauded as being 'perfection ... amongst the great
impures' and deliciously 'Lewder than all the whores in
Charles' reign', Lucy never learned to exude the slow-burning
charm that sustained Charlotte's light. She and Mrs Weatherby, who acted as a kind of manager-cum-mother-figure, rowed
bitterly and frequently. Choosing to ignore her procuress's
advice, Lucy eventually exhausted her good fortune, ending
her days in debt and destitution when Charlotte's star was
most in its ascendant. Nancy Jones's fame was also short-lived.
After only a few seasons, her handsome features were destroyed
by a bout of smallpox. Robbed of the single attribute on which
her livelihood depended, she too fell from the front row of
leading lights and into the degradation of the back streets.
From there, the grasp of syphilis is said to have pulled her into
a pauper's grave before the age of twenty-five. It required only
poor judgement or a stroke of bad luck to capsize an otherwise
profitable career as an exclusive lady of pleasure. Of the three
who began the race in that year, only Charlotte managed to
sustain her stride and amass a triumph of riches.

The more often Charlotte's face appeared in the front
boxes of the theatres, the more frequently she was seen on
the arms of her fashionable lovers, the more jewels they
wrapped around her neck, the more her name was spoken by

the raffish 'in-crowd' of Covent Garden. Gossip could be a courtesan's best friend and, if its flames were stoked appropriately, could be used to her advantage; the more she appeared to be the dish *du jour*, the more desirous wealthy gentlemen became of making her acquaintance. However, unlike Lucy Cooper and Fanny Murray, it was not necessarily Charlotte's beauty about which her admirers raved. There was something in her person far more bewitching than simply a pleasing arrangement of features.

Although none of her contemporaries would have disputed that Charlotte Hayes was attractive, if not very pretty, the words used to praise her appearance are sparing and judiciously applied. She was, according to admirers, 'buxom' and 'fair'. The poet Edward Thompson commemorates her not only for her ability to preserve her youthful features but for her admirable use of very 'little paint', while Sam Derrick, always favourable in his appraisals of her, remarks simply on her 'grey eyes and brown hair'. These attributes were only partially responsible for what the devoted believed to be her true beauty. Charlotte, as one lover wrote, 'shined'. Her composure, dignity and gentility made her unlike the majority of the foul-mouthed sisterhood. How a woman of such low birth could behave with the honesty and kindness of a virtuous wife was a mystery that gentlemen found both enthralling and sexually thrilling. One observer wrote:

> She is extremely genteel . . . all her features [are] elegant, her air is fine, her address polite, and her taste in dress indisputably genteel; she is a woman of good sense, but talks less than most of her sex, except when

she is perfectly well acquainted with her company;
then few women can be more agreeably entertaining.

Throughout her life, hardly an unfavourable word was uttered against her. To men like Edward Thompson, who fell under her spell, it was Charlotte's unaffected candour that was most enchanting, making her appear in his eyes at least 'as honest as a saint'. Sam Derrick was also hooked by this and praised her for 'never learning to deceive . . . not withstanding the varieties she has seen in life'. To him, she would always possess 'a countenance as open as her heart'.

But the flattery of lovers and pundits says more about Charlotte Hayes's impeccable professional skills than it does about her true qualities. She did not become an affluent courtesan or one of London's most influential brothel-keepers by being either kind or honest. If, by chance, one of her female associates had left some jotted memory, some scrap of her life spent in the shadowed company of such a complicated creature, a truer picture of the woman might have survived. Where her male patrons may have seen her exterior, a fellow female-traveller would have seen the inside, the efforts to slowly extinguish her sense of sympathy, to unplug her emotions and to stuff the empty spaces with false smiles and theatrical tears. Her seemingly effortless deception of men is a testament to her mother's early teaching, although, in the first decades of her career, there were many more lessons still to be learned.

# THE RISE OF PIMP GENERAL JACK

THE SHAKESPEAR'S HEAD TAVERN, even in the early 1750s, when John Harrison arrived there, had been a fixture in Covent Garden for several generations. Reputed to be the first tavern in the piazza, the Shakespear did a handsome trade and was, along with the Bedford Coffee House, one of the most profitable places with which to be connected. This was partly because of its location in the north-eastern corner of the square, within easy stumbling distance of the two major theatres, and also on account of its upstairs rooms. Private rooms enabled gatherings of men (and sometimes women) before the establishment of fee-paying private members' clubs. The society meetings they hosted were entirely legitimate and were trumpeted in local papers, the most notable being the dinners held by the Beef-steak Society. When the rooms were not let out to society members intent on satiating themselves with beef and beer, individual patrons might be permitted to do the same with any number of Covent Garden's luminary ladies of the night.

The crowd at the Shakespear was mixed and boisterous. The raucous and drunken voices of celebrities such as Ned

Shuter, Charles Macklin and Peg Woffington could be heard above the din following a performance, and aristocrats and wealthy 'Cits' (or citizens of London who had made money in trade and finance) such as William Hickey were also as conspicuous at its tables as the Garden's least savoury criminal element. The Shakespear was very much a no-holds-barred type of establishment, where no one asked questions and punters did as they pleased. Devoted patrons and local scions of the law Justice Saunders Welch and the vice-busting Fielding brothers did little to impede the activities that flourished in the more inconspicuous parts of the taproom. While enjoying their beef steaks above stairs, they feigned blissful ignorance as to what transpired directly below their feet.

Although gambling was officially banned from Covent Garden taverns, the Shakespear hosted a Hazard Club where large sums of money were lost and won. Some fortunate souls could be seen carrying hats filled with guineas away from its illicit gaming tables. 'Bucks' and 'bloods' loved the Shakespear, the biographer James Boswell among them. Taking advantage of one of the empty rooms above stairs, the author escorted two willing ladies of pleasure to the Shakespear and 'solaced my existence with them, one after the other, according to their seniority'. Those unable to afford or too impatient to wait for a private room could easily 'solace' themselves in a quiet corner with one of the 'drunken and starving Harlots', who often complained that such 'wanton embracing' on the tavern floor 'soiled their clothes'.

There were few in Covent Garden who swaggered with an air of wealth more convincingly than the Shakespear's proprietor, Packington Tomkins. His tavern had everything the Covent Garden punter desired, and more: drink, women, convivial company, celebrities, gaming and an unrivalled reputation for high jinks and debauchery. The Shakespear's popularity was enormous and Tomkins's taps never ran dry; he had one of the most extensive cellars in the area, containing 'never less than a hundred pipes of wine'. Naturally, roaring trade made Tomkins shamefully wealthy. In addition to a house in London, he also maintained a Herefordshire estate and a private coach to shuttle him there and back at his leisure. Although the owner of a disreputable business, he was able to wipe the smudges of moral taint from his person and walk the streets of London as a respectable family man. By the end of his life he had married his daughter into the Longman family of publishers, and he died with a fortune in excess of £20,000. Unlike the majority of the patrons of his establishment, Tomkins was exactingly shrewd, and sober-headed enough to steer clear of the gaming tables.

A booming business required an army of assistants, and to keep his ship afloat Tomkins employed seven waiters, including a head waiter, a cellarman and a pot-boy. He also took on apprentices and ran a kitchen noted for its culinary genius. For staff at the Shakespear, it was unlikely that a better-paid position could be found in London. Aware of the reputation he was required to maintain, Packington Tomkins insisted that 'each waiter was smartly dressed in his ruffles'. A new recruit like John Harrison would have been granted a clothing allowance to pay for his attire in the first instance but soon would have had pockets heavy enough with gold to purchase any number of fine shirts, coats and breeches. The handsome tips proffered at the Shakespear permitted its waiters to smile smugly. As 'Old Twigg', a former cook there, recalled, a porter 'thought it a bad week if he did not make £7', a sum equivalent to a domestic servant's entire annual wage. This, even for the son of a tavern-keeper, was likely to have been an enormous allowance. When coupled with his takings as a pimp, any appetite for wealth that Harrison may have harboured would have been well satisfied.

Under Packington Tomkins's roof, John Harrison would have been granted the precious opportunity of starting afresh. As a waiter at a Covent Garden back-street tavern, few but the locals would have known his name and face, but at the Shakespear, in the heart of the excitement, Harrison would become a recognized character in no time at all. The Shakespear's Head was a destination in itself, a place where men from all corners of London would gather for an evening's entertainment. As a fledgling pimp, Harrison would have understood to what degree he could expand his fortune, were he to make the most of his situation. Neither could he fail to see the dangers that success might bring. Although discreet bawds, waiter-pimps and panderers higher up on the rungs of the sex-trade ladder had little to fear from the easily bribed authorities, Harrison was under no illusions as to the legitimacy of his craft. In his line of work, an alias would be a necessity, so when Tomkins's patrons bellowed for a waiter to bring them a woman, they didn't call for John Harrison; instead, they requested the watchful, well-dressed figure known simply as Jack Harris. His father's name, however esteemed, reviled or inconsequential, was cast off in favour of an altogether new identity. No longer Harrison the taverner's son, he was free to become anyone.

According to the two contemporary texts that mention Jack Harris, *The Remonstrance of Harris* and *The Memoirs of the Celebrated Miss Fanny Murray*, the keys to his success were his cool, calculating manner, his powers of observation and his rational approach to his trade. Like his employer, Tomkins, Harris was a savvy businessman. He came to the Shakespear well acquainted with the role of waiter-pimp and, under Tomkins's direction, was able to play his part to perfection. Harris had already established his understanding of the several fundamental characteristics required of a good pimp or panderer: first and foremost, a knowledge of how to supplicate, which necessitated an aptitude for 'insinuating, dissembling, flattering, cringing' and 'fawning'. Grovelling to badly behaved young gentlemen did not suit Harris's personality, but he found that pragmatic self-control made him better able to 'answer the huffing questions of fiery Blades' and to 'deprecate ire'. Although 'ready to burst out of [his] head' with anger, he learned to fix '[his] eyes on the ground ... then raise them by degrees, speaking in the winning tone of submission'. This was a difficult pill to swallow, and Harris claimed he could not have managed it had he not cultivated a certain strength of character and 'philosophy enough to bear a kicking'. His only comfort lay in the revenge he was likely to reap at the expense of his wealthy client's purse.

Harris also found that in a larger establishment conspicuously greater requirements were made of him by patrons. A wider pool of gentlemen, comprising regulars as well as visitors from other parts of London, required a more diverse pool of women to keep them amused. Harris's knowledge of local prostitutes would have sufficed for only a short period. At a venue as well trafficked as the Shakespear, demand could quite easily outstrip supply, particularly as a number of his regular ladies might be unfit for performance due to a bout of the pox or a case of the clap. How, then, to satisfy 'the Bucks [who] still rutted and called for coolers to quench their passions'? 'Man is an animal of passions,' Harris would later claim, and 'that which is subject to its passions has no steadiness . . . nor can it like anything for a long time'. The answer to such a problem was obvious: 'provide a variety of faces'. But from where? And how could he vouch for the integrity of the goods on offer if he was unfamiliar with the history of their suppliers? To make matters worse, what if these same bucks found 'the fountains from which they drew their refreshment to be poisoned'? Certainly 'they would blame those who led them to it, especially if it were done purely for the love of lucre'. Even in the early years of his career, Harris would probably have been no stranger to physical violence. Jealous lovers, angry husbands and previously healthy clients who had contracted the pox – all were likely to have sought him out at some point. Of the three, none could be so vicious as the last: a man whose entire life might have been cast into the balance as the result of a hasty and lustful encounter. He may have unwittingly infected his wife and unborn offspring, shortened his own existence and that of his lineage due to the poor advice of a pimp. It may have been a picture of this figure standing before him that inspired John Harrison's change of identity.

Managing 'a variety of faces' required a flawless memory.

A successful pimp needed a means by which the range of varied visages could be easily recalled and summoned when requested. In the case of a high-profile pimp at the Shakespear, whose reservoir was expected to be as vast as all of London, this was no easy feat. Similarly, a clever pimp would put himself in good stead with his customers if he could remember them, their preferences and which of the ladies under his care they had already sampled. Recruitment also posed a problem and might occupy a good part of a pimp's energy. He would be constantly on the look-out for further conscripts, bearing in mind the partialities of his better-paying clients, making mental notes of who liked fresh-faced country lasses and who liked buxom older ladies. He might be given specific projects to pursue, orders from a bored peer or rich banker to hunt down a cleaner, younger mistress. At a smaller establishment, these tasks might have seemed less daunting, but now that his playing field had been widened, Jack Harris had to meet the challenge. If he did so, he would make both his and Packington Tomkins's fortune.

When Tomkins took on John Harrison, he may have known something about the Covent Garden local or he may have simply divined it from the glint in his eye. Harrison had more ambition than most. He was, above all else, exceedingly clever, a man who might have fared equally well as a merchant or a banker, but who by virtue of his birth found himself in a realm far below that. 'I saw great room for an amendment in the profession of pimping,' Harris claimed, and therefore '. . . set about cudgelling my brain, and soon perceived that in the State, so in our business there was wanting a system to proceed methodically'. Pimps, he complained, 'were men of expedients, devoid of all forecast', who managed problems only as they arose. After identifying any impediments, Harris, like any adept engineer, was determined to make some changes.

Supply, it seemed to Harris, was the major obstacle to effective pimping. The answer: 'upon an absence or defection of the established veteran troops, to bring in a fresh supply'. New recruits had to be brought in regularly from other parts of town; with demand as it was at the Shakespear, he could not draw solely from the well of Covent Garden resources. In the first instance, Harris found it easy enough to 'make excursions from the colonnades of Covent Garden to the court-end of town one day; on another into the City; on another to the Tower Hamlet, and so successively to Rotherhith, Wapping and Southwark'. There he met with the area's local 'Cyprians' and made note of their virtues and abilities. Back at the Shakespear, he was then able to put his plan into practice. When a regular patron asked to be entertained by a new face, 'Out I ran and sent for a Borough or Tower Hill whore to come with all the blowzed haste of a tradesman's wife.' Then, in order to pass the time until her arrival, 'I sat down with my gentleman, or noble cull, drank his claret, smoaked a pipe with and told him lies till I almost tired myself.' This was a scheme that worked wonders, as Harris boasted: 'I used to dispatch my court-end of the town ladies of pleasure, who with fine quality airs would make their city-culls, or country bumpkins just come to town, so happy, as nothing could be like it.'

While this worked for some, it did not please all of Harris's clients. Complications forced him to remain inventive.

As he soon discovered, much to his embarrassment, a number of his patrons did not restrict their merrymaking to Covent Garden alone. A few were prone to wander further afield in order to sample the delights of the infamous brothels in the City and in Southwark. They were hardly gratified to find the same faces there as Harris had presented to them across town in the Garden. Moral critics and social reformers of the era often complained that women found their way into the channels of prostitution because profligate men demanded constant variety – what the pimp's patrons might call 'fresh game'. Harris (or the pen that spoke for him) agreed. The quest to satisfy his customers' tastes and to replenish his stock of women seemed never-ending. There were a few tried-and-tested methods which purveyors of prostitution could fall back upon in order to catch unsuspecting prey. None of these was more mythologized in the era's stories and engravings than the lure of the register office. Like job centres, register offices contained advertisements placed by those in need of domestic servants and were frequently the first port of call for an immigrant to London, and this lent itself perfectly to the inveigling of wide-eyed country girls by pimps and bawds posing as respectable citizens in search of housemaids. Like his competitors, Harris claimed to have employed this method of recruitment, although he disappointedly alluded to the fact that few who came to London via this route were as virginal as his clients might have liked.

Servants and female labourers such as street sellers, seamstresses, washerwomen, barmaids and apprentices were Harris's primary targets for enrolment. It was unusual, he believed, if such specimens hadn't already compromised their

THE RISE OF PIMP GENERAL JACK

virtue. In the unforgiving eyes of eighteenth-century society, women forced to labour for a living could be bought and sold in any number of ways. A working woman, whether she had been formally trained as an apprentice in millinery or hosiery, whether she was a laundress, a kitchen maid or an apple seller on a street corner, might sell herself for money. She could never be a lady or an individual of any real value in the world, and men, particularly those of a higher social status, knew this implicitly. Harris found that women such as these were by far the most pliable of all his converts. He was constantly on the prowl for them as he went 'lunging thro' the streets', keeping 'a sharp look out at every door'. He continued: 'wherever I decried a pretty wench, I repaired immediately to the next public house, called for a pint of liquor, and there got all the necessary informations'. After arranging a meeting, Harris found that most of them were easily swayed by a frank discussion of their circumstances and 'soon gave into the doctrine of preferring a life of luxurious happiness to one of drudgery. Which at best, according to the usual course of things, could only end in marrying with some serving man, or else with the journeyman of some laborious trade.' In fact, according to contemporary accounts, many whom Harris might have approached, particularly those holding positions as domestic servants, would not have been strangers to prostitution. Poor pay induced many to spend their lives in circulation, seeking work in bawdy houses as well as below stairs in more reputable ones.

Aside from female labourers, there existed another inviting reservoir from which to draw resources. Harris claimed that his experience with the fair sex taught him never to discount the possibility of bringing married women into his fold. Certainly, these would be new 'pieces' that no man (barring their husbands) had sampled before. In terms of adding to variety, it made perfect sense. When looking to snare this species of recruit, he made a point of visiting the theatres:

> My practice there was to nuzzle in amongst the women of not uncomely features, whom I discovered had no male friend accompanying them. I complimented them with fruit and other little civilities usual in such places. By indirect and not over eager questions, I soon learned the situation of most of them.

Like labouring women, the unhappily married woman required only an honest description of how he might 'make her present state more agreeable to her'. An offer of financial independence from 'an ill-natured surly husband' who 'was totally remiss in his conjugal duty' was generally all the encouragement required. Harris boasted: 'By this scheme I drew in several married women, particularly a packer's wife, who lived not far from the Royal Exchange; and that of a drug vendor near Crutched Friar's, both remarkably handsome women.'

In addition to creating a veritable menagerie of available London women, Harris also gained a reputation for his 'fine nursery of Irish whores'. In both *The Remonstrance of Harris* and *The Memoirs of the Celebrated Miss Fanny Murray*, he claims to have drawn upon these women in order to swell his numbers. In both cases, Harris recounts that he actively went in search of 'Irish recruits'; he not only 'ply[ed] all the Chester-waggons

from Highgate to St. Alban's', but, as he became more successful in his enterprise, took 'a trip every Summer to Dublin' in
order to import ladies. In his travels, Harris had stumbled upon
a rich vein of potential conscripts. He found that many Irish
prostitutes, as a result of being 'rarely paid and frequently
beaten', enthusiastically embraced the opportunity to escape to
London. Others, upon his approach, he found to be so 'light in
purse' and 'strong in appetite' that they were willing to follow
his direction at the promise of a hot meal. Both tracts go on to
mention that Harris had ingeniously established a type of
school for his Hibernian girls, in order to 'break them of their
Irish wildness and civilise them a little', ensuring that they
were 'perfect adepts in their art' before setting them loose
on the public. Such practices were not unknown within the
profession; London's more elite procuresses were noted for
schooling their newer girls, teaching them how to speak and
move alluringly before proffering them to the wealthy male
clientele. Harris claimed to be as skilled at refining their rough-
ness as any bawd, boasting that after some training he was able
to 'pass them upon some of our very own sensible English
gentlemen as charming creatures, as goddesses; in short as
Venuses for beauty, and as Minerva for understanding'.

However, even when scrubbed up and disciplined, not
all of Harris's acquaintances were eager to accept a nymph of
the pimp's indiscriminate choosing. Instead, a number of his
wealthier, titled customers approached him directly for a
more select service. According to his story, Harris was frequently instructed to pluck specific girls for the enjoyment of
his clientele. The crooked tales of bawds and pimps scheming the entrapment of an unsullied young lady was the meat

and potatoes of eighteenth-century literature and, as contemporary court cases attest, such scenarios were not the sole preserve of fiction. Not surprisingly, Harris's name makes an appearance in several such tales. It was claimed that the pimp kept a number of rented rooms and 'little lodges' dotted throughout the capital. Here he perpetrated many of his foul deeds against young women, 'seducing' them and then 'maintaining' them on the premises so they could be 'prepared' for a particular patron. This, according to *The Memoirs of the Celebrated Miss Fanny Murray*, was how a woman who went by the name of Charlotte Spencer was first initiated into her profession.

It was one of Harris's classic coups, executed at the height of his influence. While visiting Newcastle, Lord Robert Spencer spotted a desirable young lady dancing at an assembly, with whom he fell instantly in love. Charlotte, as it soon came to his attention, was the daughter of an eminent but tight-fisted coal merchant who, in spite of his vast wealth, offered little in the way of a dowry for his child. In an age when the suitability of a marriage partner was frequently determined by the size of one's promised settlement or inheritance, women with pretty faces and charming manners but no money almost always lost out. They were, however, ideal candidates for titled men on the hunt for attractive, accomplished mistresses. Unable to cure himself of his lovesickness but unwilling to court a woman with so meagre a dowry, Lord Spencer appealed to the talents of Jack Harris. For a considerable fee, Harris was hired to go to Newcastle and woo the object of Spencer's affection until she consented to elope with him to London. Posing as a gentleman of good family, Harris won Charlotte's trust, and she agreed to a clandestine wedding performed by a man who claimed to be her betrothed's brother in his apartments near Temple Bar. After the ceremony, Charlotte and Jack Harris took to their bed in the adjacent chamber. The candles were blown out and, as she stated, 'he came to me as I had thought'. Upon awakening the next morning Charlotte received the shock of her life. A strange man occupied the space beside her. Her screams of terror eventually brought Harris from the next room to offer his explanation. After he 'frankly acknowledged the whole plan of villainy', she recounted that 'Mr. Harris, the pimp . . . had been employed by Lord Spencer to seduce me to town, under pretence of marriage; that the ceremony performed was not lawful; and that he had received five hundred pounds, besides the reimbursement of all expenses to let my Lord, who was secreted ready in a closet in my chamber, till such time as the candles were extinguished, possess me the first night in his stead.' Charlotte was a reluctant recruit. Harris instructed her that, from this point, she should 'endeavour to get into the good graces of My Lord Spencer', so that 'His Lordship will make a handsome provision for you'. Although his new mistress was well rewarded for her service, we are reminded that any triumph Harris secured was for his and his client's benefit alone. Charlotte ends her story on a bitter note: after 'cloying his lust with my constancy', Lord Spencer 'turned me off, and my supposed husband put me on his list, for the advantage of himself and my destruction'.

Were it not for Jack Harris's skills as a manager of information, he might never have won such acclaim for his resourceful pimping. No matter how large his bag of tricks, no procurer could have governed his trade or his army of ladies without a methodical system. A truly successful pimp would either have been blessed with an ingenious memory for names or the ability to write. In this case, Harris had literacy on his side.

By no means did Jack Harris invent the pimp's list. It is likely that anyone contending with a large volume of sex workers did what other tradesmen and women might: they kept a record of their inventory. It may also be imagined that as general literacy rates rose among the British population, information which was previously stored in the archives of the mind was transferred to paper. Whether committed to memory or scribbled down on parchment, a personally held list, frequently updated and as detailed as possible, was the most essential implement in a negotiator's trade, as indispensable as a chimney sweep's broom or a knife grinder's wheel. Not every pimp would have maintained a list, but those like the waiter-pimp, who occupied a more genteel station than the slum bully and who presided over the venereal pleasures of a large tavern, would have required some form of administration in order to perform their role satisfactorily. By the middle of the eighteenth century, at least among some of the more trafficked public houses in London, the practice among waiter-pimps of accumulating a handwritten list of the known prostitutes in the area appears to have been fairly common. Jack Harris mentions that lists were used by his 'brother pimps' and that names were regularly 'marked on our catalogues' or 'razed out of our books'. Similarly, a writer for the *London Chronicle* in June 1758 commented that during a visit to a tavern his waiter '. . . pulled out a List containing the names of near four hundred [prostitutes], alphabetically ranged, with an exact account of their persons, age, qualifications and places of abode. To me ... this list was more entertaining than the real objects of its description and I perused it with great attention.'

A handwritten list probably took the form of a small ledger or bound notebook. In it, a pimp would record a woman's name and where she might be contacted. This might be the street where she resided or a drinking establishment where she was known to pay regular visits. Then, depending on the extent of a pimp's written skills, might follow some description of the woman and the services she offered. Her age, physical features and sexual specialities, in addition to a price for her labour, would assist either the pimp or the punter in making his choice. The same *London Chronicle* hack noted that the pimp's list he inspected consisted of a basic roll call of names with commentary written in the margins: 'Ann Gill – aged 19 – has been in company two years – Bow Street. Elizabeth White, down in a sal; ditto – Mary Green, going into keeping, sees company till the end of the week, ditto.' No doubt the savvier procurer embellished his entries, citing the names of the woman's favoured customers, something about her past health and sexual history, as well as a scale of prices charged at various times to different clients. Just by virtue of the size of Jack Harris's empire, his trade would have required a handwritten list to beat all others: a veritable encyclopaedia of ladies of pleasure. Constant annotation and alteration would have required clerk-like attention to detail and an ear for the gossip that provided it. If Harris's claim to be tirelessly chasing conscripts is to be believed, his list would have bulged to mammoth proportions during his reign at the Shakespear. It is likely that its size alone contributed to his notoriety among the pleasure-seeking revellers of the Garden and was responsible for the inspiration behind the intention to publish it.

Jack Harris's handwritten list was not the only thing to be growing fat as a result of his pimping expertise. Packington Tomkins had from the outset held a stake in Harris's ability to do trade. At around the time Harris gained employment at the tavern, he claimed that his master had designs on establishing a 'practice in procuring pleasure' to his patrons by providing 'ladies for their recreation'. Tomkins had drafted Harris in as part of this plan. Through 'supplying his house with the newest and gayest of game', the pimp claimed he became instrumental in enabling his master to make 'a very competent fortune' within a few years. Whatever their arrangement, Tomkins skimmed a certain percentage off the takings Harris acquired through plying his trade under the taverner's roof. The agreement would obviously have been transacted in secret, although Harris may not have been shrewd enough at the time to realize what implications this 'special understanding' might hold if the law came calling. Jack Harris had no objections to visibly fronting this side of Tomkins's business and came to enjoy the fame it attracted.

There is also evidence to suggest that the bawd next door, Mother Jane Douglas, was in on Harris's game. The establishment of her brothel in 1741 beside the Shakespear appears to have fostered an amicable arrangement. Initially, Jack Harris's enterprises would have threatened to impede the natural flow of drunken, sex-hungry punters from the

Shakespear into her adjacent parlour, so we might assume that a financial settlement was made to appease her, which may have also included an agreement to proffer her girls to the Shakespear's patrons. In exchange, Mother Douglas offered to sell some of the first published editions of *Harris's List* along side her 'cundums', aphrodisiacs and other sex-shop paraphernalia.

Organizing and maintaining his empire was only one aspect of Jack Harris's work. Reaping the financial harvest was the other side. True to Harris's style, there was an observed protocol for this as well. Like all pimps, Harris displayed an acute talent for making money by every possible means. From the moment a woman's name was entered into his list, to the moment a punter demanded her presence, and once again after she had performed the required services, Jack Harris was there to collect his share of the profits.

Fanny Murray's *Memoirs* provide an insightful glimpse behind the curtains of Harris's operation. According to the author (or, more likely, her ghost writer), the enrolment 'upon his parchment list as a new face' was subject to a certain degree of ceremony. Having no cause to trust his votaries of Venus (as they undoubtedly did not trust him), Harris insisted that they undergo an examination by a medical practitioner before he accepted them into his corps. Only after 'a surgeon' undertook 'a complete examination of her person . . . to report her well or ill', did Harris call upon 'a lawyer to ingross her name, etc. after having signed a written agreement to forfeit twenty pounds, if she gave the wrong information concerning the state of her health in every particular'. Once satisfied that his conscript was clean, the pimp would have 'her name . . . ingrossed upon a whole skin of parchment'. Although a degree of poetic licence must be accepted, the author of the memoirs claims that the handwritten entry would have then read something like:

*Name: Fanny Murray*

*Condition: Perfectly sound in wind and limb*

*Description: A fine brown girl,[1] rising nineteen years next season. A good side-box piece[2] – will shew well in the flesh market – wear well – may be put off for a virgin any time these twelve months[3] – never common this side of Temple-Bar, but for six months.[4] Fit for high keeping with a Jew merchant. – N.B. a good praemium from dittos[5] – Then the run of the house – and if she keeps out of the Lock,[6] may make her fortune, and ruin half the men in town.*

*Place of Abode: The first floor at Mrs.—'s, milliner at Charing Cross.*

The twenty-pound bond taken as a security of her health was only the first fee of many that Harris's ladies would find themselves owing to their pimp. 'Poundage is the pimp's long established tax of five shillings out of every guinea [The Sportsman's pound] which pretty ladies receive for favours granted to gentlemen,' the pen that spoke for Jack Harris wrote. It was standard practice for Harris's ladies to clear their debt with their pimp each Sunday evening when they convened in Covent Garden. At that point they might also find themselves reaching into their purses to provide him with what was referred to as 'Tire-money'. Tire-money, Harris explained, 'is what I make the ladies pay for equipping them with all the necessaries fit to appear in. There are other folks in the town who do the same and are called tally-people, but they can shew nothing like my wardrobe.' The unfortunate girls who fell for the enticement of lavish clothing would have been hit hardest by this tax. Along with the bawd or pimp's percentage, this method of exacting money from a prostitute was one of the oldest. As any recent recruit would most likely have fallen upon hard times in order to have consented to her new profession, it was unlikely that she possessed a store of clothing appropriate for attracting men to her side. Fine gowns, lace cuffs, dainty hats with ribbons and shoes with glittering buckles were given to a young lady as she was pushed out of the door to solicit business. Nothing more would be said about the 'gift' made to her until her procuress or pimp asked for their weekly percentage and the young woman found that she had been charged for the hire of her clothing. Frequently, this left a girl with virtually nothing to show for her unpleasant labour. Fanny Murray realized that 'by the end of the week she had picked up five pounds, ten shillings and sixpence' but after she had paid her dues 'she was sixpence in pocket'.

This finely honed programme of fleecing did not end with charging tire-money. Harris managed to squeeze one final fee out of his wretched volunteers. After the pimp's dues had been paid on Sunday, many of Harris's ladies would choose to meet for a night of drinking. Officially, they had dubbed themselves the Whore's Club, in imitation of many of the male drinking and dining clubs that frequently met in the taverns and coffee houses around Covent Garden. Like any society, the members of the Whore's Club were liable to pay dues and, in this case, women were asked to spare a half-crown. While one shilling of this sum was 'applied to the support of such members as may be under a course of physic, and not fit for business, or can not get into the Lock', another sixpence went 'to the use of our negotiator for his great care and assiduity in the proper conducting of this worthy society'. The remaining shilling, not undeservedly, was 'to be spent on liquor'.

Although it may appear as if the prostitute was in receipt of the sharp end of Harris's stick, a thought should also be spared for the punter, whose purse was bled to the point of exhaustion. An intoxicated man at the mercy of his erection was a procurer's dream. Pimps and bawds invented seemingly limitless schemes designed to part desperate men with handfuls of their cash. While his recruits were charged poundage and tire-money, their cullies had to pay chair-money:

> Chair-money, is when I charge a chair for a girl who had been in the house [the tavern] when called for; or living not far off, walked to the house: or when there is a necessity from the badness of the weather of coming in a chair, to charge double the fare, saying that the lady, a kept mistress, lives a great way off, at Berkeley Square.

If this was an additional charge that could be tacked on to straightforward requests for women whose names appeared on his list, a man who demanded the services of a more exclusive Cyprian might find himself an unwitting donor to what Jack Harris referred to as his 'humming fund':

> The humming fund is when we pretend to a rich cull, the mighty difficulty there will be to get such a girl for

him, who is a kept mistress; or one that will grant her
favours only where she likes – we bleed him from time
to time of a few guineas; now giving hopes, now diffi-
dent of success. We play him off a thousand ways, and
at last stipulate in the lady's name for a good round sum
to be paid ere the consent . . .

It was a practised trick of the trade for a woman and her
pimp to then conspire in an attempt to eke even more money
out of the client. If a customer began to betray a certain partiality for a lady, it might be arranged that:

After a night or two's cohabitation, off she goes in some
pretend pique and retires; no-body knows where. Then
we are employed to find her out – But . . . we advise him
to think no more of her – which advice whets his desire
the more, till he decides he will have her at any rate.

The punter having played directly into the pimp's hands,
Harris then closes in for the ultimate clinch: he informs his
client that his inamorata has been located, but that restoring
her to him will cost not only a cash fee of '30 pounds or so', but
that she will only agree to the reconciliation on the condition
that 'he make gifts of trinkets, etc . . . to her'. Naturally, the
pimp will save the cully the bother of making such purchases,
if he would be so kind as to simply hand over the money.

The range of ploys used to extract money from punters
varied from pimp to pimp and from tavern to tavern. Casanova, who was doing the rounds in London in 1764,
complained bitterly of his treatment by a waiter at the Star
Tavern in the Strand. The great lover had called for a woman
and much to his frustration learned that he must pay a

shilling for each one he viewed, whether he chose her for his bedfellow or not. The pimp marched a string of unappealing prostitutes by him, leaving the most attractive until the very end. Twenty shillings later, and still without a woman to show for it, Casanova left in a huff. If Casanova had been one of Jack Harris's clients, there would still have been no guarantee that the lady he elected to accompany him above stairs would perform her duties undisturbed. In order to screw the maximum profit out of a prostitute's company, Harris regularly double-booked his ladies; he referred to the practice as arranging 'a Flier'. He was loath to turn away any request for one of his women, especially if a punter had asked for her by name. Although engaged in the act with another man, Harris would coyly interrupt the couple and 'Tell Miss a lady wants to speak with her in another room. Those who are ignorant of the tricks of the town, let her go.' The woman smooths her skirts, adjusts her hair and enters the next room, where her eager paramour awaits. A quick sexual interlude follows and she once again 'returns to her company as demure as if nothing had happened'. This, Harris conceded, could prove to be a rather fraught manoeuvre, as the girl ran the risk of contracting the pox from lover number two and passing it straight on to lover number one. 'Thus,' he explained, 'a girl who has often come clean into company, by these short digressions gets herself infected.'

Systems, procedures and regimentation were the order of Jack Harris's ever-expanding empire. Like a true imperial ruler, he also ensured that his subjects lived by an established code. Laxity in his leadership, Harris would have learned, was a sure path to the encouragement of trouble. There was to be no indulgence of his listed ladies' personal difficulties, and no transgressions of behaviour would be tolerated. Although Harris (or Harris's literary interpreter) never mentions that he resorted to violence in order to enforce his authority, other punishments could be implemented with equal effectiveness. Harris recognized that if a woman was 'struck off his list', she had little chance of 'repairing her fortune'. A good many of Jack Harris's ladies were a mere cut above the lowest of the low: the destitute streetwalkers whom Tobias Smollett describes as 'naked wretches reduced to rags and filth', who 'huddled together like swine in the corner of a dark alley'. A thrust down the stairs, from being a listed prostitute to a friendless pariah, required only the blackening of a woman's healthy reputation. Unfortunately, it did not take much to incur Harris's wrath. All a woman need do was to lie. More than anything, Harris would not stand for being 'bilked', or cheated out of his percentage. The repercussions for this were severe. The ruthless pimp erased her name from his list and 'whenever after she is called for by any company, we say she is down in a salivation and so stop the channel of her commerce – many have starved in consequence, which was a necessary expedient in *terrorem* for others, to make them behave honest.' According to the author of Harris's *Remonstrance*, a similar fate awaited those who refused to share his bed if he desired their services for the night.

The knowledge that Harris's Covent Garden ladies were, for the most part, exposed to any whim their pimp might impose upon them might very well have been the impetus behind the creation of the Whore's Club. Whether or not this was a tongue-in-cheek invention of the brains behind Fanny Murray's *Memoirs*, it seems likely that listed women would under the circumstances band together for companionship and protection, just as their streetwalking counterparts were known to do. Not surprisingly, the roll of club rules appears to indicate that the society's immediate function was the intoxication of its members, but its more enduring design was to raise support for the sisterhood.

By definition, the only women who qualified for membership were those who were 'upon the negociator Harris's list; and never have incurred the penalty of being erased therefrom; either on account of not paying poundage, making proper returns of her health, or any other cause whatever'. It further stipulated that: 'No member of this society must have been in Bridewell above once,' and that 'Any member of this society that may have been tried at the Old Bailey, for any crime except picking of pockets shall not be objected re-instating, if acquitted, upon condition that she did not plead her belly.'

One can imagine the Shakespear's Head on a Sunday evening, perhaps the only slow night of the week. It was a time where Harris's ladies might be able to enjoy something resembling a night off from their normal travails. Some arrived by chair, lowered to the ground with grace. Others arrived half inebriated, leaving a trail of gin behind them. As they greeted one another, gossiping excitedly, expostulating, embracing, the handful of drinkers raised their eyes to watch a flutter of cheap silk and lace caps disappear above stairs. Before the hard drinking began in earnest, any serious business would be addressed. Principally, this would relate to raising financial support for those who found themselves in prison or suffering with the pox. This fund was amassed through club dues, and also through nominal donations made by members who became 'modest' women 'by going into keeping'. The Whore's Club anticipated generosity in this case, insisting that the money given be 'in proportion to her settlement allowance'. Once the business was dispatched, the fun could begin.

In spite of its members being foul-mouthed and tipple-loving, the club rules recognized that a certain degree of civility and decorum should prevail. Evidently the meetings (not unlike those held by men's clubs) degenerated somewhat by the end of the evening. There were, however, rules in place to deal with any unfortunate alcohol-related mishaps. It was established that if 'any member by an overcharge of liquor, should in clearing her stomach, spoil any other member's cloaths, she shall be obliged to take the same off her hands, and furnish her with new ones, or in some other manner compensate the damages'. Penalties were also exacted from those who broke 'glasses, bottles, etc. or behave[d] in a riotous manner' and for others 'not able to walk' at the end of the meeting. Throughout, Jack Harris would have kept an eye on the proceedings, periodically tugging at the sleeves of those whose names had been called from down below.

In the rise and rise of his fame, Jack Harris may have lost sight of the fact that while he had come to know a vast number of names and faces, so a vast number of names and faces had also come to know him. The more people who had Jack Harris's name on their lips, the more exposed his position became. As his dominion expanded, so would the volume of gossip among patrons of the Garden. Second-hand stories about his past and present exploits would have been swapped by a cross section of society, from the lowest bunter to the aristocratic heir. Like all names that attract notoriety, legend would have accompanied him like a shadow.

For the most part, Harris believed that he had nothing to fear. In spite of the Shakespear's proximity to the headquarters of the local magistrate on Bow Street, hardly a shout's distance away, neither Packington Tomkins nor his head waiter ever experienced any trouble from the law. The Shakespear and its activities were well known in the area yet, remarkably, no concerted effort had been made to quash its illicit business. The law was explicit in the eighteenth century; the open solicitation of sex and the keeping of bawdy houses were illegal after 1752, but the enforcement of these two edicts was entirely haphazard. The night watch, the closest London came to a police force before the advent of the Bow Street Runners, were more interested in maintaining calm on the volatile London streets than proactively enforcing the law. While streetwalkers might make a nuisance of themselves, calling out lewdly from doorways and grabbing at men, those who conducted their business quietly indoors ensured that they were inconspicuous enough to be almost impossible to prosecute. This was particularly the case for those who occupied the upper tiers of the sex trade: waiter-pimps, more expensive prostitutes and brothel-keepers. These individuals, due primarily to their discretion, to the high rank of their clientele and to their false appearance of gentility, were rarely fingered by the long arm of the law. Their illusory immunity from prosecution provided them with a sense of security upon which they might build their fortunes.

By 1758, Harris was feeling invincible in his dominion of the Covent Garden sex trade. At the height of his influence, he boasted that from pimping alone he had acquired a fortune of 'four or five thousand pounds in about a half dozen years', a sum comparable to the salary earned by the First Lord of the Treasury. His list was rumoured to have stretched to four hundred names, including women from all parts of London, from Southwark to Shoreditch, to Bloomsbury and Chelsea. In addition, he had in his employ a staff of 'under-pimps', young apprentices recruited to learn the trade and to manage the outposts of his empire. Unfortunately, Jack Harris's sense of pride was growing too. Where once John Harrison had acted with calculated discretion, now Jack Harris swaggered in defiance, unconcerned about the extent of his exposure. Pride would be his weakness. As the self-proclaimed 'Pimp General of All England' stepped out into the piazza attired in his ill-gotten finery, it was not just his neighbours and patrons who noticed the glint of his shoe buckles and bright buttons. The gaze of Bow Street had also affixed itself to him, and much more closely than he imagined.

## 6

# SLAVE TO GRUB STREET

Sᴀᴍ Dᴇʀʀɪᴄᴋ'ꜱ ᴇꜱᴄᴀᴘᴇ ꜰʀᴏᴍ linen-draping had been years in the planning. In all the care he took to dupe Mrs Creagh, in all the relationships he had nurtured across the Irish Sea, in all of the letters he had written to those he had hoped to impress, not once did he contemplate the possibility of failure. His convictions drove him headlong towards Fleet Street, London's 'Street of Ink', where he believed his laurel wreaths awaited. It would be only a matter of time before he was crowned by the kings of patronage and publishing as a reigning genius, another Dryden or Pope. When Sam scrutinized his work he saw only excellence, but when those patrons and publishers read his verses and examined the small, eccentric man who produced them, they saw something far less auspicious.

Sam was drunk on the promise that London, and Covent Garden in particular, offered him. Bursting with enthusiasm for his new liberated lifestyle, and with money enough in his pocket to sustain him, he threw himself into the capital's manifold pleasures. He loitered in the watering holes of the literati and attended the theatrical performances of his friends. In the hours between and afterwards he drank, gambled, spent his money like an heir and, occasionally, found time to write. Sam canvassed his acquaintances for roles in their plays and, when they had none to offer him, he thrust his dramatic works into their hands. These were usually returned to him with the curt response of 'not calculated to succeed'. One theatrical manager with whom Derrick had cultivated an acquaintance told him that although he had managed to lose the unmemorable tragedy Sam had written, he was welcome to put his hand into his bureau 'and take two comedies and a farce instead of it'. When not buzzing around backstage at the Covent Garden and Drury Lane theatres, Sam was continuing his campaign of subscription-raising for his collection of poetry. Although no one seemed especially interested in reading an entire book of Derrick's verses, his cautious supporters were intrigued enough to endow him for the printing of one poem: 'Fortune, a Rhapsody'. It may have helped matters that the work was dedicated to David Garrick, who had stumped up part of the money necessary for its publication. Although the poem expressed some cogent sentiments about the fickleness of success and the difficulties of being an artistic genius whose talents no one recognized, neither was 'Fortune, a Rhapsody' 'calculated to succeed'. In fact, at some points his writing borders on the atrocious:

*For he who can the purse command,*
*Must ev'ry science understand;*
*Or tell him so – and it agrees,*
*As well, as with a Welchman's cheese . . .*

Regardless of what the general public must have made of his first foray into literature, the subject and date of Derrick's work is quite telling. 'Fortune, a Rhapsody' appeared in 1752, a year after Sam's move to the capital. Disillusionment had already begun to set in and, one year on, the accolades that he had anticipated receiving were nowhere to be seen. The reservoir of linen-draping money on which he was surviving would have been running thin, and while he would have received a small sum for the publication of his poem, it would not have been enough to successfully subsist on for long. Nevertheless, the difficulties he faced did not deter him entirely. Sam had numerous irons in the fire and he felt that these temporary setbacks would only slow his path to glory, not impede it altogether. As he reminisced in conversation with his friend and fellow aspiring thespian Francis Cooke, he had seen many like himself 'abandon their parents or forsake their masters to starve . . .', but in spite of the occasional disappointment, London and 'the diversion we met, answer'd for all the trouble'.

As the wolf neared the door, Sam began to gain some perspective on his situation and turned to Grub Street for assistance. In the eighteenth century, Grub Street was not so much a location as a type of existence. Today, the mythical street that gave a lifestyle of literary misery its name lies below an office block near the Barbican Centre, but in Sam Derrick's era the presence of Grub Street stretched far beyond its geographical borders. Up the main thoroughfare of Fleet Street and down Ludgate Hill to St Paul's Cathedral, shoved into the narrow alleys snaking off it and pitched against church walls, stood row upon row of booksellers' outlets. Some were merely stands offering pamphlets and a few titles; others were prominent shops with bow windows that displayed their wares to passers-by. Behind the shopfront and shelves, in the back room, the cellar or the floors above, came the incessant thump of a printing press, rattling out pages that would shortly find their way into the public domain. Elsewhere in this creative factory (most likely in the garret) would sit, diligently working, a writer, or two or three in threadbare coats, with holes in their shoes and fingers black with ink. Here lived and toiled the subclass of petty authors that Dr Johnson defined as 'writers of small histories, dictionaries and temporary poems'. They shared the same colloquial name as the well-ridden horse, the tired beast that would do anyone's bidding: the hackney writer, or simply, the hack.

The hack wrote to eat. It was not from any great artistic urge that catch-penny pamphlets and puff reviews appeared on the booksellers' stalls, but from necessity. The bookseller, who doubled as publisher, would hire a hack to write to specification anything that would sell. There were no bounds: total falsehood masqueraded as true confession; odes, sermons, scandal, reviews, opinions and hearsay were typeset and run off indiscriminately. The author Richard Savage, through the pen of Iscariot Hackney, confesses: '. . . I wrote Obscenity and Profaneness, under the names of Pope and Swift. Sometimes I was Mr. John Gay and at others . . . Burnet or Addison. I abridged histories and travels, translated from the French what they never wrote, and was an expert at finding out new titles for old books.' While some hacks worked independently of booksellers, choosing to peddle their manuscripts after completion, labouring under the umbrella of a bookseller who could provide a steady stream of commissions appeared to be the more secure option. Those who chose this route often found themselves living in a state of indenture to their publishing masters. Booksellers paid for the hack's basic board and lodgings in return for a constant turn-out of material. The notorious publisher Edmund Curll had his 'translators' lying 'three in a bed in the Pewter Platter Inn at Holborn', where 'they were for ever at work to deceive the public'. In exchange for his services, the hack received a demeaning rate of pay. By mid-century, eighty pages of reviews poured out by one of his writers on tap might have cost a bookseller no more than two guineas. Such work might have taken weeks, if not months, to produce, toiling around the clock, leading James Ralph to comment in 1758 that 'There is no Difference between the Writer in his Garret and the Slave in his Mines . . . Both must Drudge *and* Starve; neither can hope for Deliverance.' Grub Street could be a graveyard for ambition, a pit of quicksand that swallowed authors whole, pulling names and the works attached to them into a well of anonymity. While a handful, such as Henry Fielding and Oliver Goldsmith, managed an escape into literary fame, many more languished there, forgotten.

In the beginning, the prospect of a writing life had thrilled Sam Derrick, but after a stint at the grist mill of Grub Street the unsavoury face of his chosen path emerged into full view. It was here that Sam's momentum began to grind to a halt. The slush of inconsequential articles, puff pieces and essays he churned out was, in his eyes, only another temporary expedient until an eager patron came to his rescue. Although much of what Derrick produced would have appeared in journals under pseudonyms, making it virtually impossible to extract a full catalogue of the pieces that he authored, a handful of his early works can be identified, including a dramatic critique of *The Tragedy of Venice Preserv'd* (1752), translations of two French dramas, *Sylla* (1753) and *A Voyage to the Moon* (1754), a translation of the *Memoirs of the Count du Beauval* (1754) and the translation from Latin of the *Third Satire of Juvenal* (1755). As a poet, Sam may not have excited many positive responses, but as a translator his skills were more valued. What he had not yet come to recognize was that his true talent lay not in twirling words into rhymed verse but in analysing, observing and documenting the peculiarities of human nature.

It was only down to Derrick's tireless subscription-hunting that any of his worthier works made it into print. To add to his frustration, Sam soon learned that patrons tended to favour his translations above his poetic productions. So, the endless soul-destroying rounds of subscription-raising continued, a practice that compelled prospective authors to '. . . wait upon the nobility and the gentry with proposals for printing books . . . soliciting the honour of their names to the work'. Even then, after the initial flattery and lock-tugging had taken place, it was only with '. . . perseverance and frequent teasing' that 'many gentlemen will give a guinea to get rid of an impertinent fellow'. The cultivation of patrons could be a slow and arduous process; it could be years before the costs of printing a work were raised. Eighteenth-century Britain abounded with aspiring poets and essayists, novelists and satirists, and not every gentleman or lady of means was interested in supporting them.

Although Sam's relationship with Grub Street may have begun with a tentative dip of the toe, after several years its constant tide would be the only force bringing him income. Sadly, Derrick's name had made no more of an advance into the pantheon of English authors than those of his friends and fellow hacks David Mallet, Soame Jenyns, Aaron Hill, or even Francis Gentleman. The pecuniary rewards were sparse and, when they did come, were quickly siphoned off by shop-keepers, taverners or creditors. In keeping with his unfailing faith in the size and impending receipt of his inheritance, Sam refused to temper his spending. While he was enjoying himself, debating the merits of Charles Macklin's theatrical abilities or Samuel Johnson's opinions in the booths of the Bedford or the Shakespear's Head, he lost himself in the present. As his circle of acquaintances began to swell, so his purse began to shrink. He boasted to his new comrades, whom he watered liberally with drink and nourished with food, to whom he loaned money and made gifts, that he was an heir to a fortune. People took him at his word and were not especially forthcoming in making good on their debts. Sam was never able to recoup the sum he had advanced to friends such as the theatrical manager Thomas Harris or his young, rakish correspondent Tom Wilson. Like a true man of means, Sam took great pleasure in sending tokens of his esteem to potential patrons, such as the large and expensive wheel of cheese Sam had delivered to Lord St Leger at the height of one of his more impecunious periods.

The difficult truth was that Sam was no more a man of means than any other struggling hack. His boasts, however, did succeed in convincing merchants and shopkeepers to extend his credit, at least until the larger bills required pay-ment. In keeping with his profligate lifestyle, Sam harboured an unfortunate penchant for expensive clothing. Any portions of his inconsistent earnings that weren't squandered on entertainment went straight into his tailor's coffers. He adored elaborate coats rimmed with gold frogging, intricately wrought buttons, silk waistcoats and well-cut britches. He wore only the most recent and foppish fashions, but never wasted a penny on those items that couldn't be seen hanging on the outside of his person. Samuel Foote found Derrick's peculiar preferences for dress to be wholly irrational. Why would anyone opt to own 'five embroidered coats', while possessing only one clean shirt to wear underneath them? The practicality of owning fresh underwear never served his purposes as well as did a variety of 'sumptuous cloaths' in which to promenade. Derrick dressed as he lived; he had no interest in sensible choices. As a result, his wardrobe ebbed and flowed with his unpredictable fortune. A promise of publication yielded a celebratory new suit of clothes, which, invariably, after only a few months' wear, ended up in the window of a pawn shop. On one occasion, seeing that Derrick had neglected to invest in appropriate legwear and was struggling to maintain decency beneath his hole-riddled stockings, Tobias Smollett 'slipt a guinea into his hand, to equip his legs and feet for the next day'.

Increasingly, and not surprisingly, Sam's prodigious spending began to adversely affect other areas of his life. No longer able to afford comfortable lodgings, his residences became increasingly downmarket. The fire in his hearth became smaller and then, as he was unable to afford the coal necessary for even the shallowest glow of warmth, non-existent. At times, when he had not been able to sell a poem or was in the midst of writing his next review, food became scarce. Although Sam had always been small in stature, Smollett began to notice that he had also grown 'lank'. During such lean times, he saw fit to call in a number of favours owed to him by his Covent Garden associates, but his destitution made him the grudging guest of fellow literary lights, such as the author and scientist Dr John Taylor. Desperate enough to sleep anywhere, Derrick's visits to the Taylors' cottage in Highgate were not deterred by the lack of a bed. In a pinch, he was willing to doze in John Taylor junior's cradle with his feet propped up on a chair. When acquaintances had not even a cot to offer him, Derrick found himself on the street. On his way back to his own apartments, the author Thomas Floyd was quite startled to stumble across Sam asleep against a shop hoarding. 'My Dear Floyd, I'm sorry to see you in this destitute state,' Derrick was rumoured to have said as the actor stood over him, a bit worse for wear after a night of drinking. Sam then gestured to the filthy patch beside him: 'Will you join me at my lodgings?' Although, as Dr Johnson claimed, his wit in such situations lent him a reputation for a particularly resilient 'presence of mind', the reality of Sam's predicament, heightened by his irresponsible behaviour, was beginning to exact a toll on the estimation others held of his character.

Even when he was down on his luck, the distractions of Covent Garden made starving in London preferable to living a comfortable, dull existence as a Dublin linen draper. George Faulkner, who worried frequently about his friend's prospects, was not averse to reminding Derrick that he could always 'quit the Muses for sordid pelf', adding that he wouldn't mind seeing Sam back 'in Ireland, and at the Linen

Hall, buying vast quantities of Irish Manufacture to be exported to England'. This, however, would never happen as long as the roar of the taverns and playhouses could still be heard from the piazza. In spite of the hardship Sam suffered, the bitter edge of his lifestyle was sweetened by the presence of many underfed and poorly paid kindred spirits, from struggling actors, dancers and musicians to impoverished painters and dramatists. Unlike the linen hall, Covent Garden was also a place dominated by youthful energy. While home to a number of established veterans, the majority of those drawn to its flame were in their teens and twenties. The abundance and influence of aspiring players and poets, in addition to 'greenhorn' apprentices, fresh-faced 'votaries of Venus' and hot-blooded young heirs, cannot be underestimated. What lent Covent Garden its vigour and its reputation for high-spirited fun had as much to do with its activities as with those who partook of them. All the drama of adolescent angst, the emotional outbursts, the infidelities, the romances and the complicated friendships, when brewed with large quantities of alcohol, made the piazza's establishments the centre of some of London's best unscripted performances, as well as being the ultimate precursor to the modern student union bar. With a keen eye for both observation and histrionics, Sam Derrick could not have found a more suitable or inspirational home.

When not writing or attempting to gain access to a patron's drawing room, Sam was generally to be found in the watering holes of the piazza, more specifically at the Bedford Coffee House or the Shakespear's Head. Whether for the purposes of drinking or seeking shelter, Covent Garden's coffee houses offered respite. In the worst of times, they provided protection from inclement weather and the opportunity to be bought refreshment by some passing acquaintance. There he remained, presumably until he was shunted along, reading the newspapers, writing and receiving letters, chatting and warming his notoriously bad-smelling feet by the fire. In quiet moments, he sat and took in the surroundings. Coffee houses and taverns were, as they are today, delectable venues for people-watching, and he was in a prime position to catch snatches of gossip as they blew in his direction. He became a master of scandalous information, scribbling down anecdotes and tales of carnal conquest. If his works for the stage 'were not calculated to succeed', then Sam resolved to record rather than to create drama. As he watched a certain renowned waiter transact his business with his gentlemen clientele, and silk-clad young ladies with heavily painted faces flounce up the tavern stairs, an idea started to germinate.

It helped, of course, to have more than a passing acquaintance with the noted female faces of Covent Garden. The borrowed money that Sam generously spent on food and drink and merrymaking was not solely for the entertainment of his male companions. A large quantity of it was lavished on women. If Sam had one weakness which far exceeded his passion for fine velvets and silk brocades, it was his insatiable attraction to the female sex. Derrick adored women, both the tavern harlot and the blushing lady, although, given his usual situation in Covent Garden, he was more likely to meet with the former than the latter. In the midst of a loud evening, when the audiences of both theatres had emptied into the surrounding watering holes and the 'Cyprian Corps' were busy plying their trade from booth to table, singing bawdy songs and supping porter with their swains, Sam Derrick would have been just another cull whom they flirted with and occasionally honoured with a favour, whether he could pay or not. With Sam, it was often a quid pro quo arrangement. Poets and playwrights were shamefully bad clients and more likely to bilk a girl than even the rowdiest 'buck'. Unlike the buck, who was simply a disrespectful young womanizer able to afford the services of a prostitute, the tender-hearted, struggling author who wooed his moll by eulogizing her beauty or promising her a lead role in his play was perpetually penniless. With a skilled tongue that flowed with Shakespeare and Milton, he often succeeded in acquiring sexual encounters for free. But Sam Derrick's success with the votaries of Venus could be attributed to more than just his seduction technique. He offered the ladies of Covent Garden something that the majority of their fee-paying patrons did not: empathy.

Hacks and ladies of pleasure shared much common ground and were likely to see through each other's constructed veneers and into one another's despairing hearts. Interestingly, the traditional home of the hack writer around Fleet Street and Temple Bar was also that of the streetwalker. While one group loitered in the doorways and byways around Fleet Street, the other stared down at them from their garrets. Each occupied these positions out of necessity, compromising their integrity because of desperate financial need. Dr Johnson, who lived on Gough Square, cheek by jowl with nests of hacks, commented that such authors were simply 'drudges of the pen' who 'have no other care than to deliver their tale of wares at the stated time', not wholly unlike 'the whore', who mechanically produced her sexual offerings upon payment. Indifferent and detached from their labour, hacks parted with their intellectual principles as readily as the streetwalker shed her physical honour. Sam Derrick was not the first, nor would he be the last, of his kind to feel a distinct compassion for the plight of the downtrodden girl who peddled herself to the public. However, true to the spirit of his age, he never advocated that prostitutes should abandon their calling: instead he appealed to society's wealthy patrons to lift these 'frail and fallen women' into 'high keeping'. Under such protection, and with a generous cash allowance, they would enjoy a liberation otherwise unavailable to them. In Sam's view, all that those in either profession required was someone to pay their bills.

As Sam perched on his tavern chair through the daylight and evening hours, avoiding the slanting rain that wetted his street-corner bed or the prospect of returning to a fireless hearth, he would have seen many of his night-time companions baring their 'after-hours' personas. He would listen gallantly to their tales of woe and share in their small happinesses. In addition to friendship, Sam's protection would have been solicited by women whose vulnerable position on occasion required a male supporter. A gentleman defender may have been called upon to speak on a woman's behalf, whether her persecutor was a magistrate, a bailiff or a vengeful lover. The better connected a man, the more benefits he could offer, and Sam had managed to insinuate himself into the company of a variety of influential men. A friend of Sam Derrick who regularly popped into the Shakespear or the Bedford might also find herself in a position to further her own interests. Most ambitious sex workers sought to choose their own clientele. Naturally, the most favoured were those handsome young men with large estates and allowances at their disposal. The ever-roving subscription-hunter and the ever-enterprising Cyprian were stalking the same prize, and who better to provide the tip-offs and the introductions than a well-connected acquaintance?

Due to his approachable disposition and chivalrous manner, Sam became quite a favourite among the higher orders of the sisterhood. He was, more than anything, a true friend to women such as Kitty Fisher and Lucy Cooper, who, even at the height of their influence, experienced periods of utter loneliness. For his kindness, Sam was handsomely rewarded by his meretricious companions. Lucy Cooper took it upon herself to feed Derrick whenever he was in need of sustenance, which was quite a regular occurrence. After Sir Orlando Bridgeman installed her in a set of elegant lodgings, Sam became a feature at her table, eating and hobnobbing with the most fashionable profligates of the mid-eighteenth century. It was whispered that Derrick was repaid horizontally as well; the roles of male protector, friend and client were frequently defined as one and the same by most who sold sex.

In later years, once he had attained a degree of celebrity, Sam Derrick looked back on his youthful days in Covent Garden with some trepidation. Perhaps he had been too ubiquitous in the taverns, too immoderate in his habits, too interested in 'the company of the daughters of Venus'. With hindsight, he admitted to indulging himself with 'large draughts of pleasure', supping too greedily on the available delights when he could have been cultivating his talents. By the time of this epiphany, however, it was too late. Although Sam had been networking his way around the piazza even prior to settling in London, his subsequent behaviour had the effect of souring the faith of many of his contemporaries. Sam was friendly and entertaining, a jester and a wit, but he displayed these qualities rather than any tangible proof of his poetic skill. He was merely one of many, one more hack without a patron, one more among the legions of the mediocre, one more tempted by the lifestyle of Covent Garden. What lay in Sam's favour, however, and what would be the making of his career, was that the more hours he spent around the tables of the Bedford and the Shakespear, the better known his name became and the better he came to know others.

It may have been Sam Derrick's constant presence at these locations that provided him with the few literary breaks he received. In 1755, after approximately eighteen years in the devising, and due to the generosity of his friends in Covent Garden, Sam was able to see his *Collection of Original Poems* in print. The list of subscribers prefacing it reads like a *Who's Who* of eighteenth-century Britain. As well as gaining support from his friends Garrick, Johnson and Foote, Sam had collected subscriptions from Charles Macklin, John Cleland, Tobias Smollett, Ned Shuter, George Anne Bellamy and Peg Woffington. This roll call also included the noble support of the earls of Chesterfield and Hillsborough, the Dean of Durham, Sir Francis Dashwood and several noted Covent Garden 'ladies'. Through his minor successes, Sam was able to cultivate further relationships with a number of those mentioned as subscribers, including Dr Johnson, who hired Sam to assist him with his *Life of Dryden*. Unlike some,

Johnson always claimed to have 'a kindness for Derrick' and was able to see beyond those characteristics that so irritated others. Tobias Smollett also championed Sam and provided him with employment writing for his *Critical Review*. Perhaps one of the most unlikely alliances to blossom from Sam's endeavours was his collaboration with the poet Christopher Smart. The partnership, formed over a mutual interest in the bottle, appeared doomed to failure from its outset. Both men brought out the worst of each other's excesses at the card tables and at the tailor's shop. Matters were complicated further by the unpredictability of Smart's mental disorder, which threw him into sudden fits of religious ranting. The coupling produced little in the way of memorable work besides inspiring the sniping of a punster:

> *Contradiction we find both Derrick and Smart,*
> *Which manifests neither can write from the heart;*
> *The latter, which readers may think somewhat odd,*
> *Tho' devoted to wine, sings the glories of God:*
> *The former lives sober, altho' no divine;*
> *Yet merrily carrols the praises of wine.*

At times, it may have seemed to Sam Derrick that he was the only person who truly believed in his merits as an author. Neither Johnson nor Smollett nor any other leading figure in England thought his writing exceptional. His critics saw in him something absurd, a dissipated, puffed-up Irishman with assumptions that outshone his abilities. The antiquary and friend of Johnson Dr William Oldys found Sam and his 'familiar conversation' offensive. 'Oldys thought him a flippant fellow and never spoke to Derrick when he was in the room,' and if addressed, the doctor gave him only 'short discouraging answers'. James Boswell was far more treacherous towards a man he once considered a friend. After successfully ingratiating himself into Johnson's circle, Boswell promptly discarded Sam and then began to ridicule him. Johnson would have none of it, but Boswell found a willing conspirator in the poet John Home, who, after a dinner at Eglinton Castle, mocked the lines of Derrick's 'Eblana', replacing them with something he believed more apt:

> *Unless my deeds protract my fame,*
> *And he who passes sadly sings,*
> *I knew him! Derrick was his name,*
> *On yonder tree his carcase swings!*

While Boswell and Home may have sniggered at their mean-spirited ditty, sadly, even a number of Sam's more sympathetic contemporaries would have been inclined to agree with the assessment of his future prospects. Unless he changed direction, Sam Derrick was heading towards the rapids.

# 7

# THE COMPLEXITIES OF LOVE

O F THE MANY BAD influences within Sam Derrick's circle, not every character leading him down the path of temptation was either a wanton woman or a bohemian reprobate. Sam's popularity and his willingness to gamble and whore made him a choice companion of high-born rakes, with whom, as an heir, he felt an affinity. But what he neglected to consider when sitting down for a game of cards or making purchases from his tailor was that the lives of his associates, men like the debauched Sir Francis Dashwood, were supported by a deep well of family funds. After the bottles were emptied, the games of whist lost, the cold suppers ordered and the harlots paid for, carousing with the eighteenth century's young bucks was a costly business.

During the period of some of his worst excesses both in expenditure and judgement, Sam had by his side a person considered to be 'one of the most dissipated men of his age': Robert Tracy. As the grandson of the esteemed judge, also called Robert Tracy, his origins lay not with the established Tracys of Stanway Park but with a more recently created limb, fairly new to the amphitheatre of conspicuous wealth.

Due to the untimely death of his father, his grandfather's fortune as well as his Gloucestershire estate of Coscombe (or 'Coxscombe', as his friends later dubbed it) were passed to him as a child. Tracy had grown up as an heir, denied nothing and, as the only surviving son, spoilt rotten. Blessed with all of life's advantages, 'Beau' Tracy, as he was known, was not only rich but strikingly handsome and unbearably self-obsessed. By his early twenties, he had emerged into society ready to sharpen his full set of degenerate traits on every temptation available.

By the time Sam made his acquaintance, Tracy's bulging purse had already gained a reputation for leaking money all across London. He had established a trail which ran from his set of chambers in the Middle Temple through the doors of Covent Garden's watering holes and brothels and into the boxes of both theatres. Needless to say, a devil-may-care approach to spending, combined with his devastatingly fine features, earned Beau many friends of both sexes. Actors and writers were especially keen acquaintances and Tracy, who one suspects concealed a desire to go upon the stage himself, whiled away much of his time at the Bedford Coffee House in the company of the thespian set. He counted among his closest friends the theatrical celebrity Arthur Murphy, who, as well as Sam Derrick, benefited from his generosity on a number of occasions.

As much as it would have suited moralists to paint such a wastrel as an empty-headed ninny, Tracy was nothing of the sort. Like his grandfather before him, he had been trained as a barrister and had received the classical education of a gentleman. Contemporaries thought him to be 'a man far above mediocrity with regard to sense and learning' and commented upon his sharp scholastic ability and 'very pretty library'. Tracy also subscribed to the tenets of self-improvement and made a point of never succumbing to idleness; even 'whilst he was under the hair-dresser's hands' he took the opportunity to 'peruse some favourite author', later remarking that 'whilst the outside of his head was embellishing, the interior region of it should be polishing; or else the powdered fop could be considered in no better predicament than a barber's block'. But in spite of feeding his mind on literature and the rhetorical quandaries of the law, Tracy still suffered from the unavoidable affliction of those who have everything. Beau was bored. There was nothing he couldn't buy, no one he couldn't charm and, with his father long in his grave, no one of any consequence to reprimand him for his reckless behaviour. In fact, as far as his mother's relations were concerned, if Beau managed to 'destroy himself by his vices before he had attained his thirtieth year', all the better. His maternal cousin and sole heir, Robert Pratt, was poised in the wings, eagerly awaiting the arrival of his fortune.

Of all Tracy's vices, none cost him as much as 'his weakness with regard to the fair sex'. Dominion over the objects of his attention was straightforward enough, as most women found it rather difficult to resist his appearance. 'He was,' as the author of the *Nocturnal Revels* writes, 'about 5 foot 9 inches high, of a Herculean form with a remarkably agreeable countenance'. Many gave their hearts as willingly as their bodies, a grievous mistake for any lady of pleasure, as Beau tended to weary quickly of his conquests and cast them off as readily as the unwanted items of his enormous wardrobe. As an inveterate philanderer, his ego dictated that he was entitled to the choicest 'pieces' as they arrived on the market, so by the time of his premature death in 1756 he could lay claim to having loved his way through the bedchambers of virtually every fashionable thais in London. For most of 1750 he had been seen dangling Covent Garden's current reigning lovely, Fanny Murray, off his arm, but by the early part of the following year ennui had begun to get the better of him. His lusts had already strayed in the direction of another impure *du jour*.

How long Beau had designs on Charlotte Hayes no one can say. While he was parading Fanny Murray through the boxes of Drury Lane and Vauxhall Gardens, Charlotte was being maintained in her elegant Pall Mall residence at the expense of her keeper, Edward Strode. Strode, like Tracy, was a restless lover, but without a fortune of his own to squander he had little reservation about raiding his wife's. As his divorce proceedings later state, in order to fund his exploits he beat Lucy Strode until she yielded her jewellery, which he then pawned to pay his debts and keep Charlotte in comfort. Just as Robert Tracy's interest in Fanny Murray had gone into decline, Strode had entered the market in search of another mistress. As it happened, whether by accident or intention, Strode ended up with Fanny and Tracy with Charlotte. For whatever havoc he had wrought upon ladies' affections in the course of his womanizing progress, Charlotte was about to reap the ultimate revenge. Fickle by nature, Tracy was not in the habit of falling in love with his meretricious companions, but Charlotte seemed to have worked her magic on his senses and, by employing her renowned charms, ensured that Tracy became enthralled to her. Charlotte would be the last woman he ever pursued, his great love and, consumed by his adoration of her, she would be a conspirator in his ruin.

Several years earlier, Beau had found himself in a similarly compromising situation. Alcohol had combined with urgent passion and induced him to make a quick 'Fleet marriage' to Susannah Owen, the daughter of a washerwoman. Before the union was annulled, the debacle had made Tracy the laughing stock of his more experienced rakish set. Any gentleman of his standing should have known better than to let one's emotions prevail over reason in such circumstances. Male commentators could never comprehend how a man far from being 'devoid of parts and understanding' could possibly allow himself to become the fool of a woman. After this, Tracy took pains to evade the snares of love, although he found himself incapable of avoiding those laid by Charlotte. He was young, and had more money than sense; Mrs Ward could not have invented a better keeper for her daughter. His susceptibility made him an ideal lover, one who spared no expense on a mistress he adored and was too absorbed in his own vanity to concern himself as to whether his affections were reciprocated. Although she may have flattered Tracy and done her best to convince him that her pulse raced at the sight of him, for Charlotte this was yet another straightforward mercenary arrangement. Not even Tracy's handsome face could sway her passions, and his famous allure left her cold.

Every lady of the town would have wished for a lover as pliable as Tracy. As Charlotte soon learned, a smitten keeper tipped a relationship's balance in his mistress's favour. With her basic needs addressed and no real ties of affection to her paramour, a small window might be opened through which she could manoeuvre just enough to follow her own desires. However, in order for the scheme to work, the business of intimacy could never be confused with that of love. Charlotte's duty did not lie in loving Tracy but in convincing him that her devotion to him was felt as deeply as his to her, a skill for which the most renowned courtesans were famed. Charlotte had tuned her repertoire of coquettish expressions finely enough over the years to lead any of her patrons in a merry dance. As might be expected, Beau followed along willingly and allowed his mistress absurdly extravagant liberties at the expense of his purse and his reputation. According to *Nocturnal Revels*, 'she had him so much at her command that she could fleece him at will'. Furthermore, Tracy openly permitted it 'without upbraiding her'.

Beau had fallen prey to the protocol of the day, which demanded that a modish gentleman keep his mistress fitted out in suitable luxury. In a vain, consumption-driven society, the appearance of a man's lover spoke volumes about his own status and wealth. The agreement to retain Charlotte in a state of high-keeping would have involved the provision of a number of requisite 'extras'. Like all thaises of the highest order, Charlotte jolted over the cobbled streets in her own 'chariot', driven by her own horses. Whether these were purchased for her by Tracy or by some other admirer, these extravagances required maintenance and upgrading where necessary, as did Charlotte's personal appearance. Her position as a 'nymph of the highest order' demanded a constant supply of new clothing: stylish gowns for the theatre, for strolling in the park or for entertaining her lovers at home. Each carefully planned ensemble was the sum total of numerous equally expensive parts. It was not simply her variety of frocks that displayed her radiance but her aprons, underskirts, decorated stomachers, ruffles, ribbons, gloves, stockings, shoes, buckles, capes, hats and muffs. This was before her jewels, snuff boxes and dainty fob watches, most of which she would have expected to receive as gifts, were taken into account. Anything else Charlotte required for her extravagant lodgings – the vast amount of food consumed at her table, the bottles of port and wine, the servants to manage her kitchen, a hairdresser to fix her coiffure, maids to light the fires in her grates, to squeeze her into her stays and sew her into her bodice – were paid with virtually unlimited credit drawn on her lover's name. Beau's mistress could match his profligacy, purchase for purchase. She took advantage of his generosity to run up enormous bills all over town for silks, tableware and haberdashery. After shopping to her heart's content, if the rare occasion arose when she found herself without immediate funds, Tracy again made himself her pliant poodle. According to the *Nocturnal Revels*, Charlotte was frequently seen 'calling upon Bob at his chambers in the Temple, dressed to the greatest advantage'. Her ploy was to:

> pretend to be in a violent hurry to go to the play or some other public diversion; when having by these artifices ... influenced his passions she would not stay a moment unless he would toss up with her for a guinea each time. To this he readily yielded, for the sake of her company. Whenever she won, she always took it; when she lost she did not pay. By these means, in about a

quarter of an hour, she would ease him of all his ready money then bounce away and laugh at him.

If Mrs Ward had warned her daughter against growing too complacent in the arms of an indulgent keeper, Charlotte had failed to listen. During the years of her youthful bloom, she chose to live only for herself and her pleasures. While she harboured no love for the man who had purchased her her freedom, her heart was not entirely devoid of affection for others. Although it may not have been advisable for a woman of Charlotte's occupation to fall in love, this did not mean she was not susceptible to it. The undiscerning heart was the curse of ladies of pleasure, as it was liable to fix its sights upon the wrong sort of man. If she was foolish enough to allow it to interfere with her judgement, she could find herself thrust into poverty or an abyss of heartbreak. Unfortunately for most prostitutes with ambition, their lives were peppered with unsuitable candidates who often proved too great a temptation to avoid. These were usually men who, not unlike them, had little claim to any fortune. As younger sons with no inheritance, struggling half-pay officers, clergymen with insubstantial livings and members of the precarious middle classes, wealth and its acquisition governed their lives. For many, their only hope of leading a comfortable existence was by making a good marriage to a sufficiently financed woman. They would never be adequate keepers for expensive Cyprians. The most enticing beauties, the Kitty Fishers and Fanny Murrays, were simply out of their league. This, however, was no deterrent to genuine affection taking root where it shouldn't. Impecuniousness did not make them any less

110

physically attractive or kind or humorous or irresistible to professional ladies who should have known better.

Charlotte Hayes certainly should have known better when chance threw the impoverished Sam Derrick in her path. The circumstances of their initial acquaintance are, and will probably remain, entirely unknown. It is likely that they would have recognized one another in passing for some time before their fates intersected. As frequenters of the piazza's attractions, they may have greeted one another below the signs of the Shakespear's Head and the Bedford Coffee House, exchanging pleasantries and flirtatious jests. Sam had arrived in London at the height of Charlotte's glory and undoubtedly he, like other gentlemen, would have watched her holding court in the theatre boxes. Together, he and Tracy would have admired her, dissecting her beauty and speculating on her accessibility. When the wheel of fortune spun in Beau's direction and enabled him to purchase her favours, Sam glowered with jealousy. Of all the celebrated beauties with whom he nurtured friendships, he could lay claim to none of them exclusively. While Lucy Cooper humoured, fed and occasionally honoured him with carnal privileges, he could never attain the title of being her sole keeper. Nor was this to be the case with any of the ambitious votaries of the piazza.

As a companion of Tracy, Sam would have been brought tantalizingly nearer to his friend's mistress as she accompanied him on his public outings. Charlotte's friendship and affection for Sam, who cut an otherwise unremarkable figure next to his dashing companion, would also have been given the occasion to ripen. How Sam could pose a challenge to wealthy lotharios like Robert Tracy for the attention of women like Charlotte

Hayes remained an endless source of mystery to male acquaintances. In spite of being described as 'of a diminutive size, with reddish hair and a vacant countenance', Sam's record for intrigue was impressive. 'It might be supposed, from the universal partiality of the ladies to him, that his person was so comely and elegant as to be irresistible,' wrote the author of a piece in *Town and Country* magazine: 'But this was far from the case.' Where the male eye saw only an unwashed, penurious and puffed-up peacock, women admired something entirely different, commenting that he was 'a pretty little gentleman, so sweet, so fine, so civil, and polite, that . . . he might pass for the Prince of Wales'. Sam's appeal was not so much his dress or his physical appearance but his charm. His gift of the gab was unrivalled, so enchanting that his manner and words could sway both men and women alike, or, as Tobias Smollett gushed: 'He talks so charmingly, both in verse and prose, that you would be delighted to hear him discourse.' It was those who had seen Sam at his worst, comrades with whom he shared many a bottle and had spied him sleeping on the streets, who could not conceive of the attraction. In the company of women and potential patrons, however, Sam could fashion himself into another person, one whose ambition it was to be recognized as 'a man of the most gallantry, the most wit, and the most politeness of any in Europe'. An actor by nature, he had no difficulty playing both roles.

Sam's gallant side was, without doubt, responsible for winning Tracy's mistress away from his friend's handsome company. How, precisely, their relationship evolved from polite friendship into a full-blown love affair will remain a story that both have taken to their graves. They have not so much as left a clue about the duration of their romance; we know only that it smouldered between the years of 1751 and 1756. For at least some of this period, Sam's love for Charlotte was fervent. Long after their ardour had burned out, she remained his one great passion, the woman whose tender memory haunted him even in the final hours of his life. In his eyes she would always be 'as desirable as ever', irrespective of age or the deterioration of her beauty. When they parted, it was as friends. Sam Derrick never said a word against her and always wished her well. Looking back, he remembered his 'old friend and Mistress Charlotte Hayes' not only with adoration but with a gripping sense of remorse.

But what did Charlotte feel for Sam? How deep her emotions ran and how sustainable they remained over the course of their romance is also unknown. Her behaviour, however, leaves some evidence as to the sentiments of her heart. At the outset of their relationship Charlotte was prepared to risk her income and possibly even Sam's life by entering into a liaison with him. Their very willingness to conduct an affair under a roof financed by Tracy's money demonstrates a certain hot-blooded heedlessness. Although duelling had officially been outlawed, it was not unusual for gentlemen to find themselves drawing pistols over lesser breaches of honour. Neither Sam nor Charlotte could possibly have known how Tracy might react to their betrayal. As it happened, it seemed her keeper was lenient. It seemed that the liberties Tracy permitted his mistress with regard to her expenditure also extended to her private passions. Love had once again immobilized Beau's powers of reason. Inevitably, when the gossip of Charlotte's escapades reached Tracy's ears he refused to acknowledge it. While the rakes and harlots of Covent Garden laughed at his expense, he simply shrugged in disbelief.

While Tracy looked the other way, Charlotte flaunted the rules of intrigue, tentatively at first and then with flagrant abandon. While it was commonly understood that women in her position always kept an eye on future possibilities, it was generally perceived as good form for those in high-keeping to exercise a hint of prudence when pursuing additional amours. With rented lodgings in Pall Mall and a household to maintain, it was best to have a list of ready candidates for the position of keeper, should she happen to find herself suddenly out of favour. Between visits from Tracy, Charlotte would have been able to pursue a relationship with a 'favourite' or 'favourites' of her own choosing. Her favourite in this case happened to be Tracy's friend Sam Derrick. Men who occupied this honoured position were made to follow a discreet protocol. Sam would have found himself in a similar position to William Hickey, the favourite of Cyprian Fanny Hartford. Although Fanny was in keeping by another man (whose name she refused to reveal), Hickey made himself a regular visitor when his rival was not around and on one occasion found himself having to slip out of bed and into the adjoining closet when Mr— popped in unexpectedly. Although keepers would have demanded fidelity from their mistresses, few would have trusted the object of their passion to maintain it, making jealousy and suspicion a common feature of such relationships. Provided a mistress's indiscretions were conducted behind closed doors and not in the public gaze, there might exist a possibility of forgiveness, but when she took her pleasures openly her behaviour became an act of gross defiance.

Observers of the convoluted triangle that had evolved between Charlotte, Sam and Robert Tracy blamed only Beau for the feckless management of his mistress. The situation took a spiteful turn when Charlotte began to publicly parade her romance with Sam. Her experiments with Tracy's tolerance had degenerated into a campaign of humiliation. As one gossipmonger wrote: 'When she had an inclination to enjoy the company of her favourite man, she would take him to the Shakespeare or the Rose, and regale him at the Beau's expense in the most sumptuous manner.' To add insult to injury, she would then present Tracy with an exorbitant bill. On more than a few occasions, after 'having very simply given her credit at those houses', Tracy was accosted by taverners for sums of thirty or forty pounds, 'when he thought there might be a score of four or five'. What precipitated Charlotte's attack on her keeper's reputation can only be imagined. Her behaviour speaks of resentment or revenge. Although the details of their sexual arrangements are never revealed, even women of Charlotte's elevated standing could find themselves the recipients of violent beatings and degrading sexual practices. Charlotte's fashionable contemporary Ann Bell was a victim of her wealthy lover's abuse. After being anally raped, she was repeatedly slashed with a penknife and had her hands broken before being dumped in one of Covent Garden's most up-scale bagnios. She would not have been the first, nor was she to be the last, who suffered such treatment at the hands of a keeper. While it is possible that some degree of foul play may have been responsible for encouraging Sam's participation in

Charlotte's scheme, it is equally probable that jealousy alone drove him to it.

Upon entering into a romance with Charlotte, Sam would have been forced to recognize that theirs could never be an exclusive relationship. Not only was Charlotte bound by circumstance to share her body with his friend Robert Tracy, but she had to cultivate the interest of other possible keepers in the event that Beau should tire of her. Sam's position would not have been threatened so much by the existence of these peripheral admirers but rather by the unavoidable reality that Tracy owned Charlotte. With the ability to buy her security and affection, Beau would always possess the upper hand. In spite of Sam's faith in the receipt of his inheritance, his wealth would never match that of his friend, nor of Charlotte's other admirers. This was a contest Sam could never win. He could only take a back seat in Charlotte's life, and be her protector. According to the *Nocturnal Revels*, Sam's presence in his mistress's house was felt by all who visited there. Sam Derrick was quite regularly to be found lurking somewhere under her roof or 'enjoying the run of Charlotte's kitchen'. When there was no danger of Tracy appearing to demand her company, Sam bedded down with Charlotte, living partially as her lover and partially as her green-eyed lodger.

Whatever Sam offered Charlotte in terms of genuine affection, she repaid in comfort and kindness. She shared what she could, providing him with companionship, support and sustenance, 'when he had not shoes for his feet'. Aside from his persistent hope that his inheritance would one day arrive and alter his needy circumstances, it is unlikely that either of them harboured any illusions concerning the future of their affair. Although it was not an ideal arrangement, neither she nor Sam was in a position to enjoy any other alternative. He could never hope to support her in the luxury she required, while she, as a first-rate lady of pleasure, would never condescend to exchange her existence for one of impoverished misery simply to follow the ephemeral joys of love. It is easy to picture the destitute Sam lying in his lover's arms, fraught with anguish and unworthiness at his inability to buy them a suitable future. Charlotte, too, must have succumbed to a certain degree of despondency – although, with less patience and trust in the promises of men, she eventually would have tired of Sam's empty assurances. Many years later, he was still unable to forget what he felt he owed her.

Forced to adore his mistress from the sidelines, it was not long before hostility sprang from Sam's feelings of impotence and envy. As a poet, his natural inclination was to turn to the might of his pen rather than the force of his sword. Either way, his action was hasty and ill considered. In the end, its repercussions would be detrimental to Charlotte's well-being.

In 1755, when relations between Beau and his mistress were beginning to wane, Sam could conceal his emotions no longer. 'A Defence of Female Inconstancy', dedicated to his friend Robert Tracy 'of Coxscomb, in Gloucestershire', appeared in print. Derrick had thrown down the gauntlet. If Tracy had ignored the rumours of his friend's treachery with his mistress in the past, now he had no cause to doubt them. The epistle not only carried a confirmation of Charlotte's irregularities but offered a justification for them. Women were inconstant by nature, Sam explained, and were prone to wandering affections. He reasoned:

*Why to one man, should woman be confin'd?*
*Why not unfetter'd, like his freeborn mind?*
*Is it not better she should the numbers bless?*
*All smell the rose – but are its sweets the less?*

He then ripped the seams out of Tracy, the celebrated paragon of perfection:

*Besides, restriction palls the jaded taste;*
*And in one man few virtues can be trac'd;*
*If all should in one prodigy unite,*
*Could such a monster give the least delight?*

No, Sam concluded. Tracy's handsome physique, his charm, his mind and his money were not sufficient to maintain his mistress's affection. Women know what is in their best interest, and 'if worthier objects arise', then 'You can not blame them, to withdraw the prize.' In spite of owning Charlotte, Beau needed to recognize that his mistress defied her own nature if she did not look elsewhere for someone she truly desired. That someone, of course, was Sam. Finally, he implores his friend to loosen his grip and let Charlotte follow her heart, concluding:

*Henceforth, uncensur'd, then, let woman range,*
*And due reflection be a friend to change.*

How Tracy reacted to Derrick's proclamation is, frustratingly, unrecorded. Certainly, the code of gentlemanly honour would have demanded the satisfaction of a duel at such a public insult. As Sam is known to have been involved in at least two other exchanges of fire, it is not improbable that this incident may have precipitated a third. Could this have been the culmination of the unfortunate triangle? If so, then all three managed to come through it alive, but it is unlikely that Tracy and Derrick found ample time to repair their injured friendship. A sudden turn of events shortly after the poem's publication was about to alter their lives.

By 1755, Beau's finances were in an appalling state. Years of unbridled expenditure and gambling, exacerbated by Charlotte's efforts at the pump, had come near to draining his resources. Even to the casual observer it had become apparent that 'by pursuing such a line of conduct, Tracy might in time have squandered away the most ample fortune in England'. Charlotte, too, had not failed to scent trouble in her keeper's circumstances, but unfortunately, finding a candidate as generous and as easily manipulated as Beau was proving difficult. She had been so distracted by her quest to locate a replacement keeper that she was taken entirely by surprise when, without warning, Robert Tracy died.

The ailment that gripped Tracy, a man not yet thirty, is unknown. His will was drawn up in haste on 14 May 1756, only a few days before he expired. Beau, who until then had lived only for his own pleasure, left a wake of debt behind him. The *Revels* reports that 'his affairs were much disordered', and his will records that he was even in arrears to his manservant, William Morgan, for 'about one hundred pounds'. Knowing that his creditors would be baying outside the door of his chambers, he entrusted a fellow barrister with the task of selling 'all the said goods, furniture, books, watches, rings' to pay off what was owing. As was traditional, a small sum was then set aside for the purchase of mourning rings, tokens of remembrance worn by those closest to the deceased. Tracy specifically left five pounds 'to my laundress Charlotte Ward' for this purpose.

In death, Beau had exacted his much-belated revenge. By the conventions of Charlotte's profession, such a bequest was nothing short of an insult. The gift of a mourning ring would have been a suitable gesture only had it been accompanied by a pension to remunerate Charlotte for her devotion. It was through such bequests and pensions that a courtesan might gather an ample living for herself, so that in old age her security could be assured. Tracy, however, was not about to reward his mistress in death for her offensive behaviour while he lived. He owed her nothing she hadn't already taken.

Beau's departing deed devastated Charlotte, not because she loved him, but because through his calculated reprisal he had set into motion a chain of events that would ruin her. Furious at his betrayal, Charlotte would one day boast to his friends that she had never loved Tracy, or 'any man in her life'. After more than ten years on the town, and as seasoned as she was, her former keeper's actions were entirely foreseen. Charlotte had used his name to secure goods on credit from a multitude of shopkeepers and merchants; now she was unable to pay her bills. Everything she had won by her service to Tracy – all her plate and jewellery, the fine furniture and silk gowns – had to be pawned. Even then she was not able to make up the shortfall. She could no longer maintain either her carriage or her horses, she dismissed her servants, gave up her expensive lodgings and sought refuge with her mother. Unable to make good on the remainder of her debts, it was only a matter of time before the bailiff traced her whereabouts to Mrs Ward's front door. Then, as the winter set in, they came for her. As she languished in the spunging house, a kind of halfway holding pen between freedom and the extreme discomforts of debtors' prison, friends and family took what steps they could to have her exonerated from the charges. Unfortunately, these measures failed, and by early 1757 she was in the Fleet.

Sam was more disconsolate than ever. Having no funds with which to rescue his mistress, he employed the only gift of use to him in such situations: his infamous charm. According to *Town and Country*, he had done what he could to spare Charlotte from her creditors in the period prior to her arrest. He made appeals to those whom she owed the most money, pleading her case in person, begging them not to foreclose on her debts. Sadly, his persuasive words were not able to move their hearts. Once these methods had failed and Derrick could do no more, he fell back on the tradition of collecting a subscription for the incarcerated. This approach had worked for the imprisoned Lucy Cooper, who had had funds raised on her behalf when she 'was almost naked and starving, without a penny in her pocket to purchase food, raiment or a coal to warm herself'. The thought of Charlotte enduring similar misfortunes would have plagued Sam. He would have blamed himself at least in part for her troubles: had poverty not bound his hands so tightly, the woman he loved would not have had to suffer.

Over the years, Sam had come to see Tracy only as an obstacle to his happiness; now it seemed that Tracy had been

the lynch pin in Sam's complicated relationship with Charlotte. Tracy's much-desired elimination had proven nothing
short of disastrous. At this juncture, Sam was unable to provide
Charlotte with anything, neither stability nor even reassur-
ance. In the sinkhole of the Fleet, Sam's only offerings – his
wit, his charm and his gallantry – were useless to her. In her
hour of desperate need, she required now, more than ever,
the one luxury Sam was never capable of giving her: Robert
Tracy's money.

# 8

# INSPIRATION

IF CHARLOTTE HAYES HAD left an impression upon Sam Derrick's heart, there was another woman who had left one upon his spleen. Even before his poetic outburst of 1755, Sam was coming to recognize that his relationship with Tracy's mistress was untenable. Irrespective of his passion for her, Sam was not the type of man who would confine his interests to one woman alone. By the end of 1755, the complexities of his situation had become emotionally exhausting enough to prompt him to begin solacing himself elsewhere.

Around this time, Sam had made the acquaintance of a young Covent Garden prostitute. Like so many others, Jane Hemet claimed that she had been abandoned and left destitute in London by her husband, a naval captain. She had been no more than sixteen when she had made the foolish match and now, alone and penniless, she had no other choice than to 'see company' in order to survive. It was a likely story and one that Sam had heard many times before. Whatever she called herself in those early days, whether Jane Hemet, Jane Stott, or some other pseudonym, in later years it would be the name Jane Lessingham that identified her as one of

123

London's better-loved comic actresses. It is unfortunate that those men who recorded the effects of Jane Lessingham's life upon her era seem to have nothing pleasant to say. According to John Taylor's *Records of My Life*, Jane's nature had been corrupted by her prettiness. In addition to entertaining 'as many lovers as Anacreon boasts of mistresses', Jane was unappreciative, amoral and possessed 'no restraint of delicacy'. Taylor denounced her as a 'common whore through and through', with few redeeming qualities. Other contemporaries of Mrs Lessingham agreed with this assessment and declared her to be 'a plump lascivious harlot' and 'a tasteless milksop'. Sam Derrick, however, probably for these very reasons, found her enchanting.

In the future, and not without a good deal of bile, Sam would remember Jane as she was when he first met her, a desperate and impoverished teenager in urgent need of a friend. In exchange for protection, food and kindness, Jane willingly provided her services to him. Taylor's memoirs seem to suggest that before she met Sam, Jane had not considered a career on the stage, but that he, with his theatrical eye, saw in her the makings of an excellent performer. He reasoned that if he personally 'was not calculated to succeed' upon the stage, then certainly he was capable of training someone to do it for him. Only three years earlier, Sam, in his capacity as observer and critic of dramatic technique, had compiled an assessment of contemporary players and drama in his work *The Present State of the Stage in Great Britain and Ireland*. Jane was to be his first disciple, the first beneficiary of his knowledge, and so began a concerted campaign to make her stageworthy. With pretty Jane staring at him adoringly, following his every direction, Sam's ego stood to benefit enormously. Love was bound to blossom, and Sam, always prone to thinking with his heart rather than his head, determined rather unwisely that the two should take up lodgings together.

Loving and coaching Jane filled Sam Derrick with a sense of renewal. As a result, the years 1755–6 proved to be a fairly prolific period in his literary career. Not only did he finally manage to see his *Collection of Original Poems* in print, but also his translation of *The Third Satire of Juvenal* and his *Memoirs of the Shakespear's Head*. Although Derrick was still unable to 'afford an expensive habitation', his recent publications enabled him to rent a set of rooms 'on a floor two pairs of stairs high in Shoe Lane, Holborn'. A neighbourhood composed largely of thieves and prostitutes, Shoe Lane was not exactly a salubrious address in the 1750s, although in the first few months it suited the needs of the couple well enough, providing them with a rehearsal space and a home. Jane's devotion to Sam and her gratitude for his faith in her abilities showed no sign of abating. At the height of their romance she doted on her lover, proclaiming 'she had so great a partiality for him and his talents, that nothing could have ever weaned her from him'. Jane also began referring to herself as Mrs Derrick, a name which Sam used to introduce her to his friends. But his taking up with an uncouth fallen woman and calling her his wife without actually marrying her did not sit well with many whom he was keen to impress. To further complicate matters, it is possible that Jane also bore Sam a daughter during this period. It was at this point that his otherwise hospitable friends, the Taylor family, broke off relations with him. To those of the comfortable middle class, from which Sam also came, this sort of behaviour rendered him unfit to be received by respectable company. Where periods of living on the street made him pathetic, living with 'his whore', begetting an illegitimate child by her and then lying about it to his close associates made him dishonourable. According to some, Sam's better judgement had been suffering at the hands of Covent Garden's sharpers and dissolutes for too long. What may have seemed harmless to his set of young rakes, thespian friends and meretricious companions with their multiple lovers was not acceptable to the more refined element of society.

Towards the end of his life, after he had achieved a degree of respectability, Sam Derrick inevitably found himself in a position to lament a number of the actions of his impetuous youth. His love of Jane Lessingham was one of them. Jane, even more than Charlotte Hayes, was responsible for disordering Sam's state of mind most enduringly. By 1756, he had spent a year educating his prodigy and boasting of her talents to all who would listen; now she was ready to be revealed. Shortly before the start of the 1756–7 season, John Rich, the manager of the Covent Garden Theatre, was looking for a new face to take on the role of Desdemona in a production of *Othello*. After some consideration, he approached Jane. In the short period of time between Rich's engagement of her and her debut in November of that year, the good fortune of her position began to turn her head. Overwhelmed by the adoration she was now receiving from Rich and other members of the theatrical community, she became a different person. Now that she was to be a luminary of the stage, she no longer required anyone to coach her or make her introductions. Even those indifferent to her when she was escorted through the theatres and taverns by Sam noticed a change in her behaviour. With her newly acquired confidence, Jane sought to shine at the centre of every social gathering, and even resorted to 'assuming men's attire and frequenting the coffee houses' in order to cause a stir. It was only a matter of time before her little garret on Shoe Lane and the poor poet who lived there no longer suited her life.

Before the curtain rose on her first performance, Jane ran off with another man. He had more money than the penurious Sam Derrick and was able to place her in high-keeping. To add insult to injury, she had no qualms about shedding the surname of her devoted tutor in order to make a debut under her lawful title: Mrs Stott. It was a gesture of mean ingratitude, and Sam smarted about it for years to come. It was also rather ill timed and misjudged. No sooner had Mrs Stott appeared on the London stage than a gentleman calling himself Captain John Stott appeared in town after a three-year absence. In spite of their estrangement, the captain was mortified to learn of his wife's public indiscretions during his period at sea and filed for divorce. By this time, however, Jane had already moved her affections elsewhere and was enjoying the attention she received as the mistress of her husband's commanding officer, Admiral Boscawen.

In the following years, Jane progressed through as many keepers as she had starring roles. Throughout the 1760s and '70s, she reinvented herself as a comedic actress. As her fame continued to rise, so did her demands on the men in her life. Although she bore two children by her admiral, Jane's allegiances shifted to that of the new manager of the Covent Garden Theatre, Thomas Harris. With Thomas Harris accompanying her about town, the two became the eighteenth-century equivalent of a celebrity couple. Together they reigned as the 'King and Queen of Clubs', their stories appearing in scandal sheets and newspapers, their names on the lips of all Covent Garden. But Harris had no sooner bought her a house in fashionable Mayfair than Jane was off again, this time with Justice William Addington, who was richer still than the stage manager. In a short time, Addington, too, was cursing her after he gave her a house in Hampstead and was then promptly replaced by a strapping young actor.

In the eyes of many an injured party, Jane Lessingham was poison. Justice Addington vowed never again to speak her name, while Thomas Harris and Sam Derrick passed their evenings discussing her demerits over cards and cold suppers. Unfortunately, Sam's name had been the first on her list of lovers and not one of the later ones. Had he known what havoc she was liable to wreak in his life, he might never have stopped to flirt with her on the evening when they first met. Had he never seen a spark of talent in her or a flicker of love cross her face, he would have lived his life a richer, if not a more respectable, man. Had he never set up home with such a woman, had he never attempted to fool his friends as to their marital state, had he not insisted in living in sin and leading his life in the depravity of Covent Garden, he would never have had to author *Harris's List*.

Sam's last gesture before he departed from the shores of Ireland in 1751 was to successfully bamboozle Mrs Creagh into believing that he was about to establish himself in

London as a linen draper. What had begun as a small falsehood gathered mass like a ball of yarn. Sam had been spinning lies for five years, penning letters filled with deceptions and requests for advances on his inheritance. His aunt may have been an old woman several hundred miles away, but even from that great distance she could scent a rat. Mrs Creagh had heard frustratingly little of her nephew's life and it is likely that she suspected he was withholding information from her. She may have heard rumours or tittle-tattle, filtered across the water by way of letters and gossipmongers, that her nephew was living in sin, that he was sleeping under bulks, or existing hand to mouth from gaming table to pawn shop. Whatever the situation, her suspicions had been raised.

A heavily edited letter in the National Art Library, preserved just enough to be legible today, attests to the event that changed Sam Derrick's life. In it, an unknown Irish correspondent reveals to Sam that his aunt had 'sent one of her emissaries' to London with a specific mission in mind. 'Apprais'd of your conduct,' the writer continues, 'she [then] set her spies on your behaviour.' It seems that one day a stranger had come to call upon Sam and Jane at their lodgings in Shoe Lane. Sam had been out, but 'Mrs Derrick' invited the visitor inside. The visitor sat with her for some time, making polite inquiries about their lives and about Jane's 'husband'. With further prompting and some investigation, the spy was able to confirm what might have been suspected all along: that the two were unmarried, perhaps even raising an illegitimate child. Furthermore, there was no evidence that Sam was earning his living by the linen trade. The spy saw only indications of a depraved existence, one that had been hidden from Mrs Creagh for years. Wasting no time, the spy reported back, 'in consequence of which,' the letter continues, 'she has made a will and disinherited you'.

Condemnation was heaped upon Sam from friends and family in Dublin. 'I would be sorry rightly to censure or condemn anyone, much more a man for whom I had a regard. Now I never imagined that you wanted sense and prudence to direct your conduct (Religion I leave out of the question) and to embarrass yourself with such vicious and ruinous connexions is a piece of frenzy,' one of his correspondents rails. But by the time Sam had received this news the damage had already been done. The inheritance he had lived for and lived on, on which he had secured credit and good faith, had been whisked out of his hands. The entire pattern by which he had lived his life until that day would have to be changed: his anticipated saviour would now never arrive. This was a blow to end all blows. He could not expect the few handouts he had received from Mrs Creagh's purse any longer and, once those friends from whom he had borrowed caught wind of this change of fortune, he would be ruined. Sam was simply too far in debt to pay anyone. Towards the end of 1756, as the storm clouds were mounting, Sam looked to Jane and her future prospects for hope, and what did Jane, dear 'Mrs Derrick', the source of much of his woes, do? She left him.

In later years, when the white hat of the Master of Ceremonies at Bath sat comfortably on his head, when Sam Derrick had plenty of coal for his fire and food on his table, he must have looked back on the events of 1756–7 and shuddered. It was to be his *annus horribilis*, one of his darkest periods. The loss of his inheritance and his unrepentant betrayal by Mrs Lessingham, two calamities in rapid succession, would have exacted a toll on his normally resilient spirit. To exacerbate matters, early 1757 found him more destitute than ever. He had been counting on receiving some recompense for Jane's tutoring through whatever earnings she would be bringing home. Without her financial assistance, he was no longer able to afford the poor attic lodgings they had rented together and turned once again to the streets. Additionally, his creditors were closing in. With his usual abandon, Sam had made a number of improvements to his wardrobe during his brief period of financial security. Towards the end of his relationship with Jane, an angry unpaid tailor had already appeared at their door and had succeeded in having him arrested for debt before 'Mrs Derrick' bailed him out.

Sam was in dire straits when he encountered Tobias Smollett at the Forrest Coffee House in Charing Cross. The author of *Nocturnal Revels* records that, at the time, 'he had neither shoes nor stockings that were wearable'. Painfully aware of the deficiencies of his dress, Sam made numerous trips to 'the Cloacinian Temple' (or water closet) in the attempt to adjust his stockings, 'which wickedly displayed every few minutes such conspicuous holes ... as put [him] out of countenance'. 'Why Derrick,' asked Smollett, 'you are certainly devilishly plagued with a looseness or else you would not repair so often to the cabinet?' Sam replied pitifully, 'Egad, Doctor, the looseness is in my heels as you may plainly perceive.'

Smollett must have sensed that Sam's circumstances were far worse than he had revealed and not only took him home to Chelsea, where 'he gave him a good dinner', but allowed Sam to reside with him for the next several months. Smollett, who was known for coming to the aid of starving hacks with offers of work, engaged Sam to write for his *Critical Review* and may also have provided him with some employment working on his *Complete History of England*. By pulling Derrick off the streets and providing him with a temporary refuge from his hounding creditors, the author had granted Sam an immeasurable favour. For a brief spell, he was able to catch his breath and add a few pennies to his purse before the bailiffs caught his scent.

In the eighteenth century, there was no quibbling about debt. If a person found themselves unable to pay their bills, they went to prison. It was as straightforward as that. Where they were kept, how they were kept and who saw that they remained there, on the other hand, was a complicated affair. On the whole, debt collection was a lucrative business run by an assortment of bounty-hunting bailiffs hired by creditors to pursue and retrieve as much of the outstanding sums as possible. The chase, however, could continue for quite some time; Derrick's relocation to Chelsea was all part of the game of wits. The bailiffs wasted several months turning over the back alleys of Covent Garden and Fleet Street until someone pointed them in the direction of Smollett's home. When eventually they did alight upon him, Sam was escorted to a 'spunging house'. Here the debtor was kept until the final few pennies were exacted from their possession. As spunging houses were privately operated enterprises run from a bailiff's home, a bailiff could do what he pleased in order to compel the prisoner to cough up the debt. While this might include physical coercion, it more frequently entailed allowing a prisoner to work outside the confines of the spunging house in order to earn some money. Ironically, in spite of having no funds, a bailiff's captive was charged for their accommodation, so whatever the debtor managed to earn through honest work generally never got beyond the spunging house's coffers. Any sum left over tended to be swallowed up in legal fees. Once the bailiff tired of this vicious circle and the last few coins were emptied from the debtor's pocket, he or she was handed over to the authorities, who in turn sent them to the Fleet or the Marshalsea.

In spite of these challenging circumstances, it was not wholly impossible for a prisoner in a spunging house to make good on their debts, although this would have required exceptional luck, wealthy friends or a healthy dose of ingenuity. Sam Derrick had ingenuity on his side. In the confines of Bailiff Ferguson's spunging house he was left to simmer in his own thoughts and contemplate a possible remedy. His mood would have been black indeed. It must have seemed that he had tried his hand at everything and failed. As an actor, he was abysmal. No one was interested in the plays he had written. He had not received the reception he had anticipated as a poet. He had no produced no major literary works to speak of. He had no income, no home, no mistress and no inheritance. The only thing he did have was friends in Covent Garden.

By 1757, there were virtually no faces in the piazza that Sam Derrick didn't recognize. He knew every actor, every bully, buck and bunter. Years of wearing down the benches at the Shakespear, the Bedford Coffee House, the Rose and the Piazza Coffee House meant that he was never short of a drink or of somebody with whom to converse. As an inveterate subscription-hunter, he excelled at ingratiating himself and making introductions. James Boswell was to learn that no one knew better than Sam Derrick the needs of the wealthy wastrel and the wandering wanton and what both were likely to be seeking on a night's excursion. He had personally inaugurated Boswell into the 'sportive' delights of the capital. Johnson's biographer was duly impressed and, later, with hindsight, thoroughly disgusted at the breadth of his associate's knowledge. He chose his epithets carefully when referring to his former host, calling him 'a little blackguard pimping dog'. It was a term that acknowledged, much to Sam's discomfort, the fine line that existed between himself and those seasoned professionals of the piazza.

Rather than turning his hand to professional pimping, a vocation that Sam Derrick would have deemed far beneath his calling, he deployed his knowledge of local characters in another direction. In 1751 a small, witty volume called *The Memoirs of the Bedford Coffee House*, written by someone who referred to himself simply as 'A. Genius', appeared in print. Whoever A. Genius was, he was a man who had passed a good deal of time taking in the melodrama of Covent Garden's most renowned drinking spot. Whatever the author perceived around him – actors drawing blood in drunken brawls, jilted mistresses bursting into tears and practical jokes being played on the unsuspecting – he gathered together in a collection of amusing tableaux. In order to protect vulnerable reputations, the names featured on the *Memoirs*' pages were disguised, but any of the regulars to the Garden would have easily recognized the antics and true identities of characters like Errato the poet and Mopsy the inveterate womanizer. Packed with tittle-tattle and retellings of drunken revels, the stories would have raised a storm of hilarity among those who were able to identify their exploits in print. The book proved amusing enough to warrant a second edition, shortly before the appearance of another work, intended as its companion piece, *The Memoirs of the Shakespear's Head*.

It is quite likely that Sam Derrick, who was responsible for the creation of *The Memoirs of the Shakespear's Head*, was also the enigmatic A. Genius. The vantage point he enjoyed as a permanent fixture in both establishments would have provided him with ample opportunity to document the whirl of activity. Sam may have viewed himself primarily as a poet but in many respects his true flair lay in journalism. Like the hack writer Ned Ward a generation earlier, he was especially accomplished at describing the eccentric mix of characters that inhabited his patch of London. Writing the *Memoirs of the Shakespear's Head* would be an easy feat for someone so accustomed to soaking in the scenery of his favourite tavern. Sam certainly wouldn't have had to travel far for inspiration. Comfortably ensconced by the fire, he would have set his eyes and ears to the task of information-gathering.

Not unlike the *Memoirs of the Bedford Coffee House*, the *Memoirs of the Shakespear's Head* recounts tales of its patrons' amorous conquests and general bad behaviour. On the whole, the characters that colour its narrative are of the same basic stock, except for one, whose presence on an average evening might have otherwise gone unmentioned. 'Jack, a waiter . . . who presides over the Venereal Pleasures of this Dome' features prominently in Derrick's account of the Shakespear. As

Sam sat in his corner during the early months of 1755 and observed Harris conduct the movements of Packington Tomkins's establishment with the ease of a master of ceremonies, the pimp's organizational skills left a strong impression on him. Whether or not Jack Harris was aware of it, Sam Derrick had been studying the pimp's science intently, listening in on transactions as they occurred in private booths or around the tavern hearth. The result, which appears in *The Memoirs of the Shakespear's Head*, reads like a tour through 'good pimping practice'. The reader follows Harris as he moves from table to table, assisting women into the company of men, enrolling recruits on to his list, promising variety and smoothing ruffled feathers. Derrick records the discussion surrounding the 're-branding' of one of Jack's listees and his decision to bestow her with a more alluring appellation. He also shares with his readers the intricacies involved in palming off one man's discarded mistress on to a waiting patron, much to the satisfaction of all parties concerned. Far from casting an unwelcome light on Harris's secrets, much of the account pokes fun at the punters while demonstrating a quiet reverence for the pimp's abilities.

Although Jack Harris and Sam Derrick would have maintained at least a passing acquaintance in the years before 1755, it is quite probable that the idea to publish Harris's compendium of names had its genesis at about the time Derrick was documenting the happenings at the Shakespear's Head. Whose idea precisely it was to lay the work in print will never be known. Either the entrepreneurial Harris planted the seed in the author's mind, or Sam, after espying the ordered entries of the pimp's personal catalogue, became fascinated by its contents. From behind the bars of the spunging house, the pimp's list, this rambling notebook, the product of Harris's hand, with its many pages of detailed descriptions, came to occupy Sam's thoughts. In his mind, it was a ledger that glittered with gold. Although he would never renounce his calling or social aspirations to lead the life of a professional panderer, the temptation to cash in on the knowledge he possessed, the information he shared with Harris, was too great in his time of need to be ignored. In taking such a step, Sam was entering Jack Harris's playing field and, in doing so, he would become everything of which Boswell accused him.

Even if Harris's handwritten list had been unavailable for consultation, Sam could have easily scribbled out his own prototype drawn from his extensive experience with Covent Garden's ladies of pleasure. It would have been as simple as jotting down the names and descriptions of his neighbours, his drinking companions, his friends and his lovers. While Harris's personal inventory would have formed the inspiration for the work, it was Sam's plan to make the published version of the pimp's list more literary. Here was an opportunity to flex his poetic muscle. He would add embellishment to what was, in its original form, not much more than a 'little black book' of names, addresses and brief descriptions. A pimp's list on its own would not necessarily have made titillating reading, but with the trained mind of a hack, he would be able to spin straw into gold.

His task would be to create a truthful yet colourful and witty romp of a work, not unlike the *Memoirs* of both the Shakespear's Head and the Bedford Coffee House, a publication that delighted in chronicling the area's characters and their scandals. *Harris's List*, as reworked by Sam Derrick, would have appealed to the same readers as his tavern and coffee-house memoirs, vain men hoping to see some mention of their exploits or those of their mistresses and friends in print. Like the *Memoirs*, Derrick's *Harris's List* is filled with snippets of local knowledge, references to waiters, to the area's watering holes and to incidents that had unfolded on particular evenings. But unlike his earlier productions, it offered more than a one-off laugh and the gratification of seeing a friend's name emblazoned in ink. Its primary function was always to serve as a practical catalogue to the sexual goods on offer in Covent Garden. The beauty of the scheme was that now, rather than relying solely on a pimp to secure the wares, the customer could cut out the middleman and go straight to the supplier. Such a plan on its own, devised by an outsider to the trade, was bound to have incurred the wrath of the area's waiters, had not Jack Harris, the undisputed 'Pimp General of all England', put his name to the endeavour. As for Sam, he was more than pleased for the pimp to receive top billing. Regardless of how lucrative or popular the publication might prove to be, this was one literary undertaking with which he would not wish to be publicly associated. Although he was content to receive dividends from his ghost-written work, once he moved into a higher social sphere he would spend the final years of his life attempting to outrun its shadow.

While the decision to use Harris's name as a kind of brand formed part of the agreement negotiated between the pimp and the poet, it is impossible to know exactly what type of bargain was struck between them or how the profits from the published list were divided. Certainly, Harris would have been promised his share, either by Derrick or by his publisher-bookseller, the mysterious H. Ranger. It is probable that this amounted to a one-off payment, as no one, and especially not Derrick, could have possibly predicted a thirty-eight-year print run for what looked on the surface to be yet another piece of Grub Street dross. Either way, Harris would not have done badly out of the arrangement. Regardless of how well the published version of his list performed in the public domain, his longstanding pimping practices remained the same. Harris would have continued to charge his women a fee to have their names inscribed on his personal handwritten list, and all the usual agreements concerning percentages and dues would have remained. However, greater publicity spelled increased custom for the listed ladies, while a wider clientele equalled a better return for the procurer as well as the prostitute. In financial terms, both stood to benefit. Of the two groups, those who gained the most were the ladies who worked independently of either a bawd or a pimp. Favourable exposure on the *List* would broaden the range of patrons requesting a woman by name, a situation which might then allow the much-desired thais some discretion in her choice of bedfellow.

The true genius of Sam Derrick's plan was that, for his version of the *Harris's List* to prove useful to anyone, it had to remain current. If it were to take the form of an annual register, as he may have originally proposed, it would require constant updating, thereby providing him with a reliable stream of work. To be effective, it would have to keep in step with the frequent movements of the working girls of the Garden. The nature of the sex trade was one which lent itself to perpetual change and variety: a harlot who was deemed 'sound in wind and limb' one night could the next week find herself 'down in a sal'. Additionally, any procurer or punter knew that women bounced in and out of exclusive keeping on a frequent basis and that London-bound wagons replenished the capital's stock of recruits almost daily. Recording every new addition to the legions of Venus, or confirming the location of an elusive veteran, was a difficult task to master at the best of times. For this reason, Sam Derrick's version of the panderer's 'little black book' would never offer any real challenge to the supremacy of what remained in Harris's pocket; the pimps who kept up-to-date inventories of their wares would always maintain the upper hand. But in order for the printed *Harris's List* to offer some credibility, it would have to be an ongoing project, requiring Derrick, as the editor, to revise and research names, addresses and stories on a regular basis.

Although he may have borrowed a few choice bits of information from Harris's compilation, by and large, the names listed in his publication were collected from a variety of sources. The 1761 version, the earliest extant edition, makes it clear that the ladies featured were not only those with whom he had a personal acquaintance but '. . . the personages whose intrigues were most universally spoken of, and whose celebrated names were in almost everybody's mouth'. Unlike later issues of *Harris's List*, published long after Sam Derrick was in his grave, the early versions are earnest in their desire to create a truthful picture of the women within.

Derrick strenuously insists that 'the present work cannot be looked upon in light of romance or novel, merely to draw the attention of the idly curious ... for we can assert that the facts herein contained have been most authentically proved to us', and reminds the reader that his circumspect quest for the truth 'has cost no small trouble and enquiry'.

While mentally matching faces with their associated scandals and sexual skills may have helped to pass the time inside the spunging house, repeating the task later when he was at liberty would become an altogether different venture. For support in his enterprise, Sam deferred to the input of his Covent Garden comrades and turned the act of compiling *Harris's List* into a community undertaking. He appealed to the eyes and ears of the Garden's patrons as well as to the ladies themselves for his information, encouraging them to '... send us the anecdotes of their private engagements and places of abode'. In this manner he (or 'we', as Derrick writes from behind the mask of Jack Harris) could be everywhere, seeing everything and keeping himself fully abreast of what was happening in the area. Like the editor of *Playboy* magazine's letters page, Sam also sought his readers' stories to flesh out existing descriptions or to remind him of an omitted name or clarify confusion. In the 1761 edition he thanked his 'correspondent at the Cardigan Head, Charing Cross' for informing him 'of another Irish girl, bearing the same name [Polly Gay], who has lately appeared in his precincts, and who has not yet reached the Garden'.

In order to avoid confusion and preserve authenticity, Derrick would have maintained a system of notes not entirely dissimilar to those kept by Harris. However, in spite of his

record-keeping and the assistance of his readers and inform-
ants, following every movement of the listees was a
complicated endeavour. Unlike the pimp, he was not in the
business of preventing some of the more requested names
from disappearing. He candidly confessed that he was incapable of unearthing every punter's lost paramour. Women like
Poll Edmonds, he was forced to admit, 'we know not where
to trace . . . for she has left Long-Acre about a year ago'. Jack
Harris's job, it seemed, was more difficult than Sam had ever
imagined.

And there were other problems. In authoring *Harris's
List*, Sam Derrick recognized that he was skirting the boundaries of complete social disgrace. The recent debacle with his
aunt would appear minor compared with the repercussions
he was likely to suffer should some of his supporters catch
wind of his activities. In circles of polite society, any mention
of his project would be taboo. While Sam maintained his
aspirations to succeed as an author of legitimate literature, he
would have to preserve his anonymity as the *List*'s creator.
Unfortunately, all those who knew the Garden would know
whose efforts lay behind it. Sam had left his paw prints all
over the publication. His unmistakable voice, peppered with
his unique brand of personal observation, witticisms and toilet humour, could be heard throughout. It is the informal and
brusque sound of Georgian London, the inappropriate male
chatter otherwise confined to the tavern back room and
coffee-house table.

By 1757, when Derrick first touched his pen to paper in
the process of committing his *List* to ink, Covent Garden had
become his home in every sense of the word. He wrote

confidently and from a position of complete familiarity with his surroundings, as one who knew each bagnio, brothel and quiet tavern corner and had paced its every street and byway. The short biographical entries he composed said as much about the locality in which they were written as they did about the women they profiled. Based upon an amalgam of collected observations, he alternately bestows jeers and praise beneath each listee's name. About 'Mrs Hughes, in the Strand', he writes with personal scorn: 'This matron ... keeps a house of entertainment, much frequented by the bloods and bucks, who gives the sign the title of the Cat, although in fact it looks more like a lion; but which of her good qualities bear any resemblance to that animal, I could never learn.' He praises 'Nancy Howard, near Spring-Gardens', who he claims after meeting 'appears at least ten years younger than she is in reality' and always seems 'chatty enough when she pleases'. He also takes the opportunity to wag a finger at acquaintances of his, like Miss Clarke, who he had observed 'breaking the glasses at taverns and the windows of hackney chairs', or Bet Davis, who not only could 'damn a waiter with . . . grace' but whom he had spied smashing bottles 'with the air of a bully'. Such behaviour, he warns, 'will never recommend' these ladies 'to OUR notice'. In taking such a tone, Sam Derrick went beyond any service a pimp might perform by simply compiling a list of available names. Instead, he succeeded in creating an animated record of Covent Garden's personalities which appealed to a more literate class of patron.

If his intention was to secure his liberty through the creation of a printed pimp's list, then his endeavours were an unmitigated triumph. Even before it arrived on the shelves, *Harris's List of Covent Garden Ladies* had earned him enough 'by its sale to a certain book seller' to absolve him from his debts. For the first time in his life, Sam's pen had bought him something truly worthy of merit: his freedom.

9

# AN INTRODUCTION TO
# HARRIS'S LADIES

O N 2 JUNE 1757, the readers of a short-lived satirical publication called *The Centinel* were in for a treat. Its savvy
editor had identified his readership as the type who liked
prostitutes and chose to tip them off to a new work that
might be of interest to them. In keeping with the flavour of
the periodical, the announcement was written in the style of
an auction advertisement:

> For Sale by the Candle At the Shakespear's Head Tavern
> Covent Garden: The Tartar and the Shark Privateers with
> their Cargo from Haddock's, Harris, Master; Square
> stern'd, Dutch Built, with new sails and rigging. They
> have been lately docked and refitted, and are reckoned
> prime sailors. Catalogues with an account of their Cargo
> may be had at Mrs. D[ouglas]'s in the Piazza, or at the
> Place of Sale. To begin at twelve at night.

*Harris's List of Covent Garden Ladies* had made its entry
into the public domain. In the first instance it was available
for sale only at Haddock's Bagnio, the Shakespear's Head and
next door, at the well-established brothel run by Mother

145

Douglas. By the following year, the enigmatically named publisher 'H. Ranger' had not only assumed the printing of it but had become its primary retailer. Situated in the heart of London's literary district, H. Ranger's outlet sold a variety of reading material churned out by Grub Street hacks, most of it smutty. In addition to publishing *Harris's List*, his back catalogues included notable top-shelf works such as *Love Feasts; or the different methods of courtship in every country, throughout the known world* (two shillings and sixpence) and *The Polite Road to an Estate; or Fornication one great source of wealth and pleasure* (one shilling). Like a good tabloid editor, H. Ranger knew the value of a titillating read, and after spotting Derrick's ingenious idea it was his generous advance that sprung the author out of Ferguson's spunging house. Who precisely H. Ranger was in these early days is unknown. He, like Jack Harris, attempted to keep a fairly low profile and regularly moved his bookstall up and down Fleet Street, from Temple Bar to Temple Exchange Passage to No. 23, near St Dunstan's Church. Over the thirty-eight-year lifespan of the *List* it is likely that he was as many as four or more individuals. 'H. Ranger' simply became a useful trading name, as Elizabeth Denlinger points out: 'ranger' was a term synonymous with that of 'rake'. The 'H', it is believed, stood for 'Honest'.

For those who managed to track down the furtive bookseller (and it is claimed that approximately eight thousand did annually), the cost of purchasing *Harris's List of Covent Garden Ladies* was two shillings and sixpence. For their cash, the reader received a six-by-four-inch volume that, like any useful guidebook, could be slipped into a waistcoat pocket. It could be put to immediate use on the streets of London or taken home secretly and consumed in private. The publication's lewd prose was undoubtedly created with the purpose of solitary sexual enjoyment very much in mind. This may explain why H. Ranger's catalogue of stock regularly promotes lists from earlier years, sold, interestingly, for the same price. The devoted *Harris's List* collector would have relished thumbing through the pages of his various copies, comparing the entries of ladies they had sampled in bygone days and savouring the descriptions.

The reader of *Harris's List* need never feel ashamed of his purchase, or for that matter of his love of whoring. Once he had parted the cover in his hands and pushed past the publication's mildly arousing frontispiece of a stock-image seduction scene, Sam Derrick's preface in celebration of fornication would have assuaged all pangs of conscience. Nearly every edition from the 1760s to the 1780s begins with a lengthy sermon praising the merits of prostitution. Derrick's original essay, which appears in the 1761 reprint 'at the request of several gentlemen and ladies' after being 'universally admired', seems to have been an important feature of the *List* from its outset. In it, the cases of both the 'whore' and her keeper are exalted. To Derrick, the prostitute becomes a 'Volunteer of Venus', wrongly persecuted and shunned by the society whom she seeks to benefit. He argues that it is through her amorous embraces that the violent natures of men are distracted and placated. To 'the whore' we owe 'the peace of families, of cities, nay, of kingdoms'. To her customer and her keeper, equal regard is given. Referred to as 'gracious' and 'venerable', dealing out 'comfort to the oppressed', the male user becomes the ultimate patron, applying his coin to a good cause. He concludes with a lascivious rallying cry:

> Persist, oh ye hoary seers! Persist in the cause of keeping; in that you shew yourselves friends to charity, virtue and the state; continue it cherish these gifts of heaven; still hug to your bosom the cordial, the reviving warmth communicated by youth and beauty: to the dear girl whom you shall select, be your purse strings never closed; nor let the name of prostitute deter you from your pious resolve!

While such a preamble would have been penned with tongue firmly in cheek, it nevertheless makes a good attempt at presenting non-believers with a convincing case in favour of the trade.

Beyond its decorative merits and its introductory epistle, the entire *raison d'être* of the *List* was to conduct the desirous to the embrace of a prostitute. However, the question of what type of prostitute has never quite been decided. Sam Derrick saw his creation as worthy of containing the names of a wide range of thaises, from the most celebrated women such as Kitty Fisher and Lucy Cooper to those he called 'low-born errant drabs'. Subsequent authors chose to employ the *List* as a vehicle to warn users off certain women, while others included only genteel-mannered ladies of pleasure worthy of praise. Their prices varied, ranging from an affordable five shillings to the exclusive 'banknotes only'. Those looking for uniformity in the publication across its thirty-eight-year print run would be hard pressed to find any. The *List*'s contents and objectives changed with the whims of its authors, publishers and readership. It defies all attempts to categorize it as either exclusively upmarket or simply middle of the road.

Similarly, the social origins of the women who comprised the *List*'s roll call of names were diverse. In 1758, Saunders Welch estimated that out of a London population of 675,000, the capital was home to just over three thousand prostitutes, most of whom were drawn from the lowest ranks of the poor. Although this figure appears plausible, other commentators such as German diarist Sophie von la Roche and the reformer John Colquhoun believed the number to be considerably higher. As Welch never clearly specifies who he included in his count, it is difficult to be certain of his accuracy, particularly as the era's definition of a 'whore' was a broad and convoluted one. Along with visible street-walking prostitutes and those who plied their trade in the theatres, taverns, brothels and bagnios, there existed an entire stratum of invisible 'whores', from the outwardly respectable woman who conducted secret affairs to the labourer who offered sexual favours from time to time. The author of *A Congratulatory Epistle from a Reformed Rake*, written in the same year as Welch's tract, attempted to break down the term 'prostitute' into a 'gradation of whores' whose hierarchical ranks included:

Women of Fashion Who Intrigue[1]

Demi-Reps[2]

Good-natured girls[3]

Kept mistresses[4]

Ladies of pleasure[5]

Whores[6]

Park-walkers[7]

Street-walkers[8]

Bunters[9]

Bulk-mongers[10]

Of these ten categories, those from Demi-Rep to Street-walker were found on the pages of *Harris's List* from 1757 to 1795. Interestingly, irrespective of where they may have found themselves along this scale, H. Ranger treated all as equals, facetiously omitting certain vowels and consonants from their names as if they were members of polite society who sought to have their identities protected.

In Welch's assumption, the majority of those who resorted to prostitution entered the trade as either orphans or children of poor families. Among the poor he included those of the 'laborious poor' with offspring 'too numerous for their parents to maintain'. Justice Fielding also found this to be the case when he questioned a group of prostitutes arrested on the night of 1 May 1758.

While a considerable number of full-time sex workers came from the poorest of the poor, many of those who featured in *Harris's List* did not. In addition to those like Charlotte Hayes, born into financially comfortable sex-trade families who had been in the procuring or bagnio-keeping game for generations, was an entire range of often unseen women who moved in and out of prostitution or who exchanged an occasional sexual act for payment or protection. Were Saunders Welch to have included this sub-category of 'working girl' in his estimate, he would have found the social pool from which they originated to be much more diverse.

Much to the frustration of dedicated moral reformers, identifying all the capital's women of the town was not as easy as simply taking a stroll down the ill-lit Strand. Not every prostitute in London was engaged in openly plying her trade and not every woman that society considered a prostitute was immediately identifiable. As women of the lower classes were generally believed to have a looser sense of morality, it was assumed that their sexual services were available for sale if the right price was offered. This particularly applied to female market traders and street peddlers. Contemporary accounts, as well as ballads and engravings, suggest that these women frequently sold more than their baskets of fruit and nosegays. At times, the street seller and the prostitute were considered so closely related that little distinction was made between those legitimately attempting to make a living and those using the trade of merchandise as a front for their more lucrative sexual activities. Female workers toiling indoors also found themselves the object of similar suspicion, and not without some cause. An absence of well-paid employment for women sometimes made it necessary for those who laboured in traditional female occupations, trades dedicated to the laundering, mending or creation of clothing, to supplement their earnings by offering access to their bodies. No one profession was considered more notorious than the milliner's trade, which it was believed imparted the value of vanity to its many impressionable practitioners. The same was said of other female-dominated and fashion-oriented fields such as haberdashery, glove-making and dressmaking, all of which bore the stigma of being 'seminaries of prostitution'.

Had Welch probed his sample further, he would also have discovered that prostitution for many women was a seasonal occupation to which they turned as a stopgap between periods of employment. Notable among this type were entertainers, namely London's aspiring and established actresses, singers and dancers; the end of the annual theatrical season meant a period without income for many. Entertainers were always on the look-out for generous patrons who might ensure their comfort during 'resting' spells. But for those less fortunate, the brothels of Covent Garden and the Haymarket proved useful refuges. Not unlike entertainers, domestic servants were particularly prone to stints on the town. Even with the high demand for domestic help in London, the turnover of household servants could be quite rapid among families and individuals with ever-changing needs and places of residence. Out-of-work female servants with no alternative and immediate means of earning their keep might find it expedient to fall back on the one sure source of work available for women. As Daniel Defoe observed in 1725, resorting to such measures was quite common, causing servants to move frequently from 'Bawdy-House to Service and from Service to Bawdy-House'. In all of these cases, incidental periods of prostitution which may have lasted several weeks, months or years were integrated into life when the need to defray expenses and make ends meet arose. According to the eighteenth-century model, these women wore the label of 'whore' as much as those who practised the profession full-time. Certainly, the authors of *Harris's List* made no distinction between them.

The occupation of prostitution was not the exclusive preserve of the poor. Middle-class women also make an appearance in the *List*, or at least this is the impression that the publications' authors wanted to impart. The daughters of the precarious middle classes – those who perched on the middle-to-lower end of London's burgeoning and diversifying bourgeoisie: the petty shopkeepers, the master craftsmen, the sometimes successful artists whose fortunes rose and swelled and occasionally fell – were prime candidates for lives of high-class prostitution. Just how many girls from this level of society were responsible for expanding the legions of Venus is entirely unknown, although there is evidence to suggest that their numbers were strong. Certainly, the many young ladies trained as haberdashers and dressmakers would have come from families sufficiently well endowed to pay for their apprenticeships, a luxury that the poorest classes could not afford. Even Francis Place's own apprentice-master in the 1780s, a breeches-maker by the name of Mr French, had three daughters actively earning their livelihoods in the sex trade. 'His eldest daughter was and had been for several years a common prostitute. His youngest daughter, who was about seventeen years of age, had genteel lodgings where she was visited by gentlemen; and the second daughter . . . was kept by a captain of an East India ship,' Place explained. Similarly, James Grant, a friend of William Hickey, kept a mistress called Miss Brown who was the daughter of a successful tailor with his own shop on Ludgate Hill. Far from disapproving of her lifestyle, Tailor Brown profited greatly by his daughter's position, as she kept 'the interest of her father in view by recommending all . . . Mr. Grant's friends to employ him in this business'. Slightly further up the middle-class ladder, the lawyer and author Thomas Vaughan, lumbered with the misfortune of having fathered six pretty daughters, confided to Hickey that lack of funds meant his girls might 'have to turn out whores'. As the *List* suggests, there was a healthy market for attractive, educated girls without suitable marriage portions. In fact, they made the best courtesans.

However, not every woman in *Harris's List* originated from the respectable background the authors claimed. As Sam Derrick saw himself as a chronicler of Covent Garden characters, he preferred truth to embellishment. Unlike the authors of succeeding editions, honesty and the recounting of gossip and amusing stories were his principle aims. In later years, as eighteenth-century society became increasingly obsessed with gentility and politeness, the authors attempted to 'prettify' not only the prose used in descriptions but the stories of the ladies themselves. Editions from the 1770s through the 1790s feature more daughters of lawyers, clergymen, half-pay officers, schoolmasters, physicians and shopkeepers. The *List*'s publishers had learned that, like modern celebrities, part of a prostitute's allure was her persona: her name, tales of her escapades and, most importantly for Georgian society, her background or 'breeding'. After all, where was the glamour in bedding a streetwise orphan from Southwark? The attraction of a motherless and disowned daughter of a country parson was much greater.

The eighteenth-century middle classes loved to be scandalized by what they read. They were enthralled by suggestions that the dissolute women who lived under the roofs of disorderly houses were in fact the daughters and sisters of people they might have known, people just like them. The unsure footing of many on the margins of the middle classes meant that slipping down in society's estimation after having maintained a respectable appearance was a genuine fear. As the heroine of Fanny Burney's *Evelina* learned, little distinction was made between a virtuous young lady and a sexually available one when one's address was 'an hosiers in High Holborn'. The era's print media was more than pleased to cash in on this sense of social insecurity, and the literate public, in turn, lapped it up. Novels such as Samuel Richardson's *Clarissa* and *Pamela*, tales of seduction and rape, became instant bestsellers, while all of London thrilled to reports of the trial of Elizabeth Canning, a girl purported to have been abducted and imprisoned in a bawdy house. The era seemed unable to get enough of tales of 'virtue in peril'. Understandably, the producers of *Harris's List* recognized this and made it a noted feature of later editions.

Mixed in with the standard stories of seduction and betrayal by women claiming to be illegitimate daughters of the nobility and legitimate daughters of wealthy City merchants are genuine tales detailing the paths women took to their present situations. Love and youthful innocence are most regularly cited as the root of their misfortunes. Numerous girls are recorded as having 'absconded' from their villages with recruiting officers and soldiers who then abandoned them in London. Wilful deception and broken promises of marriage are also recounted. Many of these tales include the woes of rejection by one's parents and friends, adding a tragic but often fictitious postscript to their falls from grace. Rape, unfortunately, also figures prominently, although it is frequently veiled by the use of the term 'seduction'. Like the era's favourite protagonist, Clarissa Harlowe, many of *Harris's* listees were 'seduced against their will'.

While the romantic tendencies of teenage girls make these stories entirely plausible, few of the *List*'s authors after Sam Derrick are willing to acknowledge the more mundane routes often taken to prostitution. The search for employment in rural areas led a significant number to the capital, where prospects were better. Alone in the metropolis and left to their own devices, women fell prey to lecherous employers, gave in to the advances of admirers and were inveigled by the sex trade. The old urban legend as illustrated in Hogarth's series *The Harlot's Progress*, where country bumpkin Moll Hackabout is astutely picked from the London wagon by the insidious Mother Needham, has more than a resonance of reality. The tricks of the procuring trade were well known to Saunders Welch and his reforming companions. 'Agents are constantly employed by bawds to attend the coming and going of wagons and other carriages,' he wrote in 1758. They also lurked at the register offices and deceived the unsuspecting into hiring lodgings from them or taking sham positions as servants. It was then that, by use of 'persuasion or force', they were made 'one of the family'.

Simply because the *List's* authors filled their biographical sketches with details of young women's deceptions and rapes in order to arouse their readers does not preclude the occurrence of such horrors. They might not have been as commonplace as hacks and novelists would have the literate believe, but such schemes were not unknown. In 1768, Sarah Woodcock, a milliner, was held captive and raped by Lord Baltimore. Just over thirty years earlier the infamous Colonel Francis Charteris was tried and hanged for 'carnally knowing' a servant, Ann Bond, against her will. In both instances the men had plotted with procuresses who were closely involved in the deception of their victims. While these were quite high-profile cases, owing to the social standing of their defendants, similar crimes in which bawds were involved, such as the rape of Ann Cooly in 1758, were allowed to occur quietly in the background. Of course, in a system so stacked against them, few women of the lower and middling orders would have had the resolve to bring these crimes to the notice of the authorities. Without influential family or friends behind them, no one was likely to believe their accusations. As suggested by publications like *Harris's List*, it was easier simply to accept the tragedy and assume their new role. A life of prostitution, as the users of the *List* would have seen it, held many virtues.

To the modern reader, Sam Derrick and the subsequent authors of the *List* appear to approach the condition of prostitution quite glibly. The harsh realities of a 'working woman's' existence, the threats of syphilis and venereal disease, the fear of pregnancy and induced abortions, the implications of alcoholism, violence, imprisonment and starvation, are rarely mentioned more than in passing. Readers did not want to be reminded of these things. *Harris's List* provided men with the means of gratifying their lusts and enjoying themselves.

When a man set out to locate a wanton woman, his intentions were to bury his troubles and his conscience. When he rapped on her door or requested her company at the tavern he was only in the mood for pleasure. What mood she was in was of no consequence.

# THE *LIST*

## COVENT GARDEN CHARACTERS AND REIGNING CELEBRITIES

### Cherry Poll, Covent Garden

Any one who has been at Bob Derry's, that house of remarkable civil reputation, must be too well acquainted with the celebrated Cherry Poll, to need a particular description. How she came by the name is variously reported; but her red cheeks, her red lips, and her red something else, have all helped to the dubbing of her. She is an agreeable girl, but so frolicksome and noisy, that she often forces the worthy Bob to cry out, What a blasted house is here! (1761)

### Lucy Cooper, Parliament Street

No body, in the least acquainted with the world of amusement can be a stranger to the accomplishments of the sprightly Lucy. No woman can be a more jovial companion, or say better things. She has often true wit about her; but lards it rather a little too much with blasphemy. She was, to the astonishment of the world, kept for three years by Sir Penurious Trifle,[1] who never had before shewn the slightest tendency to extravagance, but once; and that was in giving a guinea instead of a shilling, by mistake to a coachman; which, is he never demanded, it was because he knew not where to seek for jolt. She is said to have squandered for him 14,000l. without realising 1400l. She is closely connected with an actor at the Old House; and some people say, they have tucked themselves up in the matrimonial noose; but the theatrical legends range this article under the head of apocrypha. Lucy's features are regular, her hair brown, her air easy, and her shape genteel: though she is very thin, her bones are not so sharp as a razor, as a certain noted Templar, lately deceased used to affirm. (1761)

## Miss Kitty Fisher

In our list of public beauties for last year, we inserted the name of this agreeable girl, with a promise to our readers of a farther and more circumstantial account of her, and it was actually ready for press, when the following letter was brought to us, which we shall give verbatim as an excuse for our failing in the contract above mentioned.

*To Mr. Harris.*

*Sir,*

*As I see you have advertised your List for this year, and I remember you promised the public some account of me in it, I beg for God's sake, you will suffer old acquaintance to sway so far with you, as to prevent your doing a thing which will be so grievous to me. Besides you know, Mr. Harris, though brought to misfortunes I never yet was on the common: you may, perhaps, be at some loss in complying with this request, the servant*

*therefore will give you five guineas.\* Pray consider me, and*
*believe me to be,*
*Sir, your most humble servant,*
    *K-th-r-ne F—r*
*P.S. Mr.— desires you will send in six dozen of your best burgundy.*


## Bet Davis, alias Little Infamy, Russel Street
Of all the ladies we have inserted in our List, Bet is the most
eminent, among those of her own class, who have given her
the name, Little Infamy, from her abandoned and libidinous
disposition. It is reported, she has transplanted an antique
gonorrhoea by many drunken vicious husbands, to their
innocent wives, and to the blood of posterity; and that many
a sessions paper has owed part of its historical existence
to heroes of her creating. Let this be as it may, we advise her
enamoratos to be careful. – A word to the wise is enough.
(1761)


## Mrs Cuyler, Craven Street, Strand
To trace this lady through all her mazes and wanderings, from
her first setting out in life to the time of her appearance on the
stage in the character of Miranda, would far exceed the
boundary of our limits; we must therefore content ourselves
with giving a brief outline of her character which we have had
opportunities of being well acquainted with.

    She was brought up under the Wing of the celebrated Bird
of Paradise,[2] who taught her the rudiments of knowledge from
which she soon, by the strength of her own natural genius,

* the above sum has been faithfully applied in discharging Polly Hawkins from the Marshalsea; – we scorn to pocket a bribe. (1761)

became a complete mistress of the science, in which she has cut a conspicuous figure. She is about twenty-eight, is slim and tall; has a fair complexion; brown hair; good teeth; and is upon the whole a very pretty woman. She lately behaves with a great deal of reserve in public, but in private, when she likes her company; there is not a more agreeable, good-natured convivial soul in the universe. At such times she is very fond of singing 'King David on a certain day, &c.' which she performs with a good deal of humour. She does not give her company now, but to two or three particular friends, except she chances to meet with a young fellow whose arguments are too powerful for her to resist, or an old one, who will assail her like an other Danae, with a shower of gold. We cannot conclude without assuring our readers that she is a woman of the strictest honour and secrecy, and expects prudent conduct and behaviour from those in whom she places any confidence. (1779)

## Miss Wilkinson, Coldbath-fields

*'Avoid the cup, there's poison in the draught'*

To pretend to give a description of this lady would be dictating to our readers, all of whom must have noticed her, if not at Drury-Lane theatre, where she danced for some seasons, at least at Sadler's Wells, where her whole family have entertained the town for a long time. She now and then performs the character of Columbine, but is chiefly a dancer, in which we have seen many who have not excelled her: 'tis true, her bulk is rather a hindrance to her agility, which may in some measure excuse her not being able to get off the ground (as the dancers term it) but, however, she is very decent in what she performs.

We are sorry to find she still continues to tipple too much; we thought the connexion she was engaged in (a Harlequin of Drury Lane) would have reclaimed her; but alas! Habits become second nature, and we might almost as soon wash a negro white, as conquer them when of very long standing. (1773)

## Mrs. Abbington, Southhampton Street, Covent Garden

> *'Do not venture where such danger lyes,*
> *But shun the sight of her victorious eyes.'*

Of all vices we detest ingratitude, and we are afraid this lady would accuse us on that head, if we did not acknowledge the favours we have received from her in her single state. About 13 years ago, Miss Barton did not keep her coach, but has often been glad to take her place even behind that of the celebrated Lucy Cooper, when coming from the hop[3] at Mrs. Park's in Aldersgate Street, where she was famous for singing a song, and beating time with her elbow, like Mr. Shuter in Love for Love; this expedient has got her many a shilling, which the company have club'd to reward her in some ingenuity.

Some time after she appeared at Drury-lane, in the character of Miss Lucy, in The Virgin Unmasked. After this she married a trumpeter, whose name she now bears; went to Ireland, where she staid some time, and improved herself in the theatrical way; and coming over with her favourite swain (a performer at Drury-lane), engaged again at Drury-lane; where, by her excellence in her cast of parts, (Mrs. Clive having left the stage) she stands unrivalled.

Mr. Abbington, her husband, sold her to Mr.— for 500l. and entered into articles never to molest him in the possession of her. The gentleman's death (by which she expected great things) freed him from the bargain, but they do not live together. She keeps an elegant house, and Mr. Jefferson is constantly with her. Her salary, though genteel, is not sufficient to maintain her table and manner of living; but her amour with Mr.— sufficiently makes up the deficiency. She is remarked in the company for her compassion and good-nature. Can any of our readers suppose, from so humane a disposition, that she would suffer any gentleman to die with despair for her? No: we can assure them to the contrary; but then the approaches must be made the proper way; sighs and oaths and such stuff alone will not do; a little of them may be proper, and also to convince her you really are a gentleman.

N.B. She measures gentility by the weight of the purse. (1773)

## EXOTICS

### Miss Love, No. 14, George Street, Tottenham Court Road

*'The Gods on her have well bestowed,*
*Indeed she's finely fur beloved'*

Eliza is of a dark complexion, being a downright mulatto, and intimates by the thickness of her hair and her eyebrows, that she is well furred-below. Though she is somewhat addicted to swearing, the men all swear in turn, that she is a d—d fine hairy piece; and not withstanding the jolly god now and then gets the better of her, she generally gets the better of all her bush fighting antagonists in the long run, as she has her hours of relaxation from the feats of Bacchus as well as Venus; she tells a good story, and can produce an excellent tale, which she charges little more for than it is well worth, considering the scarcity of its complexion in this country, being but very lately imported from the West Indies. She is tall and genteel, about eighteen years of age, and is said to be in keeping by an American. (1789)

## Miss Lorraine, No. 30, Goodge Street, Tottenham Court Road

*'Now by my Hood, a Gentile, and no Jew!'*

This Lady is commonly called the agreeable Jewess, for what reason those who have seen the lady can only determine; for she has not the covetousness or artifice which attends all the followers of the law of Moses; nor like them is distinguished among her neighbours for 'spoiling them of their jewels of silver, and their jewels of gold'. It may perhaps be accounted for upon other principles, for though she is genteely made, and has a very good face, yet a fine black eye, and black hair, make her look not unlike to one of the daughters of Abraham. Her mouth is small, and looks like Suckling's girl in the song of the wedding, whose nether lip, 'look's as if some bee had stung it newly'. Her conversation is pleasing, she drinks little and swears seldom; so that, as times go, she is a very desirable companion. (1790)

## Miss Robinson, At the Jelly Shops

*'Avoid the danger which you ought to fear'*

This lady is a Jew but has no objection to a bit of Christian flesh—but not in Shylock's way: she chuses her lover, and less than a pound will satisfy her. She was a long time confin'd in the Marshalsea, and during the whole winter charitably supplied the prison with firring: she is not long at liberty, and I suppose will confer the same favour on many a poor gentleman the approaching cold season: 'tis said that the Jews have no regard for the gentiles; is not this a convincing proof to the contrary? She was so very good natured to Mr. Pilstow, a young Quaker, a fellow prisoner with her, that they say she gave him sufficient to keep him warm for two or three years. She is rather tall, dark brown or rather black hair, large dark eyes and eyebrows, a slim and genteel made girl—but rather too flat. (1773)

## Mrs. M—c—ntee, No. 2, York Street, Middlesex Hospital

*'—The wife experienced dame,*
*Cracks and rejoices in the flame.'*

This lady who has some experience of the town, has profitted much of that experience, and is an excellent bedfellow. She is called 'The Armenian', but has none of their religious prejudices; for she prefers natural opinions in the daily exercise of which she is zealous and vigorous; she looks upon these opinions as the whole duty of man, and makes it her complete practice of piety.

She is of a middling size, has black hair and eyes, with a

good face, though much pitted with the small pox, and as her practice has had long continuance and has been extensive, yet she is still nevertheless, a very agreeable companion, and not much exceeding two and twenty years of age; price one pound one. (1790)

## Miss Cross, Bridges Street

A smart little black gypsy, with a very endearing symmetry of parts; has an odd way of wriggling herself about, and can communicate the most exquisite sensations when she is well paid. (1764)

## CRIMINALS

## Lucy P-t-rson, St. Martin's Lane

Her father was originally a publican in Clare Market, but being detected in some fraudulent practices with regard to his liquors, was brought in a debtor to the crown, for which he died a prisoner in Newgate. His daughter was debauched probably by some crew of that place, and to that may perhaps be attributed her exact probation of the manner of so excellent an academy. She is not pretty, neither ugly; but is as lewd as goats and monkies; and she generally has a design upon her friend's watch, purse, or handkerchief. She frequently visits Bridewell, and is in a homely phrase, a vile bitch. (1761)

## Mrs. Cumming, Bow Street, Covent Garden

This female heroine was a long time bar-keeper to the notorious Terry Masionery of the Green Rails, Oyster Street,

Portsmouth, where she soon became, under his tuition, a
perfect adept in all his villainous undertakings, of which so
sensible was he of her use, that he bequeath'd her his whole
property when he died, and truly she was justly intitled to it;
soon after his decease she engaged herself with a sprightly
young fellow well known in the purlieus of Covent Garden, as
a pickpocket, where between them it is said they have
acquired a considerable sum; she is sure to be met with at
Stirlings, and if disengaged sure to be introduced to you, as
she is a great favourite of the younger S—g, and has the title
of being his hack; she is a pretty tall woman, about thirty years
of age, pitted a little with the small pox, and a remarkable
good piece; a single guinea will be both acceptable and
satisfactory. (1789)

## Miss West, No. 14, Wild Street

> *'O! Think not that she came to town last week,*
> *The waggon straw's yet hanging to her tail'*

This lady is half sister to the celebrated Miss West, whose
abilities in the arts and sciences are so well known at every
academy in town, and we can assure the public that she is no
changeling, for though she is not highly renowned as Betsy, she
has equal merit, though she appears and behaves like an
ignorant country girl, yet those who take her for such, will, in
all probability, soon find the contrary to their cost; for she is as
light finger'd and as expert as a jugler. She is rather short, her
eyes and hair are jet black, and her complexion is very dark,
she dresses very plain, but exceeding neet, and can pick her
gallant's pocket very coolly be he ever so agreeable; for like
Jenny Diver,[4] she has other kinds of men to employ her leisure
hours with in private. (1779)

## VETERANS IN THE FIELD OF VENUS

### Kitty B—ckley, Poland Street

This lady has been at the service of every man that has a mind to her, from her thirteenth year. Her mamma was a midwife in Ireland, from which country Miss B—ckley came. No woman was ever more hackney'd from the lord to the porter; Turks, Jews, Papists; every sect, and every country have tasted her sweet body. She is really an elegant figure, and has a charming sweetness in her countenance; but she is as wicked as a devil, and as extravagant as Cleopatra. She is generally three times a year in the bailiff's hands, but still makes a figure. She is now descending into the vale of years, being at least five and thirty; and is reported to have ruined twenty keepers. (1761)

### Mrs. Hamblin, No. 1, Naked-Boy Court, near the New Church, Strand

> *'The plaister'd nymph returns the kiss,*
> *Like Thisby, through a wall'*

The young lady in question, is not above fifty-six, and according to her own confession has been a votary to pleasure these thirty years, she wears a substantial mask upon her face, and is rather short. We should not have introduced her here, but that on account of her long experience and extensive practice, we know that she must be particularly useful to elderly gentlemen, who are very nice in having their linen got up. (1779)

### Nancy V—ne alias Basket, Charles Street, Westminster

A woman somewhat turned of forty, motherly and careful, and very fit for grown gentlemen to amuse themselves with; I mean gentlemen who have been old, are grown young again, and come under the birch rod. She flays, they say with an amazing grace. This is all we know of her, she seldom coming abroad till the batt and night birds appear. She thinks she is like a certain right honourable courtezan, and therefore assumes her name. – She is called Basket from a former keeper. (1761)

## NOVICES

### Polly Jackson, Late of the above place (Rathbone Place, No. 22) and now in Scotland Yard, with Nancy St—y

*'Youth without beauty has still its charms'*

Polly is a little fluttering child, about fourteen years of age, has full dark eyes, and a projecting mouth, with tolerable good teeth; but upon the whole, nothing striking or extraordinary. If her youth, and her not being fledged, are recommendations, she is certainly possessed of them. She was debauched about ten months ago by the noted Capt. Jones, who was convicted of an unnatural crime: it seems to coincide with his love of small commodities; for to be sure Polly could not have been fit, at that time, for any man even of middling parts. She has passed for a maidenhead since that period twenty times, and is paid accordingly; and being under the direction of a very good lady, who directs her to play her part to admiration, she is in a fair way of getting money. (1773)

## Miss Saunders, facing the Lancashire Witch, James Street

Heaven gave her one face, and she makes herself another, for though she has a natural fresh bloom, yet she be-plaisters her face with paint, to the great disparagement of her features, which are most exquisitely formed in the most exact mould that nature ever made. She is but 15, and is indeed an enchanting creature; she has eyes clear and as fine coloured as the azure blue, and her hair curls in a thousand artless ringlets down her snowy neck, she is tall of her age, and has a beautiful complexion; as to her meretricious performances, though we never heard them spoken of, yet we think they cannot fail of being transporting and extraordinary. (1779)

## Miss—, No. 44, Newman Street, Oxford Street

> *'Here stop your wandering steps, thou am'rous youth,*
> *Behold this emblem of untainted truth;*
> *Her eyes declare the secret flame within,*
> *Her lovely form would tempt a saint to sin.'*

This petite belle has not yet attained her sixteenth year; and, to make amends for her deficiency of height, she is elegantly formed, nor does she lack beauty. Her sparkling eyes would warm an anchorite. Her hair is beautifully fair: and her liveliness in conversation renders her a most agreeable companion. Two guineas will bring you better acquainted with this charmer; nor will you have cause for disagreeable reflections from her acquaintance. (1793)

## PARTICULARLY UNPLEASANT

### Pol Forrester, Bow Street

The very opposite of her namesake, being disagreeable, ugly, and ill-behaved. She has an entrance to the palace of pleasure as wide as a church door; and a breath worse than a Welch bagpipe. She drinks like a fish, eats like a horse, and swears like a trooper. – An errant drab. (1761)

### Miss Adams, at Mrs. Freeland's, Bow Street, Covent Garden

*'A filthy conquest only you might boast'*

Come forward, thou dear, drowsy, gin-drinking, snuff-taking Miss Adams: What in the name of wonder could influence you to leave a profession in which you was bred, for one which you do not appear to have the least pretensions. I must own, I cannot say what hidden charms you may possess. Don't you think those arms and hands of yours had better stuck to their original calling, cleaning of grates, scrubbing of floors, and keeping a house neat and clean, than drinking arrack-punch, getting drunk, and setting up for a fine lady? But soft: we are finding fault with the wrong person; 'tis your admirers who are to blame, that are so blind as not to distinguish between the girl of beauty and merit, and a drunken, snuffy drab, who is generally to propose a question or give an answer.

First, Major Hawkins, what crimes must he have to answer for, in bringing you away? And then that old fool Mr. Whitmore, that silly Cooper of the Stamp Office, how stupid must he be not to see through your manner of living!

How choice is his taste to support you!—However 'tis well for you, you have so good a friend to your back:—'fools have fortune, and knaves have luck'.

Miss Adams is rather under middle size, fair hair, grey eyes; tolerable good skin, pock-marked a little, and may easily be known by the quantity of Scotch snuff she takes, particularly when she is in liquor, when her upper lip is pretty well covered with it, and does not badly resemble a pair of whiskers. Her breath, from drinking, has acquired a very disagreeable smell: how her friend reconciles this we cannot say; he must certainly have no nose for it:—'A toad's as good for a sow as a pancake.' (1773)

## SEX ADDICTS

### Miss Kilpin

*'Those formal lovers be forever curst,*
*Who fetter's free-born love with humour first,*
*Who through fantastic laws are virtues' fools*
*And against nature will be slaves to rules'*

We can not pretend to say where this curious oddity lives, that being a circumstance she carefully conceals; and what is more extraordinary, she never can be prevailed on to go into taverns or other houses with a gentleman. To what purpose then (some reader may say) is she inserted here, if she will not go into a house to dispense her favours, not is it known where she is to be found? A little patience, good sir, and you will be informed where she is to be found, and how to procure her favours. If you walk on the right hand side of the way, from the corner of

Cheapside along St. Paul's Church-yard, and thence to the bottom of Ludgate Hill, just after sunset, and meet with a beautiful woman about twenty, tall and finely shaped, with fine black eyes and hair of the same hue that floats in curls down her back, and worn without powder, and a bewitching dimple on each cheek, you may give a shrewd guess you have found Miss K—lp—n. Her dress is in general silk, sometimes a pale blue, but oftener a black, and a large white sattin cloak trimmed and lined with rich brown fur; her head is in general bedecked with a blue beaver, with a profusion of white feathers; and if on accosting her, you are as much dazzled with her wit, her smart repartees, and her delicate agreeable raillery, as with her person and dress, you may be then absolutely certain it is the lady. But you may say, when found, of what service is it, when she will neither take you home with her nor go into any house with you? A little more patience sir, if you please, though she refuses to go into any house with you are there not hackney coaches on every stand? We have not said she will deny entering one of them with you; that is if she likes your person and conversation. And let us here add, no frothy coxcomb, no male Adonis, conceited of his own dear person, no show stringed effeminate puppy, no insipid empty chatterer, can hope to succeed with her.

If reader, thou art neither of these and should meet with, and please Miss K—lp—n, she will take as lengthen'd a ride with you as you please; and if you have the prudence to draw up the blinds, she will be as free as you please, and you may enjoy her charms, Jehu like,[5] as long as you can. She is framed for love, and will melt like a snowball in the sun. She will embrace you with unfeigned rapture, open all her charms to receive your manly tribute, and perhaps appoint another meeting.

We have rather enlarged on this lady, on account of the singularity of her disposition; and what will add to your wonder is that she never will receive any money, but take the offer as an affront. These circumstances make us conclude that K—lp—n, the name she has assumed sometimes, is not her real name, and that she is not a woman of the town, but some married city lady, who takes this method of getting home deficiencies supplied abroad, and as she is cautious of her character, uses these precautions. By not going to any house, she avoids detection; by chusing none but those whose conservation is congenial to her own, she obliges none but men of sense and honour; and by her constantly refusing money, she demonstrates that love for love is her motto; that her love of the sport is her motive; perhaps she may have another reason for chusing a leathern conveniency as the scene of her delights. We have been told that the undulating motion of the coach, with the pretty little occasional jolts, contribute greatly to the pleasure of the critical moment, if all matters are rightly placed, and therefore as pleasure is her search, no wonder she prefers every delicate addition to the gross sum. (1788)

## Mrs. Williams, No. 65, Queen Ann Street East

'Free as light and air I walk,
And uncontroll'd my passions guide;
I eat and drink and sing and talk,
And something else I do beside;
Hither then, my followers come,
And, on the couch, the seat of bliss,
I'll strait conduct the hero home,
And shew you what this something is.'

Some from necessitous motives, some from mistaken pride, and others from a contracted laziness follow the sporting profession. But we are well convinced, that it is neither of these operates with our subject lady: it is sheer lewdness and letchery; for, according to her own confession, she has an annuity of fifty pounds per annum left by relations; therefore it is not every beau that accosts her that is conducted home. He must please her both in manners and person, and then she has not finished with him. If her sparks meet her approbation, he is shewn to her lodgings; and after the glass has circulated, and the usual preludes past, she insists on examining the more essential parts. Whether this is done from motives of fear or wantonness (which at that time is so very conspicuous in her lascivious eyes) we are not certain; perhaps both. These necessary preliminaries being settled, if the size and condition of those parts please, she then shews you the coach, and presents you with as pretty a goer or comer as the wanton hand of nature ever formed. She is a genteel figure, light hair, and such melting love-tinctur'd eyes as few can boast, which never are permitted to swim in that celestial fluid under one pound one. This lady is generally to be met with at the Hop, in Queen Street, Golden Square, three times a week, to which she is accompanied by a certain young man, who always attends her home again; that is, if she meets no other companion suitable to her fancy. (1789)

## Miss Smith, Duke's Court, Bow Street

A well made lass, something under the middle size, with dark brown hair, and a good complexion. Her behaviour is in the extreme of fondness in her love-devotions. She seems indeed of true Messalinalian breed, and so inraged by a *furor matricis*, that no masculine endeavors can tire, or variety satisfy. Some

176

gentlemen who have been in her company have endeavored to discover the cause of this excess of fondness in the act of copulation: and Dr F—s in particular, (a great connoisseur in female affairs) has made the following remarks:

'That her breasts are small but at the same time conveniently hard; that there is a profusion of hair about her privies, (which are situated high, and near the navel) and that this profusion is occasioned by the extraordinary heat in those parts; that the hair of her head, &c. is short, and inclinable to curl; her voice is shrill and loud; she is bold of speech; proud, and cruel to her own sex; that she has not her courses for two or three months together; that she does not smell so rank when she sweats, as a woman of a less lascivious disposition; that her breath is sweet, lips moist, and she delights in society and public spaces.'

These, says he, are sure indications of a wanton and libidinous inclination. But as we are not able to determine whether the Doctor's remarks are truly physical, we shall leave the decision of the matter to the members of the C—e of P—s,[6] and shall be glad of receiving their opinion on this important affair, directed wither to the Shakespear, Bedford Head, or Rose, where she may be seen and examined at any hour. (1764)

## DOUBLE ENTENDRE

### Miss W—ll—s, No. 23, Goodge Street

*'My cheeks are blushing peach outvies,*
*My skin the golden pippin;*
*My bushy grot, as black as sloes*
*Is surely worth a dip-in'*

This beautiful nonpareil was originally a retailer of fruit. Her charms are always current to any one who wishes to be a medler; she was once paired with a comical husband but now she cares a fig for nobody; she has acquired a pleasing knack of engaging anyone, though so green; and would lie buried in straw to gratify their wishes, without ever being guilty of impeaching their oddities; she is not such a goose but she can bury a secret without giving her reasons for it; she loves the laymen, because they are not so apt to range. She has a natural antipathy to divines, as they are so often crabbed; she is tall and genteel as the pine, with beautiful nut brown tresses and hazel eyes. If you enter into her garden, one guinea is the fruits of her labour. (1790)

## Sally F—m—n, At a Chandler's Shop, Fleet Market

*'Take heed how you embark'*

This delicate lady is to be met with between Temple-bar and the place of her abode; she sets sail between the hours of seven and eight, if she meets with any captures she generally sets fire to them, and bears away with what plunder she can conveniently carry off. She is Dutch built, broad bottomed, and carries a great deal of sail. Goods put on board her reasonably fraited. (1773)

## Mrs. George, No. 13; South Moulton Street

This lady has not been in business long; she surrendered her citadel to a captain of the navy, who in his attack upon her, united the seamen with the lover, and the ingenuity of the one won her heart as much as the passion of the other. As a specimen of his epistolary method of corresponding with her, we shall subjoin a part of one of his letters to her, which runs exactly thus; he tells her that he had often thought to reveal to her the tempests of his heart by word of mouth, to scale the walls of her affection, but terrified with the strength of her fortifications, he had concluded to make more regular approaches, to attack her at farther distance, and try what a bombardment of letters would do, whether those carcases of love thrown into the sconces of her eyes, would break into the midst of her breast, beat down the out-guard of her aversion and indifference, and blow up the magazine of her cruelty, that she might be brought to terms of capitulation: which indeed she soon was, and upon reasonable terms. The captain was with her but a short time, being obliged to repair to his station; and after his departure, she was kept by one in the army, who was obliged to give way to the more powerful solicitations of one of greater force. She is just thirty, pretty and amorous, has a charming lively eye and a handsome mouth; she is rather short but very delicately made, a charming colour which seems to be natural, is finely diffused over her cheeks, and sets her face to great advantage, and she has fine brown hair, is good temper'd and very free and merry.

She drives a very handsome curricle,[7] and is in keeping by a Mr. C—ns. (1793)

## BEAUTIES

### Miss Wallington, facing the Floor-cloth Manufactory, Knitesbridge

*'Nymph! More fair than Houri,*
*Poet form'd'*

If we were called upon to name the lady whom we conceive to be the most beautiful among the whole sisterhood, it would certainly be Sally; she has so many enchanting blendishments, that they are quite irresistible. It is as impossible to withstand the artillery of her eyes, as the winged lightening; then her hair, her lips, her every thing, are so transportingly charming as to fill every beholder with rapture: But, alas! Her beauties are almost lost to the public; for Sir Harry P—t engrosses, or seems to engross them all to himself.

She is just twenty-two, of the most elegant form imaginable: And as we know her to be amorously inclined, we do not think any young fellow need despair if he has ability, and understands the method of carrying on an intrigue with prudence and secrecy; for when a woman once knows that she may transgress with impunity, it is ten to one that she will transgress if she has any object in view that is agreeable to her, and what can be more agreeable than an admirer, who has the man and the lover well blended together. (1779)

## Miss Emily Coulthurst, at Mrs. Mitchell's, King's Place

As this lady is one of the most beautiful women we ever beheld, and is in very high and public estimation, the reader will excuse the liberty we take in relating some particulars concerning her, although we should lengthen the article beyond the usual limits to which we confine ourselves.

Her father is an eminent tradesman in Piccadilly, and happening one day, while Emily was in the shop, to be visited by the Earl of Loudon, who was his customer, the nobleman was immediately struck by her amazing beauty, and determined, if possible, to possess her; though he is naturally a haughty man, he found a sense of inferiority before her, for beauty has always been found to awe, even the most savage, and he found her image indeliably fixed in his heart, as if it had been stamped on it by the power of some engine.

He soon gained victory over the yielding fair one, who became an easy conquest and was kept by him six months when he forsook her, since when she has been the temporary companion of most of the first water bucks in the metropolis, and has been constantly toasted at all the polite convival tables at the fashionable end of town. Her favours are not an easy purchase, but are worth almost any sum, for the 'lovely Emily' is undeniably a real beauty. She is a constant frequenter of public places, and was in the utmost danger at the Theatre in the Haymarket last summer, by her head dress accidentally taking fire but it was happily extinguished, with some difficulty, by a 'squire Gl—n, who was with her. She has resisted several good offers of being kept, nay, it is said a country gentleman of good fortune offered to marry her, but she says she is determined not to confine herself to any man, and will not act dishonourably.

She is rather tall, inclining to the majestic in gait, and has so many voluptuous and inviting graces in her countenance, that it is impossible to behold her without admiration and desire; her teeth are as white and regular as possible, and her eyes are lightening which cannot be withstood. She is not twenty-two, and is the finest woman on the common that we know of. (1779)

## THE UNUSUAL

### Betsey B—l—w, in Castle Street, Oxford Market

*'Who so fair as lovely Bet?'*

If polished ivory has any resemblance to skin, it may be compared to Betsey's, the firmness and smoothness of which are unparalleled: what extasy it is, even to feel so delicate a creature, to one who is an admirer of flesh and blood. Her eyes are blue, and hair of the sandy colour; has some extreme good teeth, and a very fine hand and arm: her only fault is being very wide and relaxed in a particular part, which renders her but an indifferent bedfellow: if she was not to drink so much tea, (the bane of one third of our females) it would be much better for her in respect to this relaxation; but women seldom know what is salutary, and generally poison themselves by drams, or throw themselves into consumptions with slip-slops.[8] (1773)

### Miss Wilkins

*'What an angelic face!—but what a form!'*

This lady very lately resided in Princes Street, Bloomsbury, at a midwife's. She is not above twenty, and has a very engaging countenance, with fine, dark, melting eyes, and very regular teeth. Her person does not entirely correspond; she is short and very crooked; but she has a certain latent charm that more than compensates for any deformity of body. In a word, take her all in all, she is a very good piece; and, if you can forget she is hunch-backed, she is a little Venus. (1773)

## Sally Str—on, at a Grocer's in Little Wild Street

*'Nor bars nor turnpikes shall my way impede'*

The character of this lady is very singular, having been upon the town near six months without ever having been fairly entered. She is so conformed as to require a peculiar method of cohabitation with her, a bar being naturally in the way, which causes a kind of obstruction; without fixing her in a certain position, no one can perform what he would wish to do. Her face is extremely agreeable, good eyes, fine teeth, about the middling size, and inclinable to be fat. She might easily pass for a maidenhead, if she kept her own secrets; but she seems to be too honest, or rather too simple to deceive anyone in that particular. Her price is optional, consequently every thing is made very easy, excepting her commodity. (1773)

## Miss Jordan, No. 20, Little Wild Street

As a remarkable woman, we could not pass over this lady, for she is an absolute curiosity, weighing, at least seventeen or eighteen stone, and considering that this is no light weight to carry, she is very nimble—we must confess we should be very loath to trust ourselves with her in bed lest we should be overlaid, or that she should chuse to place herself in a particular posture, and we should be that way smothered; she is very fair, and has a face somewhat resembling a full moon, she is always neat and clean in her dress, and is said to have a particular natural curiosity, equally remarkable with her person, either of which are open to the inspection of the curious on reasonable terms. (1779)

## SMALL AND TALL

### Jenny Dorrington, Russell Street

This little lass is of the pigmy size; she bolts in and out of the Rose and Ben Johnson's Head, like a rabbet in a warren. Her hair, eyes and eye-brows, are nearly black: she is neatly made, but of a sallow complexion, and a face that won't bear much examining. Her limbs, tho' small, are very neat; and as her size is very uncommon, we would recommend her to some old virtuosi, to keep in a case, and produce her for the entertainment of his friends, or for his own private occasions, as he shall think fit. (1761)

### Miss Sims, No. 82, Queen Ann Street East

*'Like some fair flower, whose leaves all colours yeild,*
*And opening is with rarest odours fill'd*
*As lofty pines o'er top the lowly reed,*
*So does her graceful height most nymphs exceed'*

Miss Sims is fair and tall, and if well paired would be a very proper mould to cast grenadiers in; is about twenty, and though rather above the common height, is not ungraceful nor awkward. She knows her value and will seldom accept of less than two guineas, which indeed are well-bestowed. It is remarkable that her lovers are most commonly of a diminutive size. The vanity of surmounting such a fine tall woman is, doubtless, an incentive to many, to so unmatch themselves, that they are content to be like sweet-bread on a breast of veal. Yet, not withstanding her size, we hear her low countries are far from being capacious, but like a well-made boot, is drawn

on the leg with some difficulty, and sits too close as to give
great pleasure to the wearer; it is about two years since her
boot has been accustomed to wear legs in it, and though often
soaled[9] yet never wears out. (1788)


## SISTERS


## Miss Sells, in King Street, Covent Garden

> '*The passion love unto their fancy brings*
> *The prettiest notions and the sofest things*'

These ladies have so long figured in private that they might
arraign us of partiality if we did not honor them with a place.
'Tis true, they have often favoured us with their company, and
'twas with secret pleasure we have beheld them when we have
had the honor to wait behind their chairs at our house; with how
much composure they have stood the most indecent attacks
made upon their persons and understandings; our brother
Robinson (a pimp at the Fountain in Katherine Street) had
often remarked his agreeable neighbours to us, when they lived
in Katherine Street, and their father kept a jeweler's shop; a poor
old German, whose heart they broke, and he, in a fit of insanity,
tied himself up in his garters, when they lodged in Great Queen
Street, after having left their house in the aforesaid street. After
his death they removed to the house they now inhabit in King
Street, with their aged mother, who, poor woman, is no more
than a cypher, having no will of her own, being obliged to her
daughters for her support; she answers, however, their ends, and
I suppose they find it to their purpose to give her victuals, or

else they are so good oeconomists the old lady would long ago have been sent to the workhouse.

Were we to enumerate half their intrigues since their commencement, it would fill two pretty novels for Mr. Noble's Library,[10] and therefore much exceed the bounds of our work: the eldest of them is a good shewy girl, rather going down hill; she has, to be sure, gone thro' a great deal of service and taken some rough medicines to cause abortion, which have pretty much affected her, yet notwithstanding we give her the preference.

The youngest is not so tall as her sister, her complexion somewhat better, for the good girl let Nature take its course and has a fine daughter, who lives at home with them, tho' under the sanction of a young lady as a boarder. The eldest cannot be less than thirty, the other perhaps, three years younger; they are good company, and indeed not despicable as to understanding: they have seen a good deal of the town, and can superficially talk on most subjects, but the theatre is their favourite. If our readers will call, when sauntering by their shop, and buy a trifle, they will allow part of what we have said to be true, and a present, well timed, and a jaunt into the country will make them acquainted with all their secrets.

N.B. They understand a jilting, and will fight shy a long time, a coup de maitre will therefore be necessary. (1773)

## Mrs. Hendridge, Moorfields

*'Like Heav'n, she takes no pleasure to destroy'*

Sister-in-law to a lady in these lists, named Fowler, whose brother she married, unfortunately for him; for the poor fellow scarce ever after knew what happiness was. He got madam with child before the ceremony, as she says; and thereon she went to his house, (a brassfounder in Houndsditch), and insisted upon not quitting it, alledging it was hers and that she would remain wherever he was. Her friends by promising him a sum of money, (which they never gave him) made up the match. She launched out into all the fashionable follies, and soon melted all her husband's brass into caps, handkerchiefs and aprons; he became a bankrupt, and she has sent him into the country to his relations to graze, that she might take her swing of pleasure more uncontrouled.

She is not so lusty as her sister Fowler, whom we have mentioned; a little pock-marked: genteel, tho' not so handsome; and has a neat leg and foot; her hair light-coloured, and her eyes grey. She has a good deal of life and spirits in company, and is agreeable and chatty.

Her sister and she always hunt together, and may be often met with at the bread and butter manufactories[11] at Islington, but more especially at White-Conduit House, with the master of which Mrs. Fowler had an intrigue. As they are of quite a different make, there seem policy in their being together, as they cannot interfere with each other's swains, and it answers several other purposes which they know well to turn to their advantage.

We wish they would not endeavor at the dress of the ladies in the Stand, with such bunches of ribbons, such tawdry dresses, and boldness in their countenances. If they mean to have citizens for their admirers, their very looks are enough to frighten them from the beginning of a conversation. (1773)

## LADIES OF THE TON

**Miss Ledger, next to the Bookseller's, Mayfair**
It is impossible to account for the peculiarities of some
people, as for the different formation of fishes and animals, for
this reason we believe and shall not find one person able to
give an explanation of this lady's behaviour, for as we never
understood, that an old man was an agreeable bedfellow for a
young woman, we are exceeding surprised that she should
support one merely through inclination. She has a number of
visitors, some of them men of fashion, who enable her to live
in a very elegant manner; she dresses in a stile absolutely
grand, and is a constant frequenter of public places, especially
Ranelagh,[12] where she is very well known. She is commonly
attended when she walks abroad, by a little black foot-boy,
who carries her lap dog on a fine crimson cushion, which is
curiously ornamented with tassels. She is very fond of
reading plays, and will continue sometimes repeating passages
from them for an hour altogether; she likewise places
incoherent rhimes together on the subject of love, and is
highly pleased to hear any person commend the poetry.
She is about twenty-three, has an elegant gait and good eyes;
her face is handsome, but she uses too much paint; her
favours are very difficult to gain without a very handsome
present. (1779)

## Mrs. Deville, No. 7, Holland Street, Soho

*'Here's a lot for Sk—r, or Ch—ie fit*
*To hold up and knock down as they shall hit'*

This is a first rate Thais, who, though in good keeping by a
Count, whose name she has now taken, has no sort of objection
to a bank note as being a great patriot, she hold Britannia, even
upon paper, in the highest estimation. However, a banker's
note of only five guineas carries with it a degree of temptation
not to be refused, when out of competition with one of the
first class. Mrs. D—lle is a great frequenter of auctions, and
being a particular admirer of old china, she upon these
occasions commonly makes acquaintance with some
connoisseur, whom she desires to bid for her; the consequence
is, the lot is entered in his name, and to prevent him further
trouble, she takes it home in her carriage. This lady is about
twenty two years of age, tall, genteel and very agreeable,
though a little pitted with the smallpox, but this is not visible
at any distance, especially after she has paid due attention to
her toilet. Her eyes are dark and very expressive, her
disposition extremely chatty, and has entirely surmounted that
mauvaise houte, for which the English have by foreigners been
frequently stigmatized. Indeed, from the circumstance of her
auction manoeuvres, it is almost superfluous to mention, that
she is a woman of uncommon address, possessed of a small
share of modest assurance, very necessary to carry adventures
in the fortune of the world, of both sexes, through it with
success. Her sideboard of plate is said to be very valuable, as
she has occasionally increased it at sales, by her uncommon
adroitness in forming good connections in a hurry. We think
Mrs. D—'s intrigues may afford some useful hints to the frail
sister-hood in her elevated line. (1790)

## SELECT SERVICES

*ORAL SEX*

### Miss Noble, No. 10, Plow Court, Fetter Lane

> '*She darted a sweet kiss,*
> *The wanton prelude to a farther bliss*
> *Such as might kindle frozen appetite*
> *And fire e'en wasted nature with delight*'

She is really a fine girl, with a lovely fair complexion, a most engaging behaviour and affable disposition. She has a most consummate skill in reviving the dead; for as she loves nothing but active life, she is happy when she can restore it: and her tongue has a double charm, both when speaking and when silent; for the tip of it, properly applied, can talk eloquently to the heart, whilst no sound pervades the ear and send such feelings to the central spot, that immediately demands the more noble weapon to close the melting scene. (1788)

### Miss H—lsb—ry, No. 14, Goodge Street

> '*This Pleasant vineyard is well stor'd with fruit,*
> *And many a plant here has taken root*'

This young lady is finely made, with a prepossessing countenance, expressive dark eyes, fine hands and arms, and proclaims the woman of consequence fit for the first rate company, into which she is often introduced. Nevertheless, having got the better of that mauvaise houte, with which our ladies are so much accused, with what reason it is difficult to say, she is careless about her expressions and neither shudders

at a double entendre, or trembles at a single entendre: in fine,
she may, in more senses than one, be pronounced a great
linguist. A velvet salute of this kind, had nearly disgusted Lord
L—; but having got over the first impression, he found that
her tongue was attuned to more airs than one; but she never
admits either of her mouths to be play'd with for less than two
guineas. She appears very genteel, and is supposed to be in
keeping by a Mr. Grace of Duke Street, St. James. (1789)

## FLAGELLATION

## Miss Loveborn, No. 32, George Street, Queen Anne Street East

If we are not misinformed, this lady is one of the daughters of
fortune, having a pretty good income left her by an old
flagellant, who she literally flogged out of the world, and will
probably more, as she is an expert at this manoeuvre as
Mrs. Birch herself, of Chapel Street, Soho. Indeed she is very
happily constructed for this bizarrerie, as the French call it,
being of middle size and well set together, and never leaves off,
'till her patient, (for patient he must be in our opinion) is
completely gratified. Such gratification, good Lord keep us
from! But it has been observed by a great Philosopher that there
must be characters of every complexion and disposition to fill up
the great chasm of nature; the chain of individual existence
would not be complete if there were a single link wanting; and
Miss L—n is so attentive to her interests, that she will never let
a link escape her, to which she thinks she has any claim.

Oeconomy is seldom a virtue practiced by females of her
profession but we can produce an instance of it in this lady,
which is as whimsical as it is extraordinary. The chandler's
shop which furnishes her with brooms, her chief birchen

instrument of delight, has agreed to furnish her in turn with tea, coffee, butter, bread and all other articles sold in the shop at a considerable reduced price on condition that she does not purchase brooms any where else; and it is generally believed it is a very advantageous contract for both parties. (1790)

## Miss Lee, Berwick Street, Soho

> *'Oh pray mamma! Let me down!*
> *You will find me the best boy in town;*
> *I'll never while I live offend,*
> *I promise you, you will find me mend!'*

This young lady is tall and genteel, and about seventeen, with sandy colour hair, and fine blue eyes that are delicious; her complexion is delicate and fair, but we cannot refrain saying, she has a piece of the termagant about her, which however, she qualifies with a whimsicality of humour that renders it supportable. She was debauched by a young counsellor, from a boarding school near town, where she was apprentice. Her mistress surprising her one day with a certain naughty book, took her into the whipping room, where having tied her on a horse that is always there for the use of correction, she whipped her with a large rod, made of green birch, till through fatigue, the rod dropped from her hands; the counsellor meeting with her a few days after, she told him how she had been used by her governess for the book he had lent her; he took immediately a room for her, and visited her till he went to Ireland. She found herself for some time very much embarrassed, till meeting with a merchant of the city, who is fond of the rod, she soon appeared again at the theatres, which she frequents very much.

She dresses always very elegantly, and in the season she is very seldom without the most enormous nosegay of luscious flowers, which she generally wears very high on the left side of her bosom, having discovered that many gentlemen have a great partiality for that effeminate ornament. She is constantly visited by amateurs of birch discipline, being always furnished with brooms of green birch and of the best quality, and is always very happy to see any friend that feels himself inclinable to spend three or four guineas in her company. (1793)

## REAR-ENTRY

## Betsy Miles, at a Cabinet maker's, Old Street, Clerkenwell

### *'Which way you will and please you'*

Known in this quarter for her immense sized breasts, which she alternately makes use of with the rest of her parts, to indulge those who are particularly fond of a certain amusement. She is what you may call, at all; backwards and forewards, are all equal to her, posteriors not excepted, nay indeed, by her own account she has most pleasure in the latter. Very fit for a foreign Macaroni—entrance at the front door tolerably reasonable, but nothing less than two pound for the back way. As her person has nothing remarkable one way or the other, we shall leave her for those of the Italian gusto. (1773)

## BISEXUAL

## Mrs. Forbes, Back of Yeoman's Row, Brumpton

*' 'Tis now before you, and the pow'r to chuse'*

Mrs. Forbes takes her name from a General so called, to whom she pretends she was married; but we give no more credit to this than we should to any part of her own story, had she the telling of it. She is about 36, very much pitted with the small-pox, light brown hair, rather above the common size. How such a piece of goods first came to our market we are at a loss to guess. We have indeed heard that she lived some time servant in Wapping; and, as the tars are good natured, free-hearted fellows, and, after long voyages, are not very nice in their choice, they might perhaps have done her a good-natured action; this is the only way we can account for it, every other seems absurd to us. Her hands and arms; her limbs indeed, in general, are more calculated for the milk-carrier, than the soft delights of love; however, if she finds herself but in small estimation with our sex, she repays them the compliment, and frequently declares that a female bedfellow can give more real joys than ever she experienced with the male part of the sex: perhaps her demands in that way may be so great she never found a man able to supply her; this is but a natural conclusion when a lady is remarked for paying visits to a fellow famous only for ideotism. The proverb indeed is on her side, and perhaps she has found it true. The ingenious author of the Woman of Pleasure[13] has given us a noble picture of it in the foolish nosegay man.

Many of the pranks she has played with her own sex in bed (where she is as lascivious as a goat) have come to our knowledge; but, from our regard to the delicacy of the sex, are suppressed, but in no sort as a favour to her; our plan indeed is too confined to admit of it: but we can assure her, unless she gives over that scandalous itch of hers to sow disentions where harmony and peace should ever reign, and which she envies because she can not attain to—we shall not forget her next year, but be more explicit—and moreover acquaint her old drone of a keeper, in King's-bench Walks in the Temple, of her lewd pranks and amorous feats. (1773)

## DENOUNCED!

### Polly Kennedy, Manchester Buildings

A good likely girl of Irish birth; and they never transplant flowers of her kind in this soil, till they are rotten there. In a word, this girl has been salivated,[14] till from the constant use of mercury, it has almost lost its effects upon her; and after having been dragged thro' every kennel in Dublin, she is come over to London to set up as a first rate courtesan. There is some blockhead or other, who has now got her in keeping, is as well satisfied with her, as Ixion was with the cloud when he embraced it for Juno. (1761)

### Miss Young, No. 6, Cumberland Court or Turk's Head Bagnio, Bridge's Street

Miss Young is an adopted child to the bawd, who keeps, or more properly speaking, is kept by the above mentioned houses, and is so very fond of cutting a figure, that in a hired tawdry silk gown, she will fancy herself a woman of the first quality.

We mentioned her in the last list as tolerably handsome, but of a disposition mercenary, almost beyond example, her beauty is now vanished, but her avarice remains, and what is worse, she has very lately had the folly and wickedness to leave a certain hospital, before the cure of a certain distemper which she had was completed, and has thrown her contaminated carcase on the town again, for which we hold her inexcusable, and which was our only reason for repeating her name, that her company might be avoided, and that she might be held in the infamous light she so justly deserves for her wilful villainy. (1779)

## Mrs. Berry, King's Place, Pall Mall

*'Mercury upon most women has some effect'*

An arrant Brimstone of Irish birth, who pretends to set up as one of the first rank courtezans, and would impose upon us her stale and battered commodity for fresh fruit, but we think our judgment cannot be imposed upon at this time of day, and are of opinion she has undergone too many salivations, that the power of Mercury has lost its effect upon her: in a word she is almost rotten, and her breath is cadaverous. (1773 supplement)

## FOREIGNERS

## Madam Dafloz, No. 46, Frith Street, Soho

*'Si javois pour heritage,*
*Le trésor le plus charmant*
*Je vous en donnerois en gage,*
*Á mon coeur pour un present'*

It is only six months since this lady has left her native country, and at present speaks very little English. She is young and lively, (but still does not seem to possess so much vivacity as the majority of her countrywomen); She loves to avenge her countryman's cause on the English, by doing what the most valorous Frenchman would never effect, that is, to bring Britons on their knees; she is now twenty-two, rather short and fat, with a plump face and such a roguish lear in her eye, that can not be resisted. Several of our brave officers have spent some of their best blood in her service, and regretted they had no more to shed. Her lovely dark hair seems like a net to catch lovers, and her lower tendrils which sport on her alabaster mount of Venus, are formed to give delight. She has one qualification which many English girls want, which is a certain cleanliness in the Netherlands. They are contented to wash their faces, necks and hands; but Mademoiselle, like many of her countrywomen, thinks that not enough; she performs constant ablutions on the gulph of pleasure, and keeps it constantly fresh, cool, and clean, never putting a morsel into that mouth, till she has fully absterged every possible remnant of the last meal. She constantly mounts her bidet, and with a large sponge laves the whole extent of the parish of the mother of all saints. Some may, perhaps, think her a female spy, or a smuggler; but surely a girl, who so freely discloses her own secrets, can have no improper aim at those of government.

She dresses quite in the French stile and taste, lays on a profusion of rouge and pearl powder, and is not particularly partial to money, but will condescend to take a couple of guineas, not as payment, but solely as *une gage d'amour.* (1788)

## Mrs. Charlotte Ferne, No. 41, King Street, Soho

> *'To tell the beautie's of the place,*
> *How weak is human tongue,*
> *The noble fringes which it grace,*
> *In golden ringlets hung'*

Charlotte received a good education and was once far above the perambulating class of nymphs, and might, perhaps have remained so had not her violent attachment to the curs'd buckle and belt society, rendered her disgusting in the eyes of all her friends; Mr. Goblett, brother to a tallow chandler, of Carnaby Market, took particular notice of her, and removed her once from her hated crew, allowed her a tolerable provision, and would have continued her friend, had not her rage for the old society made him forfeit his esteem. She is now rather in the wane, having seen at least twenty-eight summers, tall and very well proportioned; her complexion is but indifferent, but being a native of Germany, is not to be wondered at; she speaks French also, but we cannot get her to confess she has been ten years on the town, unless you pay her a guinea fee for confessing. (1788)

## Madamoiselle, at Mrs. W—lp—les, No. 1 Poland Street

> *'Here I would die each blissful night,*
> *Here chase the fleeting time away,*
> *And Whelm'd in love's serene delight*
> *Rise full of life at happy day'*

Every girl with a beautiful face and a good form, must in some measure, please; but very few among this list of trading nymphs afford that pleasure in enjoyment you meet with, in this delectable piece. She is now on the verge of twenty four, with fine dark hair, love sparkling eyes, and such a set of teeth as would defy the power of a Spence to imitate, or the brush of Ruspini to improve. You may toy and kiss with this charming girl, if you please, but she does not suffer that kind of amorous dalliance long; she eagerly thirsts for more substantial pleasure, and has either by experience or instinct, a most pleasing knack of prolonging the dying moment, first as nature, by inarticulate sounds, and short fetched sighs, proclaim the coming shower, her eager grasp suddenly suspends the liquid treasure and drains, by slow degrees, the soft injection, making it almost, with Dr Graham 'the critical hour'. This enchanting game she has played for two years, and if you are her partner, she expects at least double the number of yellow boys.[15] If report speaks truth, this lady has been a singer at the Opera House in Paris, and we have no doubt that she is a native of Italy. (1789)

## Charlotte Benevent, Princes Street, the Corner of Lisle Street, Leicester Fields

### *'Novelty has its charms to please'*

This lady was born in Holland, but speaks French and English tolerably well; she is of the middle stature, fine black eyes, and eye brows, dresses in an elegant taste and seldom goes out, having a set of particular acquaintance who enable her to live somewhat above the common rate. Above, on the second floor, lodges Miss Boothby, mentioned in our last year's, with whom she has no connection, thinking herself much superior to any on a second floor, and who is continually padding[16] of it, to seek for customers; her price is one pound one, from a person she likes, but otherwise she must be paid like a foreigner and a woman of uncommon discernment. (1773)

# WORKING THE NIGHT SHIFT

## Miss C—l, No. 3, Princes Street, Leicester Fields

*'The pretty sparkler never fails to please*
*As all she does, is done with so much ease'*

This lady possess a very good shape, dark hair, fine eyes, regular engaging features, and good teeth. She is about nineteen, and tho' she has not been long upon the town, she is perfectly initiated in all the meretricious powers of pleasing. Bred to the glove making business, she still carries it on to prevent the voice of scandal, if possible from ranking her as a fille de joye; but facts are stubborn things, and it must be acknowledged she has no objections to the compliment for half an hour's amorous dalliance. Her panting orbs are very attracting, and she considers them so angelic that she never lets them be pressed to afford delight without an angel at least being presented. A certain pharmaceutic gentleman within the sound of Bow-bell, generally visits her once a week: He at once superintends her health and takes care of his own, as he never enters deeper into enjoyment than the pressure and titulation of the felons, for which he constantly gives a guinea. She has some other friends of the same disposition, which she highly approves, reserving her general gratification for Captain O'Keaffe, an Irish officer who mounts guard upon her covered way almost every night, when she is unengaged, and he is supposed to be an excellent staff officer, and to do duty like a martinet. Indeed if we may judge from the breadth of his shoulders, and the stoutness of his legs, he is well qualified for the post which he fills entirely to the satisfaction of Miss C—l. (1789)

## Lucy Bradley, Silver Street, Cheapside

A low, square built lass, with a good complexion, void of art; her face is round, and her features regular; her hair is dark, and her eyes hazel. She lived as a nursery maid with a foreign practitioner of physic, near Soho, who took first possession of her, not without some force. She gets up small linen and works well with her needle; has some good sense, and honest principles. Necessity first compelled her to see company, and she seems conscious of its not being right. (1761)

## Mrs. Quiller

*'The Specious matron, or the wanton wife!'*

This lady resides in Little Titchfield Street, Cavendish Square. She is a shewy figure, though not handsome; is a very convenient good-natured woman, and has officiated in the double capacity of mistress and procuress. If you do not like her, she has generally a tolerable good piece in the first floor, whom she recommends upon honour. At present her lodgings are empty, but she soon expects an agreeable lodger, as she has entered upon a new profession—a MIDWIFE. By this means she has given sanction to a retreat to a woman of a tender character, and either a male or female may lie in there very privately. (1773)

## Mrs. Horton, No. 3, Beauclerc's Buildings

*'Ah! La jolie de petite Bourgeoise'*

Keeps a shop and sells gloves, garters, &c. and drives on a very capital trade, considering she has no shop-woman to assist her; her customers are but few, yet they are good ones, and always pay ready money; she is short and plump, has a good dark eye, and is full-breasted; her legs are remarkably well made, and she is reputed a most excellent bed-fellow. In trying on a glove she will create desire; and in selling her garters, she will commend that pattern which she wears herself, and will make no scruple of showing her legs; she has great good nature, and we do not recollect any woman who is better qualified as a shop-keeper; her age is twenty-six. (1779)

## SOMETHING FOR THE FETISHISTS

### *THE SCENT OF LOVE*

### Miss Clarkson, No. 5, Holland Street, Soho

> '*In this limpid stream you may bathe with ease*
> *Price two guineas only – if you please*'

Miss C— is of a middling stature, with dark eyes and hair but of a fair complexion. She has not been upon the town above six months, and therefore may be pronounced in fine preservation. A certain foreign prince took a particular fancy to her when she was here, and is said to have presented her with his miniature picture, which by the bye, we do not find she is now in possession of. Those awkward relations, worse than cater cousins, vulgarly called uncles,[17] are very apt to engros the good things of this world, and they have a very attentive eye to those baubles, known by the name of diamonds, which sparkle to their fancy, and give them infinite pleasure, whenever they can obtain them for a trifling sum. Thus far we attempt to account for the disappearance of the portrait in Miss C—'s apartments, probably it may be exhibited again in a few months; but we allow this is only conjecture.

An anecdote, which is related upon the first interview between the prince and this lady, may not probably be distasteful to our readers, who perhaps may be fond of a relish in the game of gusto.

Miss C— expecting a very handsome compliment in which opinion she was not deceived from the Prince, resolved to set herself off to the greatest advantage. Not satisfied with having her head dressed by one of the best Parisian hands in town, she also consulted him upon the decoration of the other extreme of bliss; when Monsieur le friseur[18] advised her to have it dressed en aile de pigeon, and powdered a la marechalle. She accordingly underwent the operation, and was now, in her opinion, frissee au dernier gout, from top to bottom. The idea of marechalle powder struck her forcibly that a little musk would add to the odoriferous scent of the seat of bliss, and accordingly it was applied. When his highness came to action, he was so much of an Englishman to despise all fictitious aids in that quarter and turning up his nose at the poudre a la marechalle, and more so at the musk, which was quite offensive to him, he rang the bell, and sent the servant for a red herring. Miss C— was astonished at the order, but being willing to oblige in every respect, yielded to what she thought an extraordinary caprice.

No sooner was the red herring brought, than he immediately applied it to her covered way, telling her that would restore it to its natural and primitive smell. Now, Madam, said he, you have the true effluvia, before I thought you a mere doll for sale at Warren's or Bailey's. He then engaged, and expressed his satisfaction at Miss C—'s rivulet, being narrow, limpid and pleasant.

Upon the prince's second visit she appeared *puris naturabilis*, in the completest sense of the expression, which greatly pleased him, and the next time he favoured her with his company, he presented her with his portrait, as we have already mentioned, and a handsome sum in cash.

These were Halcyon days indeed! Would Miss C— could see them again, however she is not badly off, as her friend the East India Captain allows her a genteel support in his absence. (1790)

## LADIES' LAUNDRY

## Miss Grant, No. 46, Newman Street, Oxford Road

*'Strange are the passions of mankind;*
*To reason deaf, to common sense quite blind'*

No female votary of venus understands the minutiae of her profession better than Miss G—t. She twines her culls[19] as it were, round her finger, studies their foibles and caprices, and gratifies them to their full extent. She has, perhaps, a set of the most extraordinary customers of any professional devotee of the Cyprian Queen, in town. As an instance, we shall relate the following account, remarkable as it may appear. A certain merchant, near Leadenhall Street visits her constantly every Saturday afternoon, as there is little to do upon that day. No sooner does Miss see Mr. B— enter than she orders the necessary implements for the washing of foul linen, such as a kettle of hot water, soap dish, wash tub and the like. These being produced, with the maid's dirty bedgown, which he puts on, having first stript off his coat, and tuck'd up his shirt sleeves, he sets to work, and in a few seconds, gets up to the

elbows in suds. After this amusing himself till he is nearly out
of breath, he wipes his hands, changes his cloaths, presents her
with two guineas, makes his obeisance and retires. Half the
ladies of pleasure, indeed if they could meet with such handy
culls, who not only pay them well for doing nothing, but save
them the expence of a washwoman. We could mention some
other visitors, equally eccentric in the gratification of their
passions, but we shall reserve them, for some other occasions,
as Miss G—is not the only lucky female in this respect.

In her person she is rather lusty, but well made, with blue
eyes and fair hair, about twenty, very engaging in her manner,
possessing what Lord Chesterfield calls the Graces. (1789)

## HAIR-COMBING

### Miss Hudson, No. 4, Meards Court, Soho

This lady is about nineteen years old, of the middle size,
pretty, with remarkable fine dark hair, and eyes, that are very
attractive, as well as her teeth. She has been upon the town
about fifteen months, and has played her cards very well,
having a good deal of custom in the merchantile way, and
never accepting of less than two guineas for her present. She
has some good customers in the eccentric class, who pay her
handsomely, and give her very little trouble. One of the faculty
of the College in Warwick Lane often visits her, and seems to
be the immediate successor of the celebrated Dr Runastrokius
of hair combing memory. Whenever this son of Esculapius[20]
makes his appearance, she is prepared to receive him, her
flowing tresses wantoning upon her shoulders; he immediately
begins his operation, and combs them most devoutly with a
tortoise shell comb, which he always carries about him for that
purpose; after which he presents her with five guineas wrapt

up in a paper, and takes his leave. The circumstance of his carrying the comb constantly about him, created an uncommon laugh against him a short time since at Batson's, when accidentally pulling it out of his pocket with his handkerchief, it fell upon the floor. The waiter picking it up, addressed all the gentlemen in the room, to know if it was their property, none owned it till it come to this gentleman, who acknowledged it belonged to him, took it from the waiter, and put it in his pocket, a wag present (who by the bye was not unacquainted with his extraordinary concupiscence) said, 'Doctor, I never knew before that you was a barber surgeon, I always took you for a regular physician.' (1790)

## EYE-LICKING

### Miss L—k—ns, No. 15, Poland Street

*'T'eccentric vices titles fools lay claim,*
*The priest, the Cit, and lawyer do the same'*

This lady is about twenty years of age, middle stature, and rather inclined to be masculine; but as the epicene gender is adopted, in appearance at least, by both sexes, she is no ways disagreeable. Her complexion is dark, and her eyes and hair are neatly of the same hue.

Miss L— lost a very good friend in the late Lord C—, as he gave her every windfall in his department, which was not inconsiderable, for which she tickled his fancy in the most concupisential point he could devise. Strange to tell, but extremely true, his caprice was entirely out of the common road; in plain English it was to have his eyes licked with a female tongue. It must, however, be acknowledged he was not afflicted with sore eyes, and though the pecuniary sauce was exquisite, there was no gravy thrown into the bargain, Quels caprices ya'till au mande! (1790)

## APHRODISIACS

### Miss Bland, Wardour Street, Soho

This is a gay volatile girl; very genteel in her person; and has an extraordinary titillation in all her members; which she is very fond of increasing, by making use of provocatives for that purpose such as pullets, pigs, veal, new-laid eggs, oysters, crabs, prawns, eryngoes,[21] electuaries,[22] &c. &c. – She is reported to have a kind of savage joy in her embraces, and sometimes leaves the marks of her penetrating teeth on her paramour's cheeks. (1764)

## PROCURESS TO THE PARTICULAR

### Mrs. Orwell, Denzill Street, Clare-Market

> '*Two whores great Madam must be straight prepar'd,*
> *A fat one for the 'Squire, and for my Lord a lean.*'

Though this lady does business in the sportive way, yet as she is far more famous as a procuress, we shall confine ourselves to her character, chiefly in that capacity as she has some employers of distinguished rank. Lord C— is her best customer, whose gout for women with breasts full of milk is so well known; then we have Sir W— M—t, who is equally notorious for his inclination towards young girls before the age of puberty arrives, and several others of distinguished taste.

This lady is remarkably expert at decoying pretty faced children, who are left unguarded in some employment in the street: Indeed, her actions in every part of science shew her to be a compleat adept; and it may, with the greatest propriety be said of her, particularly that she lives as openly, by the sale of human flesh, as the butcher does mutton or beef, but no doubt she will answer in the language of Falstaff, 'Every person in their vocation.' She is about thirty-three, has a tolerable face and a fair skin, she is plump, but not very fat, is said to keep a person of ability as a stallion, and that she never loses a bye stroke when it falls in her way. (1779)

## 'THE WORLD IS NOT THEIR FRIEND, NOR THE WORLD'S LAW'

### Kitty Atchison, Bow Street

A middle sized girl, fair complexion, with very regular features. Her youth (being scarce twenty) and budding charms, cannot fail of getting many admirers. She is convinced her situation in life is a very disagreeable one; and has more than once endeavored to extricate herself out of it. –A variety of lovers succeed each other, the last, as welcome as the first, finds not alloy in her affections, as long as his presents are standard. One evening at the Rose, after her spark had paid the reckoning, and called his chair, being left alone, she broke out into this pathetic exclamation, which plainly shows the sensibility of her condition: – 'what a disagreeable situation is this to a generous mind! What an unhappy circle to move in, for a thinking person! – To be the sink of mankind! – To court alike the beastly drunkard and the nauseating rake – dissimulating distaste for enjoyment! – No balmy ease, no innocent comfort; but nocturnal incontinence and debauch. – What must be the end of such variegated concupiscence? – INFECTION.' – Here the waiter broke in abruptly, and obliged her to put an end to the soliloquy. (1761)

## Miss Fernehough, No. 19, Berner's Street

*'What lovely looks were lately worn by thee'*

We are sincerely sorry for the misfortunes this lady has lately met with for after the death of an only child whom she had by Sir Thomas N—, she fell sick herself, owing to the excessive grief which she could not help giving way to on the occasion, and it has impair'd her so much, that she scarcely seems to be the same woman, for the brilliancy of her eye is totally eclipsed, and every other feature is equally injured, when she is recovered, we hope she will appear as she has done, with a most beautiful and pleasing countenance, and every agreeable requisite to charm. Those who visit her, will find every thing conducted in an elegant manner, beyond the common run of genteel lodgings, and may therefore know that a mere trifle will not be acceptable. (1779)

## Hetty D—rkin, Meard's Court

A thin little girl with blue eyes, aquiline nose, and a very little mouth. She is the daughter of a reputable tradesman in Wapping, and was debauched by her father's porter. She has frequent fits of repentance, and has more than once been wavering at the threshold of the Magdalen House.[23] However, a glass of punch, or wine is sure to bring her back again. She is an agreeable companion, but having no passions, considers every man merely as a cull, and seldom scruples to pick his pocket, if she can do it conveniently. (1761)

## Miss Tamer Gordon, Near Long Acre Bagnio

*'Her chains you'll find too difficult to bear'*

Miss Gordon is of Northumberland, which may be easily distinguished by her speech. Her mother and two other sisters came with her to London about a law-suit, the success of which not answering their expectations, with some other concurrent circumstances, drove her to us about five years ago.

She has a fine round face, pleasing figure, and limbs moulded like a Venus; affable, and extremely good-natured. But there her qualifications cease, for in the rites of Venus she is as cold as a Dutch woman; from whence we naturally suppose the inconstancy of her lovers. Her other sisters are among the nymphs, but where we are totally ignorant.

We wish she would not drink so much, as nothing hurts both health and beauty like it. (1773)

## Miss C—l—d, No. 4, Glanville St.

*'Here you may gaze, if gazing will suffice*
*or for a spanker take a luscious slice'*

This lady is about eighteen, rather tall, though reckoned a fine figure; she is dark complexioned, but has a very engaging countenance with fine dark hair and expressive eyes of the same colour; she has a remarkable fine leg and foot, which she exhibits to great advantage occasionally. Miss C—d is engaging in her manners and entertaining in her conversation. She has not been long in the line of life she now moves in, and appears to have an utter aversion to it, waiting only for an opportunity of being selected by some elderly gentleman for his housekeeper or companion. She has very little of the courtezan about her, never asking for any present or gratification, by which means she is often bilked,[24] or put off with a trifle, when she has reason to expect a handsome gratuity. (1789)

# 11

# THE PIMP PAYS

I N THE DRAWING ROOMS and closets of some of London's most respectable men, a storm was brewing. It began in a pile of paper: letters with strong sentiments scratched into them, pages of inky philosophy addressed to newspapers and journals. As it picked up momentum it whirled around the houses of London's authorities, Justice John Fielding and Saunders Welch, the High Constable of Holborn. It blew in through the windows of wealthy leaders of business, upstanding men such as Robert Dingley and Jonas Hanway. Concerned parties began to gather in order to discuss what might be done. By the beginning of 1758, such a gale of good intention had been whipped up that, within the year, it threatened to sweep away Jack Harris and his empire forever.

It was not Jack Harris in particular that the founders of the Magdalen charity targeted, but rather those on his list. Their purpose was to quell the spread of prostitution through a course of reformation – their desire: 'to induce women who have lived as prostitutes to forsake their evil course of life'. For this, they proposed opening a hospital (what now might be considered a refuge or rehabilitation centre) based along the lines of the one opened for orphaned children by Thomas Coram a decade earlier. The plan took remarkably little time to put into action. They had hardly been agitating for more than a year before funds were raised and a site for the Magdalen Hospital located. Influence-wielding men had been shading their eyes from the realities of prostitution for so long that this, the first genuine and concerted public gesture towards righting the wrongs of an unfortunate lifestyle, was met with overwhelming support. In 1758, news of the charity was on everybody's lips and newspapers and bookstalls were filled with discussions and proposals on the subject. There was much debate surrounding the condition of prostitution and the susceptibility of women to its lures, but few were willing to address the male behaviour or societal beliefs that contributed to the evil, or to be so bold as to suggest a plan for its eradication. What Jonas Hanway, John Fielding, Saunders Welch and Robert Dingley couldn't say was that in order for the patriarchy to prevail, a state of prostitution for at least some segment of the female population had to exist.

Among members of the well-intentioned public, fervour for the Magdalen charity gained a momentum of its own and the onus of enacting change within the community soon dropped into the laps of the law-enforcers. Local magistrates' attitudes towards the sex trade had always been fickle and, frequently, as some neighbourhoods and religiously motivated reform societies had noticed, it required much vocal persuasion to move the authorities into action. The laws against keeping bawdy houses or soliciting sex for money were so grossly complicated that rigorous enforcement wasn't worth the watch's or the magistrate's effort. Occasionally, if public sentiment called for it, the authorities might rattle the cages of the local bawds to remind them that they were in breach of the law, but more often than not, anyone of dubious repute rounded up in the course of a night would be set free the following morning. Both prostitution and the law had settled into an almost comfortable pattern of mutual toleration. This state of affairs, however, did not sit well with onlookers, those neither involved in the sex trade nor apprised of the difficulties involved in the enforcement of the law. At some point, both Fielding and Welch must have felt the hot breath of public scrutiny on their necks. It would be difficult to advocate the reformation of prostitution without making some attempt within their own precincts to stamp it out.

In April of that year, the raids began:

> Information having been given to Saunders Welch Esq., that a great number of loose and disorderly persons, both men and women was secreted in houses of ill fame in Black Boy Alley and Chick Lane, Mr. Welch, with the City Marshal, High Constables and other officers went yesterday morning about 6 o'clock to the above places, where they found upwards of seventy such persons, forty eight of whom they secured and sent to the two compters and new prison for their examination by the Lord Mayor.

This announcement, printed in the *London Chronicle* for 22–5 April, was to be the first of many. There were further swoops targeting some of the most notorious streets in the City and the West End, including actions taken against a row of brothels in Hedge Lane and in specific locations within the parish of St Giles and along Drury Lane. However well-intentioned this may have appeared, Fielding still had a difficult time escaping the hypocrisy of residing on Bow Street, snugly tucked into a nest of brothels and bagnios. As one writer to the *London Chronicle* pointed out in his 'Congratulatory Epistle from a Reformed Rake to John Fielding Esq. Upon the New Scheme of Reclaiming Prostitutes', why should the magistrate go as far afield as Hedge Lane to arrest prostitutes 'when you may, with equal justice, dispose of those next door to you'? He continued:

> Since the constables (even those of Covent Garden) are obliged to make oath there are no brothels in their parish; and you, sir, are authorised to search and commit the prostitutes (supposing there are any); I should be curious to know, what particular act of parliament exempts the bawdy houses in Bow Street and in and about Covent Garden, from the like confinement ... it is highly incredible to imagine, that the most active justice in England would let any such houses remain under his very nose.

Increasingly, there were calls to strike at the heart of Covent Garden, the previously untouchable bastion of vice. Reformers were not satisfied with the day's minor catches – streetwalking minions, petty brothel-keepers from the City and the rancid back streets of St Giles; they wanted the big fish, the genuine perpetrators of prostitution. In June, the drag-net was cast out, and what it brought back surprised everybody.

On a warm summer's evening, no one could have guessed what a bad night it would be in the piazza. An almighty noise, more boisterous than the usual drunken revelling, began to rise. The banging of doors and shouts of the watch were volleyed against the vengeful curses of foul-mouthed women. Squealing and screaming followed as scantily clad sex workers were hauled out of their premises, their culls escaping along the back routes. A crowd gathered. Patrons put down their drinks as taverners, waiters and customers clambered to the windows and doors in the hope of observing the unfolding scene. Much to the disbelief of regulars, the watch had gone straight to the north-eastern corner of the piazza. Announcing that they carried a warrant, they boldly marched through the threshold of Mother Douglas's elegant establishment: the brothel that had only recently entertained the Duke of Cumberland. Hers was the most notable, most fashionable house of pleasure to be found, but on that night, nothing, not even a royal patron, could have prevented its pillaging. Her girls were arrested, though later set free, but Mother Douglas, who had not been troubled by the law in over fifteen years, was thrown into the clink.

After the arrests had been made at Jane Douglas's, the authorities turned their attention to the Shakespear's Head. It was there that they found Jack Harris, the Pimp General of All England. He, too, was apprehended, escorted away in front of his clients and Packington Tomkins. Like Mother Douglas, he spent the night locked away in the local compter and was then hauled up before Justice Wright, who had signed the warrant for his arrest. He would not have done so had not one of Harris and Mother Douglas's girls turned informer. Tired, no doubt, of paying a percentage to both a pimp and a bawd, the woman boldly did what few of her class dared in the eighteenth century: she spoke out for herself. According to the chronicler of Harris's tale, she went directly to Justice Wright and 'made an information upon oath . . . of Mrs. Douglas and Master Harris, having procured for her a gentleman and taken poundage from her'. This was all that the magistrate required to make the long-called-for arrest of two high-profile Covent Garden players. Fortunately, Mother Douglas, who was elderly and ill, found bail and thereby 'preserved her liberty'. Jack Harris, smug and unrepentant, was not so lucky.

In the week of 17 June 1758, *Owen's Weekly Chronicle* reported that 'A warrant being granted by Justice Wright of New Palace Yard to search the houses of ill-fame in the parishes of St. Paul Covent Garden and St Martin in the Fields, upwards of 40 persons were taken, and many of them sent to Tothill-Fields, Bridewell.' This would be news to anyone who didn't live within the precinct or frequent Covent Garden's establishments, but even before this informative blurb had appeared in print, tales of the extraordinary event would have been flying about the taverns and disorderly houses of the West End. The apparently unprovoked attacks levelled against the king and queen of the Garden's flesh market were startling. The law had unexpectedly come to life, flexing its muscles in the face of every disreputable tavern-, bagnio- and brothel-keeper. While this performance may have sent a shiver down the spine of pimps and bawds alike, it threw Grub Street's hack writers into a frenzy of excitement.

The apprehension of Jack Harris made the public ask

questions. For all his boldness and arrogance, Harris had managed to remain an elusive character, even to much of his clientele. The lascivious bucks who conversed with him at the Shakespear were more interested in the women he could procure for their pleasure than in his idle chat. In all the years he had resided under Tomkins's roof, very few were genuinely acquainted with the person rather than the pimp. Even fewer knew his real name. But now, in June 1758, the talk in Covent Garden was all about Jack Harris. In the absence of knowledge, rumour and legend filled the void. Punters would have gathered around the tables at the Shakespear and the Bedford Coffee House, recounting their stories. Some would tell of how he inveigled poor country lasses, the lies he told to bring them to bed, the sham marriages enacted to secure maidenheads; others of incidents they had witnessed at the Shakespear, or rumours about his profits or the extent of his empire.

Until this time, the personal history of the chief waiter-pimp at the Shakespear's Head had not really been of much interest, but from the moment he was thrown into Newgate Prison until the date of his release in 1761 an appetite emerged for tales of his escapades. Harris's timely arrest had made his situation both sensational and topical. For most of the year, Londoners had read the colourful accounts in Hanway and Fielding's Magdalen tracts depicting the victims of prostitution, the innocents cruelly entangled in a web. Now, due to Justice Wright's efforts, the law had clapped a glass over one of the profession's perpetrators and the perfect opportunity presented itself to unveil a picture of the spider. All that was required was for someone to reveal him, and Dr

John Hill, a man with a nose for opportunity, stepped forward to do just this.

Even Dr Hill (or 'Sir' John Hill as he was later called), with all his literary panache, could not have fabricated a character as eccentric as himself. Hill could never quite define his line of work. Trained as an apothecary, he also practised as a botanist and a physician, as well as an actor, a garden designer, a Justice of the Peace, a novelist and a hack. Of all these occupations, Hill excelled at hack journalism. There were few during his lifetime who could have matched his inexhaustible stream of articles and pamphlets. Known as 'The Inspector' to his readership, he was like a modern-day tabloid reporter, making his living from scandalizing his readers, rooting out the stories that would most horrify the middle classes. Dubbed by contemporaries a 'versatile man of unscrupulous character', nothing was off limits. His lack of judgement cost him his credibility and his bad temper involved him in constant spats, with everyone from the Royal Society to Samuel Derrick and William Hogarth. Hill was at heart an opportunist, and no one had a better nose for a good story. It is likely that he caught wind of Harris's arrest from his friends at the Bedford Coffee House, where 'The Inspector' used to meet with other members of the literati. The work that was born out of the pimp's arrest, *The Remonstrance of Harris, Pimp-General to the People of England*, is true to Hill's style: the child of both fact and fiction. For the fiction, Hill needed only to skim the circulating pool of legends that appeared after the pimp's arrest. For the fact, he went straight to the horse's mouth.

In the eighteenth century, prison guards liked visitors, especially those with plenty of coins to lay in their palms. By rubbing a few together, Dr Hill would easily have gained access to Harris's cell and encouraged him to spill his story. The doctor's face would have been familiar to the prisoner, and perhaps the relief of having a visitor may have eased the words from the pimp's mouth. More importantly, Hill would have popped a few shillings into Harris's empty hands, as was the custom, and given him a mouthpiece. In effect, what Harris did was the era's equivalent of selling his story to the tabloids. Hill knew precisely what the public wanted to hear before Jack Harris had even uttered a word. His readers were hungry for a villain, one who bared his teeth and snarled, an unrepentant, remorseless beast, a caricature of how the respectable classes might imagine a pimp. Not surprisingly, Hill quickly learned that Jack Harris was very, very angry, and that, although much of his wrath was directed against Justice Wright, even more of it was aimed at Packington Tomkins.

According to Hill, no one was more surprised at his arrest than the pimp himself. Harris had for years thrived 'un-molested' by 'the watch and constables of the night', who 'never let loose but after street-walking bunters, low wretches, and those quite beneath the protection of justice'. He acknow-ledged that due to the recent 'legislation to force modesty on the town', he and Mother Douglas had become the targets of reformation: 'they call it', he sighed, 'laying the axe to the root'. But then Harris continued in a more personal vein. While Mother Douglas, 'a venerable grey headed gentle-woman', was bailed out by her friends, he was left to rot in gaol by his one supposed protector: Packington Tomkins. 'In the hour of my distress,' he ranted, 'Tomkins (such is the base ingratitude of the man) who owes half of his fortune to me;

Tomkins, I say (hear it and hate him all ye whores) abandoned me.' Harris would never forgive Tomkins, who had made no bones about washing his hands of his head waiter when the situation became sticky. The taverner, who fought hard to appear law-abiding, had realized that there might come a time when jettisoning the pimp would become essential to his own survival. Tomkins, Harris felt, had unjustly emerged from this debacle unscathed, but from the bowels of Newgate he would use Hill's visit to attempt to sink him.

The pimp revealed all his master's dirty dealings, laying down in great detail Tomkins's dishonest tricks. If the world pointed their finger at Harris for his misdeeds, he claimed, they should redirect their reprehension towards Tomkins, whom the pimp had imitated in his business practices and whom he 'had always looked up to with eyes of veneration'. Tomkins was a cheat and a liar, a gentleman who 'bows lowly, smiles submissively and lisps' as he fleeces his customers. Harris claimed that Tomkins made a large portion of his profits from serving overpriced, substandard wine which he dressed up with different-coloured wax seals. He derided his patrons behind their backs and instructed his staff not only on how to be rude but how to be crafty. Such deceits, Harris claimed, were exercised on various customers 'five or six times in a night', while the patrons were none the wiser. Harris recalled bitterly how they all would laugh when hearing 'the taken-in young squires, run out in raptures on my master'. Certainly, this was not the kind of publicity that the owner of the Shakespear's Head sought to cultivate, and it is unlikely that Dr Hill would have concocted such libellous accusations without some prompting. Harris had every right to feel slighted by someone whom he considered to be a partner in crime, and his open attack may have been his only viable means of exacting revenge. The partnership that had been so profitable for both parties was now irrevocably dissolved.

Hill also got what he wanted from his encounter with Harris. From the grains of truth the pimp proffered about his life, his business and his state of mind, Hill created the monster that his readers longed to see. Harris the pimp emerged as an evildoer, void of humanity, boastful about the wickedness of his misdeeds. Hill's Harris rides into the countryside to abduct and debauch unsuspecting young gentlewomen. He meets the wagons on the road to London and offers food and rest to innocent female passengers before raping them. He drugs the wives of City gentlemen and inducts them into a life of prostitution. He laughs at his conscripts' misfortunes, their desperation, the deaths of their parents, their illnesses and traumas. Most abhorrent of all, Dr Hill's Harris claims to have 'received the favour' of 'initiating' (whether willingly or not) over four hundred women into 'the rites of Venus'. Were it to be believed, an assertion so bold would make Jack Harris one of the most notorious rapists in British history. In a society so recently shaken by the trial of Elizabeth Canning and titillated by talk of repentant Magdalens, Hill's tale would have been swallowed with both horror and relish. *The Remonstrance of Harris, Pimp-General to the People of England* raised enough eyebrows to warrant a second print run in 1759, the year after its first appearance.

It was not the only publication to attempt to fill in the blanks of the enigmatic Jack Harris's life. The author of *The Memoirs of the Celebrated Miss Fanny Murray* devoted at least a quarter of his work to telling Harris's history. Unlike Dr Hill's publication, the author of the *Memoirs* paints a much more sympathetic picture of Harris: a man, like his prostitutes, wronged by society and forced into a profession that he understood to be repugnant. The cruelty of the world made a cruel man, apologizes the pimp. The reality of Harrison's situation most likely lay somewhere between the two versions.

Over the three years of his incarceration, and even beyond, the name Jack Harris became synonymous with the standard image of the despicable procurer. Hack writers dropped his moniker into their stories and wrote dedications to his life's achievements in their pamphlets and journals. Jack Harris was more a legend than a living, breathing man. The prisoner inside Newgate quickly came to realize that if he were ever to resume the semblance of a normal life, his name would have to die.

# THE FLEET AND O'KELLY

WITH THE EXCEPTION OF Newgate, there were few places in London with a worse reputation than the Fleet Prison. What made it marginally more bearable than the stinking, disease-bathed sink of Newgate were the comparative freedoms granted to those committed to its confines. Surrounded by a twenty-five-foot wall and with a moat dug into the side of the now paved-over River Fleet, the prison existed like a small hamlet within a city. This, however, did not make the environs any more cheerful. The Fleet might be defined today as an open or minimum-security prison, although a dungeon did exist for those particularly unrepentant few who had to be locked into shackles. For the most part, the majority of the prison population were free to roam within the boundaries of its walls, and for the very few fortunate souls who could produce the bribes necessary, there was the possibility of lodging outside of the enclosed area within the 'rule of the Fleet'. The prison itself contained around a hundred cells, as well as an alehouse, a coffee house, a chapel, a common kitchen and an outdoor area where those interred were allowed to socialize and even play games of ninepins. Ironically, gaming, the vice that bore the responsibility for landing many of the prisoners within the Fleet's precincts, was not prohibited. Some played cards in their cells or tried their luck at billiards. Similarly, the prison's two drinking establishments gave inmates the opportunity to enjoy the same pleasures they had so heartily indulged in on the other side of the wall. But however much these few privileges succeeded in lightening the miseries of existence, they could never have eradicated them entirely. A brutal tradition of extortion and exploitation wound the mechanism of this microcosm. There was nothing about life in the Fleet that could lull an inmate into believing that they were anywhere other than in a prison.

Order in the Fleet emulated the two-tiered system of hierarchy that prevailed within society: those with money could buy comfort; those without suffered doubly. In theory, everyone inside the Fleet was there because they owed money to someone they couldn't repay. This, however, did not mean that every prisoner was without some form of assets. The unofficial objective of the warden and his staff was to shake these last pennies, shillings or guineas from the debtor's tight fists, and to make as much from a prisoner's misfortune as possible. Everything at the Fleet had to be purchased. The first fee that fell due was one of £1 6s 8d, payable to the prison for hosting the debtor's stay. Beyond this, prisoners soon learned that further sums were required to secure virtually every other item or necessity, from food to bedding to writing implements, a chair or medicine. What one ate or how one slept was determined by the amount of money or possessions a prisoner was willing to exchange for these pleasures. To simplify such matters of entitlement, the Fleet was divided into two sections: the Master's side, for those who could spare a few shillings a week for better lodgings; and the Common side, for those who found themselves with less than £5 in total to their names. Those on either side of the prison were squeezed incessantly for every possible ha'penny by cruel guards, who reaped a livelihood through extortion. Threats and physical violence came not only from the turnkeys but from fellow inmates. A sudden absence of resources could result in starvation, and an illness or an injury could often prove fatal without the requisite bribe to bring a surgeon. Although the inmates of the Common side were made to endure the worst of the Fleet's abuses, the prison's proliferation of rats, fleas and lice, its gurgling pools of effluent, its virulent outbreaks of disease and insurmountable stench made no distinction between the two halves.

Those who lived their lives in the streets surrounding the prison or strolled down Farringdon Street could not fail to be reminded of what lay inside the ominous structure near Smithfield Market. The scabby arms of Common-side dwellers reached out through the barred windows, endlessly imploring passers-by for alms. Even the most meagre donation might mean the difference between life and death. When the delivery of alms did not prove sufficient, and having been divested of all remaining hard cash, prisoners soon learned the value of what remained to them. It was possible to buy off antagonistic cellmates and prison staff with personal possessions and even articles of clothing. It was not unknown for prisoners to barter away every last stitch of fabric and to shiver naked in exchange for the 'privilege' of bread. The

Samuel Derrick. One of the only known portraits of Derrick, this image appeared as a frontispiece to his *Letters Written from Leverpoole, Chester, Corke, the Lake of Killarney, Dublin, Tunbridge-Wells, and Bath* in 1767.

Charlotte Hayes (engraving after Joshua Reynolds). This portrait would have been painted shortly after Charlotte and Dennis established their *grand sérail* on Great Marlborough Street; Charlotte would have been in her thirties.

RIGHT: Mrs Lessingham in the character of Ophelia: 'There's rue for you.' Jane Lessingham appeared as Ophelia in a production of *Hamlet* at the Covent Garden Theatre in 1772. The actress was notorious for casting off her lovers.

BELOW: Frontispiece and title page from *Harris's List*, 1761. Over the course of its thirty-eight-year print run, the publishers of the *List* changed the work's frontispiece at least three times. This title page bears the supposed signature of Jack Harris as a seal of authenticity. The handwriting is likely to be that of Sam Derrick; it bears a striking resemblance to his signature.

HARRIS's LIST, 176*1*.

HARRIS's LIST

OF

Covent-Garden Ladies:

OR,

NEW ATALANTIS

For the YEAR 1761.

To which is annexed,

The GHOST of MOLL KING;

OR A

NIGHT at DERRY's.

LONDON:
Printed for H. RANGER, near Temple-Bar.
M DCC LXI.

LEFT: Frontispiece from *Harris's List*, 1779, featuring a man soliciting the favours of a prostitute beside the colonnades of Covent Garden. The two very long objects in the man's possession, his sword and his oversized walking stick, are particularly suggestive. His companion is coyly accepting payment from the small purse in his hand.

BELOW: An entry from *Harris's List*, 1773. In many editions, entries began with a quote from a poem which reflected the story of the woman listed below it.

( 50 )

pered piece, and one that does not degrade herself by her company or her actions; she comes into our corps, in consequence of her good keeper's leaving England, and enlists a volunteer, in all the sprightliness and vivacity of nineteen, with beautiful auburn hair, and a pair of pretty languishing blue peepers, that seem at every glance to tell you how nature stands affected below; nor will those swimming luminaries deceive you; *it is ever ready to receive the well formed tumid guest*, and as the *external crura* entwine and press *home* the *vigorous tool*, the *internal crura* embrace it, and presses out the last *precious drops* of the *vital fluid*, which her hand, by stealth, conveyed to the *treasure bags* of nature, by tender *squeezings* seem to increase the undiscribable rapture, at the *dye away moment*; in short, during her performance of *venereal rites*, she is all the heart of the most inflamed sensualist can wish, or any man that has two spare guineas in his pocket, can desire.

Miss

( 51 )

Miss Gr—n, No. 32, *Little Ruffel-street*.

Strait a new heat return'd with his embrace,
Warmth to my blood and colour to my face;
Till at the length, with mutual kisses fir'd,
To the last bliss we eagerly aspir'd,
And both alike attain'd, what both alike
        desir'd.

When beauty beats up for recruits, he must be an errant coward indeed, who refuses to enlist under its banner; and when good humour, complaisance, and engaging behaviour are the rewards of service, it is shameful to desert. This lady's charms attract most who behold them; though of a low stature, and rather under the middle size, she is elegantly formed; her black eyes, contrasted with her white teeth, are highly pleasing, and the goodness of her temper rivets the chains which her agreeable form first put on. One guinea, is then, too poor a recompence for such merit; and it is to be deplored, that a girl, who should only exchange love for love, should be obliged to take payment for what is ever beyond price: in bed, she is by far the better

E 2                                    piece,

LEFT: Frontispiece from *Harris's List*, 1793. By the 1790s, H. Ranger had decided to adorn the frontispiece to his publication with frolicking nymphs and garlands, giving the work a slightly more dignified, classical appearance.

RIGHT: The owner of the 1761 copy of *Harris's List* had this image of a noted votary of Venus bound in the work beside mention of Miss Smith's name. Miss Smith had been a beauty in her earlier years, the period when this engraving was most likely executed. However, by the time Sam Derrick mentions her in 1761, he claimed that she had 'defaced her native charms' through 'too much use'.

*Miss Smith.*

Printed for Rob.' Sayer, at the Golden Buck near Serjeants Inn Fleet Street.

LEFT: Charlotte Spencer. A chapter in the *Memoirs of Miss Fanny Murray* recounts the story of Charlotte Spencer, who claimed to have been initiated into her profession through the schemes of Jack Harris. For some time she acted as the mistress to Lord Robert Spencer, thereafter assuming his surname and referring to herself as 'the Honourable'.

RIGHT: Fanny Murray. During her heyday in the 1740s and '50s, Fanny Murray was one of Charlotte Hayes's greatest rivals. Although she and Charlotte shared numerous lovers and keepers, Fanny managed to avoid financial difficulties and retired to a life of circumspect matrimony with the celebrated actor David Ross.

LEFT: Betsy Coxe (or Cox). Deposited into the care of Charlotte Hayes at an early age, Elizabeth Green had been a starving, orphaned, teenage streetwalker. Under Charlotte's 'tuition', Betsy Coxe, 'a perfect model of voluptuous beauty', was born. Betsy, like several of Charlotte's 'nuns', went on to become an actress and was particularly noted for her success at playing 'breeches parts', which required her to dress in male attire.

*The Rake's Progress*, 'The Rose Tavern'. Rough, rude and dangerous, even before John Harrison assumed the proprietorship of the Rose the establishment possessed a reputation for debauchery. In this depiction of its main room, posture molls prepare for their naked performances and pockets are picked, while the tavern's interior is defaced and abused. Hogarth depicts 'the members of the frail sisterhood' who ply their trade here in ragged dress and with terrible table manners.

Colonel Dennis O'Kelly, attributed to Johann Zoffany, *circa* 1762 (image reproduced in the *Illustrated London News*, 4 June 1932). O'Kelly is seen here posing in his Middlesex Militia uniform. This portrait was probably painted shortly after he purchased his military commission.

*A Late Unfortunate Adventure at York.* In spite of being a wealthy landowner with a stable of champion racehorses, society would never entirely forgive Dennis O'Kelly for his disreputable character. Matters came to a head in 1770, when he was accused of attempting to force himself on a 'Miss Swinbourne' while at York races. The incident gathered a storm of negative press and was the source of great embarrassment to both Dennis and Charlotte. This cartoon shows a vulgar Dennis attempting to silence a faint Miss Swinbourne with cash. She eventually received a payment of £500 and a public apology.

*Miss S—t—n, the beauty of Arlington Street.* A number of lurid engravings from a slightly later date were bound into the 1761 copy of *Harris's List.* Among them is this engraving of Miss S—t—n. At the time this work was executed she may have been one of Charlotte's Arlington Street 'bevy of beauties', mentioned by William Hickey.

Canons Park, 1782. Canons (or Cannons) as it looked shortly before Dennis purchased it. One of the estate's selling points was a particularly spacious stable block and adjoining pasture land for horses.

COVENT GARDEN MARKET, LOOKING EASTWARD. (*From a Print of* 1786.)

Covent Garden (eastward view), 1786. Covent Garden as John Harrison might have known it in his later years. The Shakespear's Head is located at the north-eastern corner of the colonnade. By this period, the area's brothels had begun to fall out of favour with the more fashionable pleasure-seekers.

Fleet's handful of female inmates learned quickly that the key to their survival resided between their legs.

Due to her connections, and the fact that she hadn't been made entirely destitute in the aftermath of Tracy's inopportune departure, Charlotte was committed to the Master's side of the prison. Although this would have saved her from the unrelenting misery experienced by those on the Common side, the realities of her situation were just as deeply distressing. Charlotte Hayes's reputation as one of the 'great impures' would have caused more trouble for her than if she had been an unknown. Those greasy, disease-ridden Fleet dwellers, both guards and inmates, who could have afforded to admire her only from a distance in her silk gowns and jewels, could now demand, through physical threats, that she yield to their desires. Never would she have experienced the implications of her profession so distinctly than during her time at the Fleet. Since the date of her initiation, Charlotte's cullies had been of her own or Mrs Ward's choosing. She had always exercised the freedom to refuse customers who appeared unsavoury or medically unsafe. The horrors of back-street soliciting and the wretchedness associated with it would have been as foreign to Charlotte as a life of chastity. In the Fleet, however, her body was subjected to anyone who might exert influence over it. Her only hope of reclaiming a degree of control would be to attach herself to a protector, someone who might defend her interests and limit the demands placed on her by the prison's lustful predators.

How much time elapsed before Charlotte Hayes made the acquaintance of a man who could fulfil this role, both inside the Fleet and in her life thereafter, is unknown. At some point during her three-year sentence, her path crossed that of an Irishman called Dennis O'Kelly. The relationship they forged while in prison, and the tales of the couple's escapades, carried out under the noses of the Fleet's authorities, were to become legendary among the more dissolute circles of society.

Charlotte and Dennis had met at a juncture in both of their lives where luck, uncharacteristically, had deserted them. Only a few years younger than her, O'Kelly, like Charlotte, had already experienced 'all the varieties of life'. Bearing a curious similarity to W. M. Thackeray's infamous character Barry Lyndon, Dennis O'Kelly had been born into an impoverished family of minor landholders in Tullow, County Carlow. With no hopes of an inheritance and no prospects of furthering a career, Dennis left home for Dublin as a teenager, where some accounts of his life claim that 'he was first introduced into bad company'. Other sources, including a posthumous publication entitled *The Genuine Memoirs of Dennis O'Kelly Esq., Commonly Called Count O'Kelly*, maintain that he arrived in London before experiencing the seamier side of existence. Described as being 'about five feet eleven inches high, very broad in the shoulders and equally deep chested', with 'legs well proportioned, and . . . hands finely formed by nature', O'Kelly was able to cut a dash for himself as a sedan chairman, exerting his strength and displaying 'the comeliness of his person' in the exercise of heaving ladies' chairs on to his strong back. Not surprisingly, his looks did not escape the notice of many of his female passengers, one of whom he supplied with services comparable to those that Charlotte was offering to men. Through his amours he was able to earn a fair sum of money, which eventually allowed him to shed his servant's 'long coat and purchase smart clothes', for the purpose of 'commencing a fine gentleman'. It was at this period that Dennis 'acquired that invincible disposition for play, which proved in the end the happy source of his good fortune'.

O'Kelly was considered, in every sense, what the folk of the era would term 'an adventurer' or a 'sharper'. His villainy was difficult to detect beneath his polished air and his fine laced coat, but his wealth was won and maintained through a fatal combination of convincing deceits and charm. Accounts vary as to how many tricks at the expense of others he was able to successfully carry out in the years before he met Charlotte. His mastery of 'the long shuffle', a highly orchestrated method of cheating at cards, was said to have begun at the gaming tables of 'the polite circle'. This group was comprised in part of the same crew of indulgent young bucks who frequented London's billiards tables and tennis courts, where Dennis had worked as 'a marker . . . and . . . attendant'. As with the other inhabitants of the sphere in which he now moved, the girth of O'Kelly's purse was in a constant state of flux, and in order to dig himself out of one particularly bad round at the tables, he began to search for an expedient method of relieving his indebtedness. According to *Town and Country*, O'Kelly and a companion established a scheme to entrap two sisters 'who had a thousand pounds between them'. After encouraging the ladies to enter into clandestine unions, Dennis decamped with both marriage portions, disappearing 'to Scarborough, where he remained for some time, and appeared as a man of fashion', gaming 'as high as any man, according to the present etiquette of play'. With his illicit proceeds he embarked upon a tour of the country, appearing first 'at York races ... at Bath, and all the other genteel watering places, where he behaved as well as gamesters generally do, a variety of fortune attending him and his different operations'. In later years, horrified by the indignity of his actions, Dennis took pains to sweep all vestiges of the disreputable incident under the carpet. Although he and Charlotte profusely denied any accusations, Dennis's previous union may offer an explanation as to why he and Charlotte never officially married.

Dennis O'Kelly had been gambling his way around Britain for roughly ten years before he met with any serious objection to his practices. By the late 1750s, he was such a master at his art that few could catch him out, although many suspected that his wins were not acquired through chance alone. One particular gentleman, a visiting officer from the American colonies who had lost his purse to him at the Bedford Arms, was convinced he had been defrauded of his fortune. In a fury, the officer marched directly over to Justice Fielding and reported the incident. According to legend, it was only through the persuasions of O'Kelly's friend Samuel Foote that the charges were mitigated, enabling the cardsharp to wiggle his way out of the Tyburn nooses and land instead in the Fleet. Another account claims that Dennis's 'disposition for dress and play', one which 'far exceeded his means', bore the responsibility for a trail of unpaid bills and receipts. Although skilled at making money, he had become shamefully adept at spending it as well, so much so that when it came time to inscribe his name into the Fleet's committal book, it was placed under the Common side.

When Charlotte encountered him, he had already succumbed to the sale of most of his clothing and the 'few little moveables' that he had on his person. According to her recollections, 'wretched tatters scarce covered his nakedness' and 'famine stared him in the face'. Remarkably, however, his spirit remained wholly intact. For most of his life, Dennis O'Kelly had been noted for possessing 'the ease, the agremens, the manners of a gentleman', as well as 'the attractive quaintness of a humourist', and it was these qualities, in addition to his ruggedly handsome features, that captured Charlotte's confidence. With his formidable build, he would have made an ideal protector, while his good humour, sharp wit and resourcefulness would have assisted in fortifying her emotionally. With Dennis at her side, Charlotte might now begin to win back some control over her position within the prison. After feeding and clothing Dennis, she was able to secure him a job within the Fleet as 'attendant in the Tap', a measure that then allowed him 'to live by carrying out porter to his fellow prisoners'. Now the tables were turned, and Dennis could exact fees for the privilege of drink, just as they had been coerced from him. Unlike others, however, he was 'distinguished for his jolly song' rather than for abusing his newly acquired position. Consequently, the downcast inmates lodging on the Master's side welcomed the singing, jocular Irishman into their fold. 'His reputation extended to the private apartments' and, not surprisingly, 'his company was frequently solicited among convivial circles'. Among the downtrodden population on both sides of the prison, he became so popular that a fellow inmate, known affectionately as 'the King', bestowed on him the honorary title of 'Count'.

While collecting Fleet honorariums was an amusing way of passing one's sentence, Charlotte harboured much more substantial ideas of how she and Dennis might improve their lot. Throughout their lives, the couple were noted for their ability to scent promising opportunities. Although Charlotte had attempted to establish a brothel on Berwick Street shortly before her incarceration, in her absence the enterprise had withered, and it had died by the time of her release in 1760. Now, contained by the perimeters of the prison, her hopes for surviving in the Fleet and building the foundation for a life beyond it were pinned on Dennis. He, in turn, placed his hopes on the gaming tables.

While the Fleet did not prevent prisoners from gambling, anyone hoping to make a profit from the proceeds of card games would not seriously consider wasting their time matching hands with the insolvents in a debtors' prison. Fortunately, as those pursuing legitimate work and seeking counsel from their legal representatives were allowed to traverse the boundaries of the prison, gaining access to the world outside was not an impossibility. The Fleet's 'day rules' stated only that debtors had to remain within a short distance of the prison walls and return at nightfall. This final stipulation would prove to be problematic. In Georgian London, dedicated gamesters could find any excuse to lay bets or sit at a card table, whether it was mid-afternoon or in the diminishing hours of darkness, but Dennis could hardly abandon a healthy rubber midway simply because the sun had begun to set. The scheme therefore required Charlotte's expert diversion tactics. Outside the prison walls, Dennis O'Kelly '. . . was now as constantly seen in all public places as if he had not owed a shilling. These day and *night* rules frequently continued for weeks,' wrote the author of *The Exploits of Count Kelly*, explaining that 'as his judgement was now matured by experience, he seldom failed to make these excursions very advantageous'. Meanwhile, back at the Fleet, the prison's grubby guards failed to notice the Count's absence, while Charlotte Hayes, 'that well known priestess of the Cyprian Deity, that love and mirth admiring votress to pleasing sensuality . . . did not forget to perform her midnight orgies or sacrifice to the powers of love and wine'.

Such a plan could not have been carried to fruition without the cunning of both parties. Of all the accounts written about their relationship, not one differs in opinion about the bond that existed between them. This was love, in the truest, most devoted sense. Although the relationship may have begun as one of mutual convenience, forged through the shared experience of hardship, it evolved into something much more substantial. The 'friendly assistance' that Charlotte was said to have received from Dennis at this period became 'the basis of her future attachment to him', while he in return 'now devoted the whole of his time to Charlotte' and concentrated on securing her happiness. It is perhaps slightly over-romantic to believe that from the period of their meeting in the Fleet, 'time passed without care', as O'Kelly's *Memoirs* suggest, but there is much to substantiate the claim that their 'attachment became so strong, that no circumstance in future life, could ever dissolve or shake the union'.

Dennis O'Kelly was Charlotte Hayes's perfect match. He countered every quality she possessed. He was as well endowed with physical and personal charms as she, and had the know-how to deploy his gifts to their greatest effect. Like Charlotte, Dennis had 'a great ingenuity and a constant eye to temporary resources'. Both were instinctive emotional manipulators and observers of human behaviour. Both were intellectually astute, and Charlotte particularly so with money: in the modern era she would have made a formidable business rival. Her survival skills, especially after a stint in prison, would have been honed to a vicious sharpness. However, 'notwithstanding the varieties she has seen in life', Sam Derrick wrote, Charlotte retained the ability to love. She had a sensitive side to which Dennis alone was privy.

Like many couples, Dennis and Charlotte passed the hours together contemplating their future. If or when they were able to secure their release, *if* Dennis was able to earn enough by his gaming to satisfy their creditors, *if* they could then raise enough money upon which to live, they resolved to throw their lots into a business venture that was certain to make them rich. While residing in the Fleet, they had begun to lay 'the plan of an elegant brothel, under the title of a *nunnery*'. It was an idea over which she had mused for some time, since first encountering the concept at her rival Mrs Goadby's establishment. Jane Goadby had taken credit for bringing this fashionable new style of brothel, in imitation of the *sérails* found in Paris, to England. She had for years been regaled with stories of lavish brothels in palatial *hôtels de ville* by young men who had whiled away their grand tours exploring the insides of such places and, according to

234

the *Nocturnal Revels*, was so taken with them that she went to France's capital city to see these seraglios for herself. What she found was a complete novelty to the British bawd. The *sérails* were ordered and operated impeccably by 'two veteran procuresses'. 'Under each of their roofs were assembled about a score of the handsomest prostitutes in the purlieus of Paris . . .' – but this alone was not the attraction. Mrs Goadby found that her French counterparts were offering more than just sex; rather, they provided an entire evening's worth of genteel entertainment, where women and their customers passed 'their hours after dinner till the evening in a large saloon; some playing upon the guitar, whilst vocal performers were accompanying them; others were employed with needle or tambour work'. Drunken behaviour, and anything other than the 'strictest decorum', was not tolerated among the nymphs or their guests. Such a concept flew in the face of London's seedy bagnios and insalubrious taverns, where riff-raff, aristocrat, bunter and courtesan mixed indiscriminately over smashed glasses, foul language and punch-ups. Even the damask-lined drawing rooms of Mrs Douglas's abode had nothing on the grandness of such places. Mrs Goadby was certain that the French 'system of brothels' would earn her riches, and upon her return to London 'she immediately began to refine her amorous amusements and regulate them according to the Parisian system'. This included fitting up 'a house in an elegant stile', engaging 'some of the first rate *filles de joye* in London' to work for her, and employing a surgeon to vouch for their health. Additionally, the enterprising procuress 'brought over a large quantity of French silks and laces', which

235

enabled her 'to equip her Thaises in the highest gusto; and for which she took care to make a sufficient charge'. Most importantly, though, 'Mrs. Goadby's *sérail* was not a seraglio for *les bourgeois*; she aimed at accommodating only people of rank and men of fortune . . . ' – and by such means secured her own.

After hearing about the success of her competitor, Charlotte was determined to create a *sérail* even bigger and more splendid. Dennis, it was decided, would assist her by 'furnishing the money' while Charlotte, with her considerable experience, would 'furnish the nuns'.

On 24 June 1760, they were given their chance. It was reported in the *Gentleman's Magazine* for that month that 'Upwards of three hundred prisoners from Ludgate, the two Compters and the Fleet were discharged at Guildhall by the Lord Mayor.' By the grace of the Insolvency Act, any prisoner who could produce the small sum necessary to secure their release was absolved of their debts and free to begin their lives afresh. This, however, did not prevent creditors with grudges from coming after the newly liberated, waving unpaid bills.

Immediately after their release, Charlotte and Dennis temporarily went their separate ways in order to re-establish themselves in their respective professions. Charlotte, it seems, was still hiding from those to whom she owed money. She took unassuming lodgings in Scotland Yard and asked her former lover Sam Derrick to write her an entry for the 1761 edition of *Harris's List*. As Derrick tactfully relays, three years of the Fleet, even on the Master's side, had noticeably taken its toll: 'Time was,' he reminds the reader, 'when this lady was a reigning toast . . . She has been, however, a good while in eclipse . . .' He then ever so gently comments: 'Were we to enter into an exact description of this celebrated Thais; that is, were we to describe each limb and feature a part, they would not appear so well as taken altogether.'

Before Elizabeth Ward launched her daughter into the demi-monde she would have warned Charlotte to make the most of her beauty while it remained. There could be no more cruel fate for a courtesan than to observe how deeply time and misfortune had worn away the face that earned her a living. Now in her mid-thirties and without the support of the annuity she had expected from Tracy, Charlotte's future security was questionable. In order to survive financially, her only hope was to build a successful business where younger women provided the pleasures that she herself could no longer command high prices for bestowing. To compensate for her inability to lure the town's most fashionable bucks into her bed, she needed Dennis to succeed in luring them to the gaming tables.

To contemporary sensibilities, the arrangement that existed between Dennis and Charlotte appears weird in the extreme, but to them, this was simply the nature of their situation. In the eighteenth century it was believed that any man who entered into a long-term relationship with a woman in the sex trade would have to resign himself to the realities of her profession and the likelihood that she would return to it when necessity dictated. Dennis never questioned what Charlotte was, or the method by which she derived her only means of income, and like Sam Derrick, who could not provide for her comfortably, he had no choice but to consent to share her, at least temporarily. As the author of the *Nocturnal Revels* explains, 'policy induced her to see them [her clients] with complaicency', regardless of the fact that 'Her affections were still centred in her hero.' Ambition for a better life meant that the pair had to use the means available to them to raise the capital that would ensure their future comfort. Both worked for their mutual benefit: he shared his profits with her, and 'on him were all the pecuniary favours, which she received from others, bestowed with unbounded liberality'.

By contrast to Charlotte's experience, after his release, Dennis appears to have hit the ground running. When he set out to do it, he had an almost miraculous ability to find money and put it to use. To many, it seemed as though the Count had never been in prison; they had become so accustomed to seeing him at all the usual places. According to one source, he 'was not released from prison many days before he appeared at the Tennis Court and some of the polite coffee houses in the west end of the Town', dressed in finery, with a sword strapped to his hilt. He had also managed to procure himself fashionable lodgings in St James's, 'and absolutely wore gold buckles on his shoes'. Once fitted out convincingly as a gentleman and carrying a few guineas' worth of winnings in his pocket, he proceeded to work his way into the best circles of sportsmen. 'He became,' as his *Memoirs* state, 'intimately acquainted with a class of beings commonly known by the denomination of *black legs*, that is those equestrian heroes who are invariably seen at every capital horse race in England.'

Not surprisingly, once 'among those, he acquired an

irresistible taste for the same avocation'. Providence had led Dennis to horse racing, the one occupation that was destined to make him more money than all his card-counting tricks and deceptions put together.

Through pooling their resources, Charlotte and Dennis were prepared to launch a small brothel by 1761, roughly a year after they had seen the last of the Fleet. They had taken a house together on Great Marlborough Street, in Soho, then a mixed bag of an area, one that played home not only to upstanding members of the gentry and the secure middle classes but to tradespeople, small merchants and artists. Even during the mid-eighteenth century, Soho was beginning to acquire what might be called a bohemian reputation: not everything that occurred there nor everyone who lived there was considered to be on the right side of respectability. Soho had been built comparatively recently as part of the westward sprawl that filled out London's edges. Its orderly, grid-based streets were lined with single- and double-fronted brick terraced houses, their insides illuminated by fanlights and generous sash windows. With front and back parlours, such abodes offered ample entertaining space for small, merry parties. This was a first step on the ladder for Charlotte and Dennis. Here, they were only a few doors down from Mrs Goadby's famous *sérail*, and in the right neck of the woods to catch the interest of those seeking that sort of entertainment. It is likely that in the first instance the couple shared their home with two or three hand-selected 'nymphs' and operated on a modest scale. At this early stage, Dennis's involvement in the business of promoting their new enterprise as well as in the duties of brothel management

would have been crucial. His gaming companions, those dissolute black legs (called so for the tall black riding boots in
which they tramped about the turf and the town), were just
the sort of cash-laden clientele that Charlotte was seeking.
Dennis, as much as Charlotte, would have been responsible
for steering them into her drawing room. The Count's other
role was equally important. Without the presence of a male
figure, female-run establishments were never truly secure
against unpredictable behaviour. Whether it was the brutality of drunken culls or the exploitative tendencies of the
night watch, it was always useful to have a 'bully' lurking
somewhere within shouting distance. Thus, O'Kelly not only
assisted Charlotte 'in the double capacity of lover' but also as
'a *flash-man*, which was nothing more than a generous protector from the violence of modern buckism'.

Even in the infant days of her operation, Charlotte had
her eye on far wider horizons. Soho, by comparison with the
elegant neighbourhood of St James's, simply did not exude
the same cultivated ambience. Having spent her childhood
at her mother's establishment near Haymarket, she would
have remembered what advantages were to be wrought
from trading so close to the royal court, where bored aristocrats longed for fleshy distractions. By the mid-1760s, the
pull of pleasure-seeking gravity had shifted westward. Many
of the Covent Garden faithful had begun to abandon the
upstairs rooms and illicit gambling offered at the Shakespear
and the Bedford for the exclusive gaming tables and assembly rooms of Almack's. St James's had become the centre of
fashionable entertainment, enticing the *bon ton* to the new
theatre on the Haymarket and to private parties held in

stone-faced townhouses along the recently laid out squares. Charlotte's vision of a grand Parisian-style *sérial*, or nunnery, was not suited to her current middle-class surroundings. In order to exceed Goadby's establishment in grandeur, an appropriate setting at the heart of the *haute* world would be necessary.

## 13

# HARRISON'S RETURN

IN 1761, IT WAS John Harrison's turn to emerge from prison into the blazing light of day. What his intentions might have been upon his release it is impossible to say; what is known about how he chose to conduct the remainder of his life does not indicate that he was moved by the spirit of character reformation. Harrison did, however, choose to live more carefully and more surreptitiously. He had been born into the world of the tavern, and that trade and everything it entailed comprised the extent of his skills. Therefore, not surprisingly, he returned to Covent Garden to pick up his life from the point at which it had been unfortunately interrupted.

When Packington Tomkins learned that the vitriolic Harrison was once again at large, it is unlikely that he slept easily. Tomkins would have known the strengths of his enemy and his scheming temperament. For three years Harrison had sat in Newgate, stewing in his anger, contemplating his next move and how he might exact his revenge. Even after the publication of his anti-Tomkins tirade, the owner of the Shakespear's Head could not have guessed whence Harrison's vengeance would come, whether through violence or some more insidious means. As it happened, Harrison sought to hit his adversary in his purse, where it would wound him the most.

The convenient and highly visible location of the Shakespear's Head tavern had always been one of its greatest assets. Its signboard would have been visible to those passing in both directions and it was almost as ideally situated as the Rose Tavern, directly next door to the Drury Lane theatre. As the two largest, most notorious taverns in the area, patrons made an evening of fumbling their way between the two in search of more enlightening or entertaining company. Like the Shakespear, the Rose played host to casts of actors hot from performances and in need of refreshment. The prospect of carousing with adored actresses Peg Woffington, George Anne Bellamy, Sophia Baddeley and the celebrity patent-holder of the adjoining theatre, David Garrick, was an attraction to many, although most would have come simply for the drink and to delight in the uninhibited debauchery of the place. Undoubtedly it was shortly after Harrison's reappearance, when the proprietor of the Rose (and Tomkins's chief business rival), Thomas Watson, took the pimp into his employment, that Tomkins genuinely began to worry.

The Rose had established its reputation long before Thomas Watson assumed his position as manager. As early as 1672, it was known for its 'constant scene of drunken broils, midnight orgies, and murderous assaults by men of fashion who were designated Hectors and whose chief pleasure lay in frequenting taverns for the running through of some fuddled toper, whom wine had made valiant'. By the beginning of the eighteenth century it had gained a reputation as a haunt for 'women of a certain freedom of character'. Even to William Hogarth, an artist familiar with scenes of misery and degradation, the Rose represented the ultimate sink of iniquity. In 1735, when painting his multi-scene moral tale *The Rake's Progress*, Hogarth chose to feature the Rose's principal room as the setting where his eponymous character, Tom Rakewell, is at one of the lowest ebbs of his degeneracy. The artist's astute eye created an image that accords with written accounts of the tavern's notoriety, depicting half-clad and poxed women picking pockets, spitting, defacing the room's decor and soliciting business. As with many of Hogarth's moral scenes, several of the figures depicted would have been recognizable individuals. The face of Richard Leathercote, the Rose's porter, makes an appearance, as does one of the tavern's infamous 'posture molls', who is seen preparing to perform her party trick, which will entail pushing a candle up her vagina while standing over a reflective pewter plate, to better enable the view. The Rose never lost its reputation as the prime venue for posture girls, who, nude, struck lewd poses on tables for the testosterone-charged clientele. Much like today's lap dancers, they titillated patrons but left the copulation to prostitutes who lay in wait after a performance. It has been suggested that before she was discovered, the inexperienced Amy Lyon, who would one day become Emma Hamilton, mistress to Lord Nelson, started her career naked and spreadeagled on a tavern table.

Not unlike John Harrison, the Rose had failed to remedy its character over the years. At the time he began waiting on tables there, its reputation was as nasty as ever. On hanging days, when the guilty were carted down Oxford Road (now

Oxford Street) to Tyburn, the Rose was where the rowdy crowds congregated to drench themselves with drink before proceeding to the execution. The same could be said for major civil disturbances; the tavern was likely to contribute a team of rough, intoxicated bruisers to any property-smashing event that erupted within the West End. Like the Shakespear, the Rose was a cavernous place with numerous upstairs rooms and plenty of dark spaces in which to fornicate or pick pockets. As a contemporary commented, its ambience and the behaviour of its patrons rendered it 'no better than a barn'.

When Harrison joined the ranks of the Rose's employees, it is likely that he had his sights on something grander than simply resuming, however cautiously, the pursuits of his former profession. In spite of falling foul of the law, he would not allow his ambition to be dampened; once he had tasted the spoils of his success, the comforts, celebrity and influence it had brought him, he was unlikely ever to be content leading a humble existence. His experience with Tomkins had taught him that the only sure way of building and maintaining an empire was to operate independently of a tavern-keeper or, better yet, to operate the tavern. As Harrison had always possessed a shrewd mind, it is unlikely that he had been committed to Newgate without managing to squirrel away at least a portion of his ill-gotten earnings. Upon his release, this sum is likely to have formed the foundation for his revised aspirations. While living quietly under the roof of the Rose for four years, he practised his trade, drawing in the punters, as he had for Packington Tomkins, and amassing a nest egg in the process. Since Jack Harris's arrest, it seemed that Tomkins was not keen to sail so close to the wind as he had before. He never replaced the in-famous Harris with anyone else of his ilk. After all, the Pimp General of All England had been a unique feature of the Shakespear's Head. Now, working under his true identity, Harrison had set up shop at the Rose and began to siphon off custom. The visible lights of the Shakespear's Head reflect-ing in the Rose's windows would have served as a constant reminder of his ultimate aspiration. Then, in 1765, the oppor-tunity for which he had been waiting presented itself.

Whatever arrangement Harrison had struck with Thomas Watson, it was his name that came to replace that of his employer's as proprietor of the Rose. Now, presiding on a level equal to that of the hated Tomkins, Harrison could mount a campaign of empire-building, more carefully orchestrated and diverse than that constructed in his previous incarnation. The Rose and its location were ideal, allowing Harrison to transform himself into Brydges Street's resident baron of sin while blending unobtrusively into the surroundings. The street, with the imposing presence of the Theatre Royal mounted at its head and a passageway to the Strand at its feet, was a channel awash with constant traffic and strangers. It was a mixed neighbourhood of terraced houses split into cheap prostitutes' lodgings and loud taverns, along with the premises of respectable milliners, grocers and pawnbrokers. Due to its proximity to the Drury Lane theatre, it was also a favourite location for thespians. Its ratepayers at various times included David Garrick and Richard Brinsley Sheridan, as well as lesser-known entertainers. On performance nights, the doors of the theatre swung out on to the street, depositing audiences into the paths of waiting chairmen, ladies of the night and pickpockets. As a thoroughfare, it could be a dangerous place, frequented by pistol-wielding robbers, gangs of muggers and violent drunks. By 1787, Brydges Street had been identified as housing four of the ten most disorderly taverns west of the city. Not surprisingly, the Rose was listed among them.

Despite its infamous reputation, Harrison managed to keep the law from his tavern door. As only a pimp would, the new proprietor of the Rose understood the importance of enforcing discipline and the methods that best brought it about. Through the use of bribes and threats of violence, the watch never reported the activities of the Rose, and Harrison's clientele were compliant in maintaining a conspiracy of silence. With the local authorities at arm's length, England's former Pimp General was able to dig himself into the neighbourhood and restore his influence with surprising swiftness. By the second half of the 1760s, he had established himself as a landlord and owned the leaseholds of a number of properties on Brydges Street. In addition to the Rose, he bought the house adjoining it for his residence, and he was also the rate-payer for a handful of other premises on the street which he held in either his own name, the name of John Harris or that of Nicholas Harrison, perhaps another alias or a relation who may have been drafted in to assist in the running of what had become a family enterprise. It was under these roofs that Harrison discreetly out-housed his other interests: prostitution and, briefly, a printing press that set obscenity into typeface.

When Harrison agreed to lend his alias to Sam Derrick's publication, he never could have foreseen its profitability. Hacks produced new pamphlets almost weekly, most of which sunk into unpurchased obscurity. There was no reason to believe that Derrick's *Harris's List* would prove any more lucrative or extend beyond one edition. At the time, Harrison most likely would have been satisfied with an initial sum, whether this included a portion of the profits or simply a payment for the use of his name. Beyond this, he in all probability would have been severed from any further involvement with the publication. His disappearance into prison shortly after its launch would have reinforced this separation. After 1757, whatever profits were cleared went to fill the purses of Sam Derrick and that of his publisher, H. Ranger. Several years on, it must have caused Harrison no end of frustration to witness the *List*'s continuous appearance in print, a new edition making its way on to the booksellers' stands at twelve-month intervals. More than any of his other circumstances, his inability to corner the proceeds of the publication that bore his name must have incensed him. By the middle of the eighteenth century, the market for lewd publications was growing and Harrison was determined to get his rightful piece of it by purchasing his own printing press. Although a short-lived venture, between 1765 and the end of 1766, 'J. Harrison near Covent Garden' produced a number of provocative publications. Of the handful that survive, Edward Thompson's *The Courtesan* was Harrison's greatest triumph in print. The epic-style poem, which set the Garden's gossip into rhyme, was updated and republished three times throughout 1765. *The Fruit-Shop*, published in 1766, documenting the lurid tales of history's fornicators, also seems to have been a work unique to the press of J. Harrison, as was another less ingenious work, *Kitty's Attalantis*.

Sam Derrick's decision to arrange the pimp's list into a format readable by the pleasure-seeking punter had required no great spark of creativity. Atlantises, as they were called, had been in existence since the end of the previous century and took on a variety of guises. Generally, they existed as compendiums of erotic stories detailing the activities of noted ladies of dubious morality. Frequently, real names were concealed through titillatingly transparent pseudonyms. Derrick had followed the well-established tradition of formatting his atlantis as a guidebook that offered practical advice on how to locate the women concerned. *Kitty's Attalantis* was no different in concept, although in execution it was of a much poorer quality. Its layout looked very similar to that of its bestselling rival, and it contained the names of sixty-one women, complete with alluring short biographies and addresses. Having already sold his name, nothing prevented Harrison from utilizing the formula that had worked for Derrick. But *Kitty's Attalantis* lacked the verve, the witty prose and agility of Derrick's storytelling. Whoever authored the work for Harrison (under the suggestive pseudonym of Nancy Laycock) fell back on misogynistic cant, littering his pages with coarse language and references to the listees as 'vile bitches' and 'blasted whores'. *Kitty's Attalantis* could not hold a candle to the now well-established *Harris's List*, and never saw more than one print run. Ironically, and undoubtedly to his great frustration, Harrison could not manage to match the success of his own name.

What happened to the pimp's publishing business after 1766 is a mystery. Any trace of it seems to have disappeared by the following year. Harrison may have decided to wind it down if it was not yielding the spectacular returns he had anticipated; it could only have served as an appendage to his more lucrative pursuits of managing a tavern, rustling up prostitutes for his patrons and extracting rents from his exploited tenants. It was these activities, and possibly other unknown and even more nefarious ones, that maintained his status on Brydges Street, and perhaps beyond.

At the centre of his rebuilt empire remained his citadel, the Rose. From his vantage point near the Shakespear's Head, Harrison could keep a wary eye on Packington Tomkins, a man who in turn may have spent the remainder of his days living in fear of some unannounced reprisal by his embittered rival. Harrison's other eye would have been fixed on Bow Street, studying it for any sign of impending confrontation. He would never again be fool enough to believe himself wholly untouchable by Justice Fielding's legions. Fortunately for the tavern-keeper, the magistrate seemed to display little interest in regulating Harrison's schemes throughout the 1760s and '70s. With few real threats to his primacy, and at the tail end of his middle age, the pimp would have welcomed the constancy of a reliable source of revenue. The Rose's future promised to be secure as long as the Theatre Royal continued to spill revellers outside its doors, a circumstance that neither Packington Tomkins nor John Fielding could possibly alter. David Garrick, however, could.

# 14

# SANTA CHARLOTTA OF
# KING'S PLACE

APPROXIMATELY SIX YEARS AFTER Charlotte and Dennis had purchased the leasehold of the terraced house on Great Marlborough Street, the couple were prepared to take on a far more high-profile residence. They settled on a site known as King's Place in a discreet passage that joined Pall Mall with King's Street, a location that had by 1744 acquired a name for sexual intrigue. Situated directly next door to Almack's, their new headquarters was as large as their ambitions. Described as being 'a very elegant house', by virtue of its very roominess it contained all the facilities Charlotte required to entertain her customers on the scale she had envisioned. A newly built townhouse of aristocratic proportions, it would have contained several sets of what were called 'apartments', or adjoining rooms, ideal for the purpose of turning a visitor's intention of a quick tumble into a drawn-out evening's event. Charlotte's ladies and their customers wouldn't be forced through lack of space to retire to the bed or the couch immediately, as would have been the case at some less well-equipped establishments. Just as in the lavish *sérails* of Paris, a visit to Charlotte's abode might begin with friendly conversation and perhaps even musical entertainment in the drawing room or salon. Drinks could be taken and a round of cards played before everyone's spirits were loose enough to proceed in private to the evening's main event. The advantages of this arrangement were great: the following morning Charlotte would have the pleasure of presenting a bill not only for sexual services but for the time a gentleman caller spent in the precious company of one of her nymphs. He would receive a charge for drinks served, music played, food consumed and a night's lodgings under Charlotte's roof (presumably when the bed occupied could have been used by another) and, of course, he would pay for any losses at cards. Through this clever scheme a customer could ratchet up a bill so high that it would require payment in banknotes rather than in coin. Many would opt for an account on credit, a request which Charlotte would willingly grant if the visitor was an established customer with a handsome enough fortune. According to William Hickey, it was possible to accrue a tab of 'near one hundred pounds for suppers and wines' in addition to sex over the course of a handful of visits to Mrs Hayes's brothel. At a time when £100 would have served as a satisfactory income for an established merchant, her house was a luxury no tradesman or apprentice could afford. And Charlotte intended to keep it that way.

In addition to the facilities of her King's Place residence, the greatest attraction her *sérail* afforded was the women Charlotte employed. According to the *Revels*, she 'took care to have the choicest goods, as she called them, that could be had at market'. 'In other words,' the author goes on to say, 'her nuns were of the first class.' If she was going to charge exorbitant fees, it was imperative that her customers felt as if they were getting services worth the price. Recruitment into the ranks of Venus was one of Charlotte's primary skills. As she traversed the streets of the West End, from her carriage or sedan chair she searched the faces and figures of the girls who composed the melee of the streets: the flower sellers, the servants scurrying from house to house, the beggars and those already initiated into the ways of prostitution. Like a modern-day talent scout, she looked not only for indications of beauty but for the sparks of light that made a young woman pleasant company. Musical ability was also a bonus and Charlotte always kept an eye on the itinerant dancers and singers who moved between playhouses and pleasure gardens in the hope of becoming famous. Within only a few years of opening the doors of her King's Place nunnery, she had launched the careers of some of the era's most successful courtesans. Clara Hayward, who was later to find fame as an actress and as the mistress of the Duke of Kingston, was introduced into higher circles through Charlotte. Sam Foote, on a visit to King's Place, was so charmed with her recitations from 'The Fair Penitent' that 'she was immediately engaged at the Haymarket' and later featured upon the stages of Drury Lane and Covent Garden. The beautiful Harriet Powell, who later married the Earl of Seaforth, began her days as one of Madam Hayes's recruits, as did 'the *rage* of the town', Betsy Coxe, who gained fame not only for her 'fine contralto voice' but through her association with a string of noble lovers, including the Earl of Alford and the Earl of Abergavenny. Betsy Coxe, whose original name was Elizabeth Green, came to Charlotte as a charity case. An orphan who had been seduced at a young age, she was taken off the street by a Captain Coxe, who deposited her at Charlotte's doorstep. With some tutelage, Madam Hayes turned a penurious waif into a heart-winning courtesan. She worked similar magic on one of William Hickey's favourites, Emily Warren, whom she had spotted on 'the streets of London when not quite twelve years of age, leading her father, a blind beggar about, soliciting charity from every person that passed'. According to Hickey, Charlotte was 'struck by the uncommon beauty of the child's countenance . . . and without difficulty soon got her into her clutches'.

Neither Hickey nor any of the other well-to-do or influential patrons of Charlotte's establishment were willing to pass judgement on the methods she employed to acquire these young women. That poor girls (and they were girls in the majority of cases) found their way into prostitution was simply a fact of life. Hickey regarded Charlotte Hayes's actions in saving pitiful creatures such as Betsy Coxe and Emily Warren from a life of destitution and brutality on the streets as commendable. The daughter of a blind beggar would have otherwise had no access to a life of comfort and splendour, had she not been pulled from obscurity, dressed like a lady and served up as a dish for a rich gentleman. But it should be remembered that Charlotte was not in the business of running a charitable organization for the rescue of young women. Whatever side benefits a life of high-class prostitution might have offered those from impoverished backgrounds was incidental to Madam Hayes's main objectives. Charlotte was a businesswoman whose very life depended upon her success. As age crept over her, her prospects became less and less certain. If she could not bring herself to sacrifice others to the lusts of men and the scorn of respectable society, then her life would surely end in the same state of impoverished obscurity from which she drew her innocent victims. Her work was selling sex. It was the only occupation for which she had ever been trained and the only reality she had ever known. Society offered no other means by which she might derive an income.

As Charlotte's King's Place establishment grew in reputation, so did the complexity of the methods she found herself having to employ in order to bring 'fresh faces' into her grasp. While she and other procuresses drew their stock largely from the vast reserves of very poor young girls who worked on the streets of the metropolis, some were lured into the web by other means. The author of the *Nocturnal Revels* claims that Madam Hayes had two primary techniques for recruitment: 'the first was by attending the Register Offices; the second by advertisement'. Lurking about the Register Offices was perhaps the oldest and most tried method available to bawds and pimps. It was at such locations that Charlotte, 'dressed . . . in a plain, simple manner, resembling the wife of a decent tradesman', would go about inquiring 'for a young, healthful-looking woman, about twenty' to act as a lady's maid for an infirm old woman. The *Revels* then claims: 'In order to carry this scheme into execution, she took a variety of lodgings in different parts of the town, and sometimes small houses ready furnished,' in order to decoy an unsuspecting girl. There is evidence to suggest this scheme was not just a fanciful tale concocted by the author of the *Nocturnal Revels*, as in both 1769 and 1775 Charlotte used the alias 'Charlotte Flammingham' to rent properties on King's Street. Entrapment stories that begin with an unsuspecting girl being plied with a dram of alcohol and lured into a set of ill-lit private rooms were not merely the preserve of fiction but a reality recognized by the era's law enforcement. The end result, however, would have mirrored that which appeared in eighteenth-century novels. Invariably, once compromised in such circumstances, a girl 'is set upon by her assailant – Lord C—n, Lord B—ke, or Colonel L—e'. Sadly, 'her outcries bring no one to her relief, and probably she yields to her fate, finding it inevitable; and solaces herself in the morning with a few guineas, and the prospective view of having a new gown, a pair of silver buckles, and a black silk cloak'. The author of the *Revels* then glibly concludes, 'Being once broke in, there is no great difficulty in persuading her to remove her quarters and repair to the Nunnery in King's Place, in order to make room for another victim, who is sacrificed in a like manner.'

If the pickings at the Register Offices seemed a bit meagre, Charlotte had other tricks up her sleeve. She found that: 'Advertisements in the Daily Papers often had the desired effect, and brought in numbers of pretty candidates (though unknowingly) for prostitution.' The applicants who approached Charlotte were seduced in the same manner as those found in the Register Offices, by the promise of a position as a household servant. The composition of these wittily created blurbs Charlotte left to some of her literary friends, who, in a manner reminiscent of Choderlos de Laclos's Vicomte de Valmont, savoured the titillating challenge of enticing the virtuous to their ruin. The renowned misogynist George Selwyn was credited with penning one of the more memorable:

> *Wanted: a young woman, under twenty who has had the small-pox, and has not been long in town, as a maid-servant*

*of all work, in a genteel family. She must turn her hand to
everything, as it is proposed putting her under a Man-cook of
skill and eminence. She must get up small things, and even
large ones occasionally, understanding clear-starching without clapping, and know something of pastry, at least to make
standing crust; and also preserving fruit. Good wages and
proper encouragement will be given, if she proves handy, and
can easily conceive, according to the instructions given her.*

As ludicrous as this advert was acknowledged to be,
according to the *Revels* it managed to 'inveigle the innocent
and unguarded'. Such was the ease with which Charlotte led
her clients to believe she could procure new talent for them.

In truth, locating suitable candidates for her nunnery, as
well as managing to keep them once they had been brought
into the fold, was more complicated than most patrons knew.
The majority of the better brothels and bagnios in London
were, like any other trade, run as family businesses. Parents
passed on their expertise to their children, and husbands and
wives manned joint ventures, much like Charlotte and Dennis. Where the management of her enterprise was concerned,
Charlotte was very much her mother's daughter. Having been
'initiated into all the mysteries of the Tally-woman', Charlotte employed the same tactics in her own business. When
it came to maintaining a lucrative trade and keeping her
ladies in line, Charlotte found that she was a natural. She had
learned through observation 'how to fix a price upon a gown,
a saque, a trollopee, a watch, a pair of buckles, or any other
trinket'. Like her mother, Charlotte 'charged them in proportion for their board, washing and lodging; and by keeping her

nuns constantly in her debt, she secured them'. Elizabeth Ward did not suffer fools or their escape attempts. The Old Bailey Sessions Papers record her name as one who wasn't afraid to prosecute 'when any one dared to elope' while in possession of what the bawd called 'prerequisites and presents'. Part matron, part landlady and part gaoler, the role of the bawd was one that routinely guarded and subjugated those under her care. Charlotte was no different. She could not afford to trust her charges or indulge them with sympathy. What affection she might have felt for these young women who lived with her and formed part of her household had to be well hidden and revealed only with the greatest caution. For her to have displayed either favouritism or too much affection would have left Charlotte vulnerable to their whims. Theirs was strictly a business arrangement – she clothed, housed and fed her girls and introduced them into the highest circles of society; they in turn provided her with an income.

Charlotte, more than any other brothel-keeper, was able to make a success of her enterprise, and those who visited her house praised it for its efficient and reliable practices. It was Chase Price, George Selwyn's partner in crime, who first bestowed the title of Abbess on Charlotte, and christened her business a 'nunnery' for its apparent order and regimentation. He also insinuates that Charlotte's 'nuns' provided the entertainment for Sir Francis Dashwood's Hell-Fire 'friars' in the caves of West Wycombe Park, the venue for his notorious orgies. In 1769 he published a satirical yet insightful article entitled 'A Genuine Account of the Monastery of Santa Charlotta' which unveiled Mother Hayes's effective management techniques. If Santa Charlotta's 'laws, constitutions, regulations and manners' for her seminary are to be believed, the situation that prevailed at her establishment was a less than favourable one for her charges. 'Sisters' in the nunnery were not permitted to 'have any favourite lover' and any 'tender attachments' were to be broken off immediately. Any such man who attempted to 'seduce or inveigle any sister out of the convent' was not permitted to visit again. Any 'presents, gifts or possessions' held by or made to members of the sisterhood were confiscated by Santa Charlotta and then 'appropriated', given as, when and to whom she saw fit, according to merit. The 'Worthy Patroness', to avoid mischief, forbade her charges from pursuing friendships 'with the sisterhood of any other seminary', and prevented them from having 'non-initiated' female visitors to call. Whether a fellow prostitute or an unsullied woman of virtue, the sisters were permitted little contact with other females. For the most part, Charlotte saw that their daily existences were structured and extremely contained. Irrespective of their varying appointments with clients, she insisted that 'they associate all together at meals', that they make frequent group visits to the theatre, that they take walks together in public and 'when the weather will not admit these perambulations, they take the air in an elegant equipage belonging to the convent'. Presumably these measures not only allowed her to keep a closer eye on her girls but fostered a sense of camaraderie that prevented feelings of isolation from taking root.

With the licentious London set singing her praises, Charlotte took every precaution to maintain the high standards of her house. So much as a whiff of venereal disease could be the ruin of her reputation. In order to vouch for the medical viability of her girls, she employed a physician, Dr Chidwick, to carry out regular medical examinations. It seems that Chidwick was well known among the elite disorderly houses in the area and cultivated a specialist practice in prostitutes' reproductive health. For his services, it appears he received payment in kind from his patients, as he is noted for taking 'neither fees nor salary'. As William Hickey records, Chidwick's consultations may have been responsible for preserving his own health, along with that of most of Charlotte's clientele. Despite his avid womanizing and fondness for votaries of Venus, Hickey was never touched by venereal disease, 'although', he claims, 'I took no particular care of myself, nor ever hesitated taking any woman that was offered as a bedfellow at [Mrs] Kelly's . . .'

Charlotte prided herself on the accomplishments of her nuns and, unlike other, more downmarket bawds, invested in their education. The Abbess's programme of tutelage was considered second to none. Teaching her recruits, particularly those who had come straight from the streets, how to behave like ladies was foremost. Not only were her girls taught deportment and elocution in the attempt to erase the ungainly reminders of their origins, but both music and dancing masters were hired to give them a further polishing. According to Hickey, Charlotte was very good at teaching her girls to walk, 'a qualification that Madam Hayes considered of importance', but other skills, such as literacy, were deemed superfluous. Nevertheless, he commented, Charlotte's nymphs were always very well spoken. For example, irrespective of her inability to read or write, Emily Warren was 'by no means deficient or awkward in conversation; nor do I recollect ever to have heard her make use of a vulgarism or a phrase that could mark her illiterateness'.

Charlotte's move to No. 2 King's Place in 1767 signified a turning point in the realization of her ambitions. Her presence in St James's was to initiate a new era for London's bawdy houses; indeed her operation maintained such an aura of elegance and sophistication that it could hardly be classed with those spit-and-sawdust sister establishments in Covent Garden like Weatherby's and Haddock's. Invariably, other entrepreneurs of the flesh market were to follow her lead and open rival houses on King's Place and the streets around St James's Palace gates. Charlotte, however, remained the reigning doyenne throughout the 1760s and early '70s.

By 1771, trade was so bountiful that she launched a second nunnery in larger premises across the road at No. 5, while No. 2 remained as an annexe in the care of a trusted assistant, Miss Ellison. Although business was booming, Charlotte's primary aim was not remain in her line of work for ever. From the early days of their relationship, she and Dennis O'Kelly had set out to earn their collective fortune, which by their terms did not simply mean an ample subsistence. They desired riches. By the era's definition, this would also include the acquisition of land, as it was only through the ownership of land that a family name might be established and wealth solidified. Land conferred status and status bestowed respect, even on those with shady pasts. With a large enough fortune and substantial enough property, even some of the grossest breaches of society's laws could be forgiven.

Dennis, as a professional gambler 'whose whole time

was, without interruption, devoted to play and chance', was able to contribute significantly to their collective wealth when the takings were good. But unfortunately, even his quick hands and mathematical mind could not guarantee a win every time he took his seat at the gaming tables. There were losses as well, sometimes on a level so great that the funds Charlotte had saved for that parcel of land intended to support her in retirement were skimmed to secure Dennis from the bailiffs. O'Kelly was an adventurer: winning and losing, spending, pawning and borrowing in constant shifts. What was taken from him in a game of hazard one night, although it may have been more than half his assets, he was certain of gaining back within a short space of time. Herein lay the problem, for as much of a wagerer as Dennis was, Charlotte was 'but a shallow mistress of speculation' and 'thought the old proverb, of a bird in the hand, the best guide of her conduct'. The lessons of her youth had taught her never again to take abundance for granted. Dennis, however, did not adhere to this code, and at times the unreliability of his actions drove their relationship close to its breaking point. She worried that Dennis, like Sam Derrick, was incapable of delivering a secure future. But Charlotte was bound more closely to Dennis than she had been to Sam, not only through deeper ties of affection but through his involvement in her King's Place business. Referred to facetiously as 'the Prior' of Santa Charlotta's Protestant nunnery, Dennis's stake in his mistress's enterprise was as great as hers; it had been a joint endeavour from the start and one that rested on the investment of both of their earnings.

Plagued by Dennis's financial inconsistencies, Charlotte

found that she had no choice but to continue in her position as King's Place Abbess for the foreseeable future. Once a reckless spendthrift of men's money, she quickly acquired the art of shrewd accountancy, balancing her own books and drawing up bills. She also learned the necessity of innovation. Charlotte's successful new brothel was being watched from all sides by her competitors. Nancy Banks, Charlotte's closest rival, on Curzon Street, had been one of her nymphs before going into business for herself. Elizabeth Mitchell, an old hand in the Covent Garden flesh trade, set up first on Berkeley Street before moving directly next door to Charlotte in 1770. By the 1770s, the entire passage was taken up with superior-standard brothels, all calling themselves nunneries. When the Baron D'Archenholz visited London in 1773, he was amazed at the 'line of Coaches which could be seen driving up to the narrow King's Place'. In order to maintain her position at the head of the queue of newcomers to the area, Charlotte had to market her attractions as actively as possible.

It was no good sitting indoors all day and night, waiting for men of wealth and prestige to call. Even the best repositories of female flesh had to advertise in order to attract custom. At any one time, Charlotte's exclusive house would have had no fewer than two and no more than five *filles de joye* in residence and, as *Harris's List* indicated, these occupants were frequently singled out for high-keeping by gentlemen. The best method by which Charlotte could promote her stock of ladies was to parade them in public, to dress them in exquisite gowns and float them under the gaze of all London. She promenaded them through St James's Park, where the *bon ton* strolled in the afternoons, displaying their fine clothing, their horses and lacquered coaches. They sat amid the most fashionable names in the theatre boxes, under the ogling eyes of the peerage and the disapproving gazes of their jealous wives. Charlotte took her nuns to any location where their beauty might be admired and the curious allowed to approach them. Pleasure gardens, assembly rooms and balls were some of the prized haunts of the great impures. Here they could display their plumage to the most artful effect, dancing in the centre of a room and moving with the grace they had learned in Madam Hayes's parlour. Charlotte and her nuns, as subscription-holders to the most glamorous of venues, appeared regularly at places such as Mrs Cornelys's masked balls at Carlisle House, where married ladies of esteemed character rubbed shoulders with their husbands' lovers beneath paste masks and veils. When her best clients retired to Bath and Cheltenham for the season, Charlotte followed them there with a travelling exhibition of her wares. Her ladies could be spotted everywhere, bobbing in the steamy waters, perambulating through the magnificent crescents and fluttering their fans in the assembly rooms. One can only imagine the anguish of a tormented wife who had hoped to leave the cause of her husband's distractions in London. Wherever the respectable world went, the shadow world of the disreputable followed at its heels, encountering only occasional protest at its presence. As Charlotte's ladies serviced the most influential men in the land, there were few who could offer any real opposition.

At the height of her renown, the nunnery of the 'Saintly Charlotte Hayes' hosted the leading lights of Georgian society in its bedchambers. The Earl of Sandwich, Viscount Falmouth, the Duke of Richmond, and the earls of Egremont, Uxbridge and Grosvenor were only a handful of the names who regularly bestowed their favours on her establishment. Scores of lesser gentry and wealthy City gentlemen of all religions, including numerous aldermen and Lord Mayors, were known customers. In later years, through Dennis's racing connections, most of Charlotte's nuns would have benefited from intimacies with the Prince of Wales and his libertine companions, an accolade that was certain to be one of the Abbess's crowning glories. There was no one of the *beau monde* to whose predilections and requirements Charlotte did not cater. In addition to the women she had readily at hand, it was not uncommon to bring in others to appease various tastes. Actresses, singers, fallen ladies of the fashionable set and other reigning 'toasts of the town' made appearances in Charlotte's salon to entertain and be seen in the highest company. It was their talents in the bedroom as much as the drawing room that were solicited for the night's events. It was Charlotte's endeavour to ensure that the needs of all her clients were addressed, even those with rather unorthodox tastes. Like Harris the pimp, the great Abbess would have kept a record of her patron's most lewd desires and ensured that the appropriate mistress of that skill was at hand on the night. The *Nocturnal Revels* records one such occasion that Charlotte had planned with meticulous care. Although the event it documents and the names used have undoubtedly been fabricated for the readers of the *Revels*, the range of delights on Madam Hayes's menu would have been accurate. As the author prefaces, this 'specimen from

Charlotte's bill of fare' was intended to 'give the reader some idea of the manner of her conducting business'.

On this particular occasion, an average night in January 1769, it was claimed that 'Alderman Drybones', with 'Nell Blossom, a maid . . . about 19' whose virginity had recently been restored to her, were 'crammed into the chintz bed-chamber, which though small is elegant'. For this pleasure the alderman gladly parted with twenty guineas. Just adjacent, in the 'high French bed-room', could be found 'Lord Spasm', who had paid five guineas to spend the night with a black prostitute, one 'of the first rate of St. Clements'. For the mere cost of ten guineas, 'Sir Harry Flagellum' was being seen to by 'Nell Handy from Bow Street' with her bunch of birch twigs in the nursery, 'Bet Flourish from Berners Street' or 'Mrs. Birch herself from Chapel Street' being unavailable. 'Colonel Tearall' had requested 'a modest woman' for his pleasure, and Charlotte accommodated him by drafting in 'Mrs. Mitchell's cook-maid, being just come from the country'. For the price of a banknote, the colonel was prepared to take 'his chance in the parlour upon the settee'. 'Doctor Frettext', a clergyman getting on in years, came to Charlotte 'after church was over' specifically to have his needs gratified by 'a very white soft hand, pliant and affable', belonging to either 'Poll Nimblewrist' of Oxford Market 'or Jenny Speedy-hand of Mayfair'. Madam Hayes had this quick piece of work completed in the servants' quarters, up 'the three pair of stairs', for an easy two guineas. 'In the drawing room and [on] the sopha' could be found the discreet 'Lady Loveitt', who had paid Charlotte fifty guineas to allow her to meet with her lover, 'Captain O'Thunder', in secret. Meanwhile, next door in the card room, 'Lord Pyebald' was charged five guineas to innocently 'play a party at piquet . . . and the like without coming to any extremity but that of politeness and etiquette' in the company of 'Mrs. Tredrille from Chelsea'. 'His Excellency, Count Alto', on the other hand, in the adjoining salon, had come for a one-hour dalliance with 'a woman of fashion' at the expense of ten guineas.

The nunneries on King's Place were known for the lengths their abbesses would go to in order to accommodate their elite guests. Virtually no request was refused, even if it came from those who were not specifically seeking the services of a prostitute. Charlotte's residence was frequently offered as a type of safe house for couples pursuing illicit affairs. The *Revels* would also have readers believe that Madam Hayes procured well-endowed men to satisfy women who were disappointed in the matrimonial bed. However, perhaps one of the strangest requests that Charlotte received came from 'a certain young nobleman' whose wife 'was having criminal intercourse' with his friend. Upon learning of his friend's betrayal and his wife's infidelity, he bet his rival 'a thousand guineas that he would once within this month be confined with a certain fashionable disorder'. He then approached Charlotte and requested that she procure for him a prostitute from whom he might infect himself with the clap. By passing the disorder on to his spouse, he claimed he could then 'be completely revenged of my wife for her infidelity, and of my rival for his'. His Lordship, meaning no offence to Charlotte by implying that she kept 'rotten cattle' under her roof, 'took out his pocket book and presented her with a thirty pound bank note'. The plot was then put into motion and the Abbess went to work rooting out a suitably diseased harlot for the job. Within two weeks, upon discovering himself infected with the clap, the young nobleman's duplicitous friend, 'in order to avoid a further discussion of the affair', grudgingly paid out the thousand guineas on the wager he had now lost.

More frequently, requests were submitted not for women riddled with disease but for clean virgins whom the best-paying clients might have the pleasure of deflowering. This presented quite a problem. Procuring an untouched girl was extremely difficult. Those Charlotte had rescued from the street, although as young as twelve or thirteen, had in many instances already been the victims of a seduction. Luring girls away from their families, schools or the households where they worked could be not only a lengthy process but a dangerous one. If the girl had a sufficiently influential or vocal family behind her, as the procuress Mrs Nelson learned, the law was liable to become involved, and her once tight-lipped neighbours might suddenly 'propose indicting the house for a disorderly one'. Nevertheless, bawds and pimps were pestered incessantly to procure 'genuine maidenheads'. In part the demand came from those who enjoyed the sexual thrill of intercourse with a young virgin, but also from those who believed that relations with an unspoilt girl would cure them of venereal disease, or ensure a 'safe sex' experience. Rather than waste time searching London for unsullied maidens, it was easier to simply recycle those 'virgins' already to hand. Those in the procuring trade stood to make hearty sums of money by passing off a very young recruit 'for a maidenhead' several times to unwitting men who might pay fees as high as one hundred guineas for the privilege. At a time when the pubescent female (and male) body was highly sexualized, such girls would have been deemed, although extremely youthful, an appealing object of lust. Given such tastes, it should also be added that in the eighteenth century what passed for the normal sexual predilections of a significant portion of men would today be enough to send most of them to prison.

In the face of such demand, Charlotte's establishment was able to forge a name for itself as a purveyor of maidenheads. When questioned by George Selwyn as to how she was able to produce so many, so often, Charlotte replied that 'As to maidenheads, it was her opinion that a woman might lose hers a hundred times, and be as good a Virgin as ever,' and assured him 'that a Maidenhead was as easily made as a pudding'. At any time, Charlotte claimed that she had enough 'maidenheads now in possession, as would serve a whole court of Aldermen, aye and the Common Council in the bargain'. This was not the idle assertion of an emboldened bawd, but rather a boastful recognition of one of the successful brothel-keeper's best-kept secrets. Even the least literate bawd would have had on the shelves of her establishment a worn copy of John Armstrong's *Oeconomy of Love*. The work, which could loosely be considered a kind of sex manual, contained poetically written advice as well as a recipe for the restoration of virginity. Armstrong had put into writing what had been common knowledge among women and practitioners of medicine for centuries. To tighten the walls of the vagina, a concoction of herbs was needed which included the myrtle's 'styptic Berries', the roots of a caper bush, oak bark stripped 'bleak and bear', in addition to 'Bistort, and Dock and that way-faring Herb, Plantain'. The collection was then to be 'boil'd in wine' so that the herbs would 'yield their astringent force', in order to produce 'a Lotion . . . Thrice powerful to contract the shameful Breach'. If applied several times a day, the desired outcome would be the illusion of an unruptured entry. Bawds added their own particular touches to this deception, some inserting a small 'bladder' of animal blood into the vagina to produce the effect of a broken hymen. Others, as suggested by John Cleland's character Fanny Hill, might use a blood-soaked sponge by 'squeezing it between the thighs' so it 'yielded a great deal more of the red liquid than would save a girl's honour'. Whatever the precise method employed, it would be Charlotte who gained the last laugh. Even after parting with copious coins and banknotes, clients could never be absolutely certain that the girl who lay underneath them had been a genuine virgin, or if she, like Charlotte's nun Miss Shelly, had 'gone through twenty-three editions of vestality in one week'.

Another contingent of well-paying patrons requiring special services also frequented Charlotte's establishment. 'The noted houses . . . in King's Place,' wrote the Baron D'Archenholz, included among their useful possessions '. . . every Device to restore old men and debauched youths' who otherwise experienced difficulties in consummating their earthy desires. It was at this feat that Charlotte truly excelled. 'She . . . Makes old dotards believe themselves gay, vigorous young fellows . . .' Chase Price boasted, in addition to turning 'vigorous young fellows into old dotards'. This expertise was achieved through the invention of a device Charlotte called her 'elastic beds'. According to the *Nocturnal Revels*, they were 'invented by that great creative genius Count O'Kelly and constructed by that celebrated mechanic and upholsterer Mr. Gale'. Undoubtedly, Dennis had been inspired by the motions felt while astride one of his galloping horses and alighted upon the idea of a spring-loaded bed frame which replicated the sensations, thereby minimizing the effort involved in the act of copulation. Charlotte, until her attempt to retire in 1778, was the sole owner of these unique contraptions, credited with giving 'the finest movements and in the most extatic moments, without trouble or the least fatigue to either Agent or Patient . . . to the amazing gratification and sensation of the Actor and Actress'. The very existence of these beds drew in some of the most lecherous ageing roués still in circulation – or, as Charlotte regarded them, 'Peers who depended more upon art than nature'. This set, which included 'impotent Aldermen and rich Levites, who fancied that their amourous abilities were not in the least decayed', were considered her best customers and 'her choicest friends'. Among these infirm rakes, none was so great a supporter as William Douglas, Duke of Queensbury, a man who through his unabated sexual appetite had earned himself the sobriquet of 'the Old Goat'.

As the Abbess of one of the most celebrated houses of ill repute in London, Charlotte had earned greater renown and a larger income than in her youthful heyday. However, in spite of her success, she was rapidly wearying of her profession. All bawds at some point dreamed of retirement, a graceful exit which would mark the official end of a long-suffered career. For Charlotte, who had been prudently counting her pennies, that occasion now did not seem so remote. By the beginning of 1769 she and Dennis had managed to save enough to make the much-desired move into the circles of landowning society. They had set their sights on the estate of Clay Hill in Epsom. While the couple had always been eager to demonstrate their wealth, there was something unusually urgent about the nature of this transaction. Something in Charlotte's physical condition had begun to change.

15

# 'THE LITTLE KING OF BATH'

With his creditors paid and his freedom secured, in the latter part of 1757 Sam Derrick was at last at liberty to roam the West End streets. The unexpected success of his *Harris's List* had replenished his pockets, and such a windfall called for a round of celebrations. In his usual fashion, Sam headed for his tailor, hired smart lodgings and spread his wealth liberally around the Garden, throwing his money at the taverns, bagnios, gaming tables and wanton women. Sam had taken nothing away from his close brush with the horrors of debtors' prison; instead of saving the dividends from his portion of the *List*'s profits, he squandered them with his usual abandon. By the following year, he was writing to his friend Faulkner in Dublin again complaining of his penury. It was obvious that any advantage he might have gained from his efforts had simply slipped through his fingers. In spite of the promise of a reliable source of income editing *Harris's List*, when Boswell encountered him two years later Sam's finances were as stretched as they had ever been. Even with the secret success he had enjoyed, little had changed in Sam Derrick's life. The year 1760 still found him in circulation around the watering holes of Covent Garden, hunting for patrons and free favours from female 'friends'.

Although it may not have been obvious to Boswell at the time, Sam's years of perseverance and prostration before potential sponsors were at last beginning to bear some fruit. The net result of a life passed in coffee houses and taverns had provided him not only with his single literary triumph but with an impressive array of acquaintances. Although many had turned up their noses at him, there remained a handful who found him charming, recognizing at least a spark of talent beyond his roguish demeanour. By the end of the 1750s, he could count among his admirers the Duke of Newcastle, as well as the earls of Chesterfield, Charlemont, Shannon and Cork – the latter, according to George Faulkner, was 'much yours and speaketh most affectionately and friendly of you'. With Faulkner actively promoting Sam Derrick's name within aristocratic circles, the gilded doors to some of the most illustrious drawing rooms in England and Ireland were at last unbolted. In the early 1760s, he found himself the guest of the Earl of Chesterfield, who undoubtedly enjoyed his ribald Covent Garden tales. Similarly, he had invitations to visit his noble patrons across the Irish Sea, one of which was followed by a commission to compose a history of Ireland. Who this particular benefactor was is not entirely clear, but for some time John Boyle, the 5th Earl of Cork, and Lord Thomas Southwell, who was in the habit of praising Sam 'with raptures and panegyricks', had been soliciting his company. A substantial advance had been paid and the business of subscription-raising had already commenced when Sam departed for the shores of his homeland in September of 1760. He had been away for nearly ten years.

Sam had decided that his long-overdue visit to Ireland would mark the belated making of him. Setting sail from Liverpool and landing in Kinsale, he would then travel over land to Dublin via Killarney, Kilkenny, Carlow and Naas, visiting potential patrons and those who had requested his entertaining company. As he travelled he scribbled furiously, taking notes for what promised to be his magnum opus, detailing the characters he met and the sites of natural beauty he observed. His ultimate destination, where he would arrive two months later, was Dublin. In the decade he had been away, the city, like him, had acquired a veneer of polish. The streets had been widened, a new crossing spanning the Liffey had replaced the old Essex Bridge, while the interiors of Dublin's public buildings had been embellished with elaborate rococo plasterwork. In his youth, Sam had abandoned Dublin for its lack of promise, but now, with some maturity, he returned to his beloved 'Eblana' in the hope that she would yield to him what he had once been denied. He had always envisioned his return to the city of his childhood – he would ride into the centre triumphantly, a celebrated bard. He had not quite arrived at that situation, but he hoped to re-establish relations with those who might assist him in achieving his goal. Unfortunately, by virtue of the season, he found many of his former acquaintances unavailable, and claimed disappointedly that 'Bath, and the vacation of Parliament' had 'robbed me of my purposed pleasure'. Nevertheless, he amused himself at the theatre, passing the hours with his friend the actor Thomas Wilkes. He also paid a visit to Mrs Creagh.

Since the day of Sam's disinheritance some three years earlier, not so much as a letter had passed between the two. After such an expression of condemnation, it is unlikely that Sam expected his words to adequately soothe Mrs Creagh's concerns with regard to his moral character. With some luck and finesse, however, reinstatement in her will might not be wholly out of the question. At any rate, Sam felt that he owed his childhood guardian an excuse or explanation, or at least an opportunity to see him standing before her as a favoured poet of the Irish gentry. In November, he appeared in his aunt's drawing room with his hat in hand. Whatever words he had chosen to effect a reconciliation had at least partially assisted in healing the wound. As the two remaining members of a dwindling family, emotional ties may have spoken the loudest, surmounting mistrust and disapproval. Derrick later wrote to Faulkner that he had been accepted back into Mrs Creagh's company. 'I am extremely glad of the good agreement between you and your Aunt, and wish a continuance of it,' replied his friend. Whether this agreement included some sort of financial reward is unknown. Certainly, if it did, not a hint of it remained at the time of Derrick's death.

Mrs Creagh was not the only person Sam managed to charm during his Irish excursion. His universally positive reception in Ireland was largely responsible for the enormous kiss of good fortune landed upon him in the following year. Undoubtedly, he had been on his most refined behaviour, playing his best-known role as the silver-tongued gallant, the one that had won him such approbation in other circles. True to his more predictable nature, however, the promised *History of Ireland*, the *raison d'être* for his voyage, never manifested itself. Instead, the material he had assiduously gathered during his travels was put to use in the one work that earned him praise in the realm of respectable literature, his *Letters Written from Leverpoole, Chester, Corke, the Lake of Killarney, Dublin, Tunbridge-Wells, and Bath*. Although judged to be an elegant collection of correspondence between himself and members of the aristocracy, it was more of an exercise in the promotion of his image as a discerning gentleman than a feat of literary genius. It appeared in print seven years after his trusting patrons had advanced him funds. Nevertheless, those in high places who had enjoyed Sam's company during his several-month sojourn across the sea continued to think and speak highly of him. The Earl of Shannon appeared to be so convinced of the gentility of Sam's character that he offered him a living in the Church. Sam had never before received such an accolade for his acting ability. The offer of the position, which he made a public show of declining as proof of his worthiness, caused him some embarrassment:

> I am not hypocrite enough to sport with sacred matters
> for a livelihood; and I think it would be a little better,
> at least I should feel it so, if I accepted a living in
> the church, when my heart dictated my being unfit for
> it: unless I was certain I could by my example enforce
> the precepts of Christianity, I would not enroll myself
> amongst its pastors.

While the Earl of Shannon may have been the only member of the titled class to have believed the author of *Harris's List* worthy of holding a place within the Church, others thought him perfectly qualified to fill an important position elsewhere.

The only other location in the eighteenth century as noted for its diversions and social interaction as Covent Garden was Bath. Tucked into the verdant hills south of Bristol, its percolating hot springs, lively assembly rooms and fashionable crowd enticed the wealthy and titled from their London townhouses and country estates in the pursuit of pleasure. Bath was as much about excess and elegance, display and theatricality as it was about curing gentlemen of their gout and women of their vapours. Like Covent Garden, it was a seat of frivolous fun, a place where the hours of the day were whiled away in parties and social occasions under the auspices of Bath's Master of the Ceremonies. Until February 1761 it was Richard 'Beau' Nash who had lauded over the assemblies in this role, reprimanding inappropriately attired ladies and leading the evening's first dances. As 'King of Bath', Nash, since the early years of the century, had been single-handedly responsible for maintaining Bath and its sister town, Tunbridge Wells, as resorts for the genteel. He had put in place a series of rules which governed with a clockwork-like regularity the etiquette and practices of the city's social whirl. Although hardly a paragon of virtue, Nash, in his unmistakable white hat, cut a formidable and respected figure as he trod the streets and crescents. By the end of 1760, however, the King of Bath was ailing, and who might succeed him was a question that no one seemed capable of answering.

As one who constantly chased the tails of potential patrons and felt compelled to keep in step with the movements of the fashionable set, Sam found Bath as natural a home as Covent Garden. When the great patrons abandoned London for the green vistas of the spa town, Derrick followed closely behind, along with many theatrical, artistic and literary personalities. At certain times of the year, it was as if the entire West End with its assorted personages had been transplanted into the assembly rooms of Bath. Still riding on the crest of his favourable reception in Ireland, Sam had decamped to the resort in the hope of building on his successes. With a clutch of letters of introduction from the earls of Cork and Chesterfield, he plied the spa's drawing rooms for potential benefactors and found unrivalled success in worming his way into the company of those who, just months earlier, would have turned the malodorous, malnourished poet away at the door. While the increasingly frail Nash had taken to surveying his kingdom from a wheelchair, Sam Derrick was engaged in his most prolonged dramatic engagement to date, wooing with elaborate artifice the good graces of those who truly ruled Bath: the aristocracy.

The death of Beau Nash on 3 February 1761 took no one by surprise; the Master of the Ceremonies had reached the supreme age of eighty-seven before retiring to his grave. After the stately progress of his funeral and interment in Bath Abbey, much of the leisured population was prepared to carry on under the rule of Nash's hastily appointed replacement, who, rather unfortunately, is remembered only as 'The Frenchman, Monsieur Collette'. Beyond his being French, there was not much in the character of Jacques Collette to which the general subscription-payers of Bath could object. He liked walking and a good game of shuttlecock. He also made an unusual show of dancing with children in the assembly rooms, although by virtue of his towering height he loomed over them rather menacingly. When compared with Nash, Collette did little to impress or annoy anyone other than the owners of the assembly rooms, who, since the day of his appointment, had kicked up a storm of disapproval at the unfair practices employed in electing him. The situation degenerated rapidly and soon, in order to sooth frayed tempers, the Corporation of Bath was forced to call a new election. 'The Frenchman' would be made to defend his title against another nominee, a dark horse who raised far more eyebrows than the long-legged Collette.

The strange turn of events during the spring of that year would be something Sam Derrick himself claimed as 'an event most improbable and most unexpected'. As he told the story, sheer accident lay at the foundation of his unanticipated rise to a position of prominence. While broadening his spectrum of patrons in Bath that winter, he had the good fortune of attaching himself to the entourage of a certain unnamed lady. After several weeks of attending her levees and waxing lyrical about the beauty of her daughters, Lady — had grown fond of him, and he, like any necessitous poet, had made himself indispensable to her. With his charm, impeccable manners and thoughtfulness, he had turned her into a devoted sponsor who sang his praises loudly to all who might listen.

Above the bickering between Bath's grandees, each of whom had their list of favourites to promote for the disputed title of Master of the Ceremonies, came a lone but quite influential voice of support for the unlikely figure of Samuel Derrick. It had all occurred quite by chance. During a social gathering at which a number of individuals charged with solving the crisis of Nash's succession were present, the talk turned to the current stalemate. The situation had reached breaking point. For weeks, lists of potential appointees had been presented and rejected and, exasperated at the mention of the last candidate's name, the husband of Lady — threw up his hands in dismay. The entire selection process was a shambles. It seemed as if every aspiring, macaroni-mannered dancing master in Bath had been put forward as a suitable candidate. The absurdity of it all! So many inferior suggestions! Why, they might as well nominate Samuel Derrick for the position!

At that moment, Lady — stepped forward 'and seriously seconded this ludicrous motion'. The room, filled with gentlemen who knew better and ladies who didn't, fell to murmuring. Sam's reputation among the wives and daughters of the gentry was immaculate: a friend of lords Chesterfield, Charlemont, Orrery and Cork, all men of taste and breeding. He had even been offered a living in the Church! He dressed well and spoke with heartfelt deference, he was a gentleman, a poetic man of sensibility: what was there not to like about him? For most of his adult life, Sam Derrick had dedicated his efforts to the female sex, charming and flattering them, and in the end, it was the women of England who provided him with the opportunities. No gentleman worth his manners would venture to explain to these ladies of high birth why Samuel Derrick was not all that he seemed. There was no appropriate way to inform Lady — that the same hand that composed verses on the virtues of her daughters ascribed similar graces to the harlots of Covent Garden. The humiliation of the situation would have been compounded by the revelation that the man whom she had come to favour as a charming, witty and talented poet had not only been disinherited for his profligacy but had made a habit of sleeping on the street like a beggar. Certainly, among the male contingent of Bath society, many would have witnessed or heard stories of his antics. The more lurid sexual tales might easily be brushed aside, along with accounts of his drinking and gaming habits; these would not be judged social sins among men of fashion. Providing gentlemen took their pleasures tempered with a degree of moderation and a helping of discretion, their public characters might remain untarnished. The problem was that Sam was neither moderate nor discreet. As Boswell had so succinctly put it, he was in the eyes of many gentlemen no better than 'a little blackguard pimping dog', a lewd, poorly washed, immoral, low-born Irishman. If his character was not in itself enough to raise dissent, then the flames were surely fanned by the whispers that circulated among those who recognized Sam as the author of *Harris's List*. Although this may only have been a select few gentlemen, it was nevertheless enough to deposit Sam's secret in the public domain. Women of Lady —'s gentle birth would never have come across even the title *Harris's List*. She couldn't have possibly understood that by putting Derrick's name forward, she had unwittingly nominated a pimp for Master of the Ceremonies.

Sam Derrick's rise to this position of prominence was assisted on the one hand by those ignorant of his unsavoury reputation and on the other by those who were fully apprised of it. Those buckish comrades who had shared his Covent Garden secrets alongside bottles of wine found the prospect of his appointment at the least novel, if not amusingly delightful. His supporters among the Irish aristocracy stood resolutely behind his nomination and influenced others of their class to do the same. As Samuel Johnson sagely explained to Boswell, Derrick owed his triumph to the contacts he had cultivated as a patron-hunting author, adding, 'Had he not been a writer, he might have been sweeping the crosses in the streets and asking half-pence from everyone that passed.' In the minds of another group of Bath society, however, the fine line that existed between Derrick and a mendicant street-sweeper was negligible. Collette, for one, was incensed that he should be made to stand down in favour of one who bore such an ignoble name. For support in his indignation, the Frenchman turned to a rather unlikely ally.

James Quin had been a titan of the stage in the days before David Garrick rendered his stiff, recitative style of acting virtually laughable. Like Derrick, Quin was an Irishman, although more senior in years. He had come to Bath, like many of the thespian set, to settle into a peaceful retirement while still enjoying the veneration of numerous admirers who looked to him as one of the resort's resident celebrities. As Bath housed a large and highly esteemed theatre which hosted performances of top London plays, Quin placed himself at the centre of this sphere, making pronouncements and passing judgements on productions with Doge-like authority. He had come to view himself as a kind of alternative 'King of Bath'. Collette therefore saw fit to air his grievances at the foot of Quin's throne. Perhaps Quin and Derrick were too similar in disposition, or Quin believed it necessary for fashion's sake to cultivate a rival, but the veteran actor never much cared for 'the little Irish poet'. So when Collette came to him venting his spleen on the injustice and 'impropriety of choosing Derrick', he found a sympathetic ear. According to *Town and Country* '. . . After expatiating upon all the errors of his conduct, and his want of knowledge in polite life' and ultimately 'concluding with an observation on the insignificancy of his figure and the disagreeableness of his smell', Collette turned to the aged actor for a word of advice. Quin memorably responded with the damning phrase, 'If you have a mind to put Derrick out, do it at once, and clap an extinguisher over him.' The battle lines had been drawn.

As many of Sam Derrick's critics had noticed, once 'the Little King of Bath' had been crowned with Beau Nash's white hat, any remaining vestiges of humility in his character vanished. 'Vanity had no small share in the composition of our master of the ceremonies,' wrote the author of his obituary. If he could not prove to the world that he was 'a man of the most gallantry, the most wit and the most politeness of any in Europe', then he also 'insisted upon . . . keeping the best company'. Sam had spent much of his life having to endure the insults and disdain of those who regarded him as nothing better than a bottom-feeding hack, an indigent lowlife bereft of breeding and morality. Enough was enough. As he had done so many years earlier when contending with his rival Tracy, Derrick chose to voice his emotions through his pen, this time exerting 'his talents in ridiculing those who had been instrumental in . . . [attempting] to dethrone him'. Unable to forgive his enemy for his vitriolic attacks or to 'forget the advice Quin had given others', the King of Bath 'wrote the following epigram upon that gentleman':

284

*When Quin of all grace and dignity void,*
*Murder'd Cato, the censor, and Brutus destroy'd;*
*He strutted, he mouth'd – you no passion cou'd trace*
*In his action, delivery, or plumb-pudding face;*
*When he massacred Comus, the gay god of mirth,*
*He was suffer'd because we of actors had dearth,*
*But when Foote, with strong judgement and genuine wit,*
*Upon all his peculiar absurdities hit;*
*When Garrick arose, with those talents and fire*
*Which nature and all the nine muses inspire,*
*Poor GUTS[1] was neglected, or laugh'd off the stage;*
*So bursting with envy, and tortur'd with rage,*
*He damn'd the whole town in a fury, and fled,*
*Little Bayes[2] an extinguisher clapp'd on his head*
*Yet we never shall Falstaff behold so well done*
*With such character, humour, such spirit and fun,*
*So great that we knew not which most to admire,*
*Glutton, parasite, pander, pimp, letcher, or liar –*
*He felt as he spoke; – nature's dictates are true;*
*When he acted the part, his own picture he drew.[3]*

Derrick's poem had the desired effect: he had offended Quin enough to make him a sworn enemy. Theirs was a mutual disgust that lasted until shortly before the actor's death in 1766, when all was forgiven over a rift-healing dinner of John Dory, Quin's favourite fish.

Upon his election as Master of the Ceremonies, Sam seemed determined to establish himself once and for all in the eyes of society as a man of importance and gentility. He sought to recast his character and invent a public persona flawless in his knowledge of propriety. Many of those whom he had duped about his moral fibre remained none the wiser, but others who knew Sam Derrick for Sam Derrick saw the transparency of his charade and found it hilarious. Not only was Sam 'very fond of pomp and show', as John Taylor wrote in his *Records of My Life*, but when his position at last enabled him to acquire a household of servants, he ensured that 'he kept a footman almost as fine as himself'. In order to demonstrate to the world that he was a gentleman of consequence, 'his footman always walked behind him, and to show that he was his servant, he generally crossed the street several times, that the man might be seen to follow him'.

Derrick now lived more extravagantly than ever, boasting of an enormous wardrobe and a luxurious 'modern' Bath townhouse filled with expensive furnishings. He travelled between his regular engagements at Bath, Tunbridge Wells and London in his own coach, drawn by his own horses. In spite of being in receipt of an income that amounted to 'upwards of £800 per annum', a very comfortable sum, Derrick had refused to change in one crucial respect: he continued to live well above his means. With his usual bravado, he gambled for significantly high stakes at the card tables. The gifts he made to friends were more lavish than ever, and the loans he issued more indulgent.

But Derrick's proud displays of puffed-up plumage served as a mask to hide something else. The more absurdly polite he became, the more mannered the airs he assumed, the more lavish equipage he acquired, the less likely it was that those whose respect he needed to maintain would be inclined to believe any uncomplimentary tales concerning his underlying character, should they come to light. In truth, Sam juggled two diametrically opposed personas, an acceptable and an unacceptable face – a situation which must have provided him with no end of trouble. Some of his friends, including his naïve correspondent Tom Wilson, believed that his position as Master of the Ceremonies meant that Sam would pack in the slightly grubby practice of writing. 'The happiest circumstance in your affairs is to be released from the vile drudgery of authorship, to be subject to the clamorous demands of devils and booksellers,' he sighed in sympathetic relief. But Sam had no intention of giving up his desire to become a renowned poet. If anything, his role provided him with virtually unlimited access to the drawing rooms of every patron of consequence in the British Isles as they came to sojourn on his doorstep. Sadly, when at last provided with a scenario ideal for creating his magnum opus, the reality of his abilities was made perfectly apparent. In the eight years of his reign, Sam did manage to produce a handful of works which might loosely be described as his most respectable: edited collections of verse by recognized poets, as well as his own letters and an attempt at epic Irish poetry, *The Battle of Lora*, but none of these publications gathered enough interest to construct a reputation of literary greatness. Of all his attempts, only one volume continued to sell year upon year at the kiosks in Covent Garden and the bookstalls that cluttered Fleet Street.

Like Tom Wilson, another of Sam's correspondents given to moralizing had wished him congratulations on his appointment to office, but also offered an interesting benediction. He 'hoped with great sincerity' that '. . . whatever you publish hereafter will be an honour to your name and character'. Derrick chose to ignore these well-intentioned words. After 1762, there was no financial need for Sam to continue as editor of *Harris's List*, and his duties as Master of the Ceremonies would have consumed most of his time. Moreover, his connection with such a publication was not an ideal one in light of his recent promotion in society. However, *Harris's List* had been not merely a money-spinning opportunity that had broken Sam out of a spunging house but, remarkably, it also became a responsibility that he owed to a community of women. His role in the *List*'s creation was one he took seriously; he regarded it as a contribution to the betterment of the lives of the women who over the years had become some of his truest friends. For all that Bath offered, Derrick felt he owed something more significant to those in the Garden. He never forgot the *filles de joye* who not only supported him but to whom he owed his first and only literary success.

For most of his reign, Sam Derrick led a double life, appearing upstanding in the eyes of his subjects and continuing in much the same vein as he always had in the company of his loose-living friends. If anything, he had become better at concealing his true nature. When not under the gaze of his public, he joined in the spirited fun of Bath's drinking and dining societies and dabbled in producing plays at Bath's Theatre Royal (much to the annoyance of its theatrical manager). Now at liberty to travel in his own carriage, he made frequent visits to London, where he called upon both male and female friends from his past. In spite of his posturing and attempts to hide his slightly rough-edged personality behind deep bows and flattery, he had no more abandoned his vices than he had gained religion. Inevitably, Sam could not prevent the wags from revealing his secret side to the public, although, thankfully, they waited until he was comfortably in his grave.

If there had been any doubt as to the true nature of the seemingly well-polished Master of the Ceremonies, *Derrick's Jests* soon put an end to it. This was the man who many of the male visitors to Bath remembered from the Bedford Coffee House: a slightly ludicrous 'beau-nasty' with poor personal hygiene and a sparkling wit. This was a man with a foul mouth who, in this compendium of quotes, revealed a disdain for the elaborate codes of propriety, who liked to abandon formality with the claim that he 'was only paid for being ceremonious in the Long-room'. This Sam Derrick revelled in his sharp retorts to dreary matrons and announced with no pretension, 'when I . . . die, I desire only a foot-stone to my grave, inscribed, *Pray don't piss here!*' What *Derrick's Jests* laid bare was that this Sam Derrick, in spite of his convincingly polished demeanour, was in his heart more at ease in the disreputable circus of Covent Garden than the glorious parade of Bath.

There were those, of course, who in spite of Derrick's elaborate posturing never failed to recognize this and shunned his company. Sam was no gentleman and never would be. On more than one occasion he complained bitterly of 'being used extremely ill' by those he believed to be allies. Friends from his long-buried Dublin past had refused to acknowledge him, and when certain individuals who had willingly subscribed to his sham politeness caught wind of his true nature they abandoned him.

More than any other treachery inflicted upon him, Sam

was unable to forgive Jane Lessingham for her behaviour on what was to be their final encounter. In the years following his appointment as King of Bath, at a time when Jane's theatrical career was flourishing, Sam thought it an appropriate moment to effect a reconciliation between them. While in London, he called upon her at her fashionable lodgings in Pall Mall. Arriving at her door, he presented his card to her manservant, who returned to inform Derrick, 'His mistress knew no-one of that name.' Sam had not expected such a curt rejection from a woman who had once adopted the name 'Mrs Derrick'. Offended and shocked, he barged into her apartments. An argument ensued; Jane burst into terrified tears, hurling caustic insults, before the constable was called and Sam, fearing a brush with the law, fled in disgrace. It was said that he never recovered from the blow.

Although a wistful coda to his story, his altercation with Mrs Lessingham was unlikely to have been the turning point which precipitated the decline of his health in his forties. A penchant for excessive drinking, careless sex and periods of living rough over the course of his life was certain to have taken a serious toll on his body. As early as 1760, Sam was complaining of illness to George Faulkner, although whether this was the same disorder that would later claim his life is unknown. It would not be unreasonable to believe that he may have suffered from a variety of venereal afflictions, not uncommon in men who chased Covent Garden's ladies around its piazza. Such was the fate of his so-called friend James Boswell, who eventually died from complications of syphilis. Whether it was the presence of one of these ailments that accounts for Sam's slow deterioration later in life is left to conjecture. Whatever his complaint, it appears to have caught up with him during the summer of 1768. Derrick suffered through that autumn and winter, supposedly nursed by a young actress called Maria Hedges, whom he had seen at the Haymarket in a performance of *The Spanish Fryar.* Not unlike Nash before him, Derrick's choice of fresh-faced mistress set Bath tongues tutting. It was whispered that she had worn him out with her extreme sexual appetite and that the poor forty-five-year-old Master of the Ceremonies was forced to take stimulants to keep up with her.

Mercifully for the Corporation of Bath, their second Master of the Ceremonies took several months to expire. It provided them with ample time to locate and elect a replacement, while Sam languished on his deathbed in Tunbridge Wells. Such was the importance of the position in the eighteenth century that the London newspapers provided their readerships with regular updates as to the King of Bath's condition. Finally, on 28 March 1769, when the pleasurable reign of Samuel Derrick had come to a close, the 'wits of Bath', who had restrained themselves so politely for eight years, took off their gloves. The satirical press had a field day exposing the shadowy side of their deceased king's character. As no one knew the true cause of Sam's fatal illness, 'the wits' were all too eager to step into the breach and offer their own explanations. One claimed that he had caught a chill in the early months of autumn when a fellow Irishman whipped off the Master of the Ceremonies' wig and exposed his delicate pate to the cold. Others pointed to Sam's notorious libido as the root cause, suggesting that he had accidentally poisoned himself by ingesting 'a surfeit of cantharides' (aphrodisiacs).

In life, Sam Derrick had never adhered to the conventional or the practical, and in death he chose to remain consistent. In spite of his handsome income, enough to maintain a household, his stables and a well-appointed table, he never bothered to file a legally valid will. On his deathbed the dawn broke over an embarrassing revelation: the King of Bath was penniless. As he lay dying, the man who never abandoned his hope of one day becoming a celebrated poet was forced to raise yet one more subscription. This one would be to pay for his doctor's bills and the expenses of his funeral. Perhaps the wealthy sojourners of Bath who had contributed to his comfortable living as Master of the Ceremonies had tired of supporting Sam Derrick and his literary flights of fancy; in his time of need, they failed to come to his assistance. The parsimonious gentry raised, in total, five shillings. By the time of his death, his borrowing had exhausted the goodwill of friends and shopkeepers alike. He had no proper assets, no land, no stock, no true wealth. He had virtually no possessions that he could lay claim to owning outright. Everything belonged to his creditors, from his silverware down to his set of false teeth. Everything, that was, but for his yet unpublished, newly updated *Harris's List* for 1769.

That belonged to Charlotte Hayes.

# 16

# 'WHORE RAISING, OR HORSE RACING

*How To Brood A Mare Or Make Sense Of A Foal-Ly'*

D URING THE EARLY MONTHS of 1769, while London's carriage wheels and shoe heels skidded across icy streets, Charlotte's thoughts were not on the usual matters of her business. As the purchase of the Clay Hill estate neared its final stage, she had a number of concerns. There were promissory notes still to be paid, bills from victuallers, vintners and dressmakers accruing rapidly. Santa Charlotta's clientele expected her ladies to be dressed in the finest gowns and to be fed at a genteelly laid table, and such lavish entertainment cost dearly. While her exclusivity entitled her to prise banknotes from her gentlemen's purses, not all of those hefty sums reached the donation box of the King's Place nunnery. 'The Friar' was known to dip his hand into the coffers before joining his cronies on the turf or at the gaming tables. The result was a precarious cash flow, one that had Charlotte frequently sitting with some discomfort on the edge of her seat. Although financial worries tended to feature with regularity in Charlotte's and Dennis's lives, this year they would merely form the backdrop to a whirlwind of affairs, both trying and exhilarating.

The year was to begin with two surprises: one death and one life. Only a few months into 1769, Charlotte heard the news of Samuel Derrick's demise. True to his theatrical nature, his expiration had been a laboriously protracted affair, dragging on for weeks and then months. For Charlotte, the final announcement at the end of March could not have been a surprise, but the events that followed it would have been. Sam was like so many other men that Charlotte had known; what little they had was spent immediately, sometimes before it was even in their hands. Men like him always left a trail of insolvency and were forever hounded by a pack of avaricious creditors who chased them to their grave. In the end, nature had swallowed Sam up as it had yielded him: with no legitimate heirs to his blood and no significant possessions to his name. While he lived, Sam had never allowed circumstances to dampen his sense of humour. As the hour of his death approached, his outlook was no different. As a parting gesture to the world he penned an unofficial will: a final piece of spurious writing by which his friends might remember the Master of the Ceremonies at Bath. Whether this was intended to be seen by anyone other than his most intimate companions is questionable. Invariably, the hands into which it fell viewed it as a fitting tribute to the true but carefully hidden nature of the former King of Bath. Upon its publication, all of England was free to learn of its contents, including his confession that he authored the notorious *Harris's List of Covent Garden Ladies*.

Among the few items to which he could lay claim were his yet unpublished writings. These he bequeathed to 'My

Old friend and mistress, Charlotte Hayes', in the hope that she might be able to profit from their appearance in print. Among these works, he included, cleverly, 'My new edition of *Harris's List*', of which 'the profits of the sale of the first impression' were reserved for Charlotte. It is unlikely that his hungry creditors would have scented this ploy: lumped in with Derrick's usual worthless catch-penny pamphlets was a nugget of pure gold. If contemporary claims are to be believed, *Harris's List* had a circulation of approximately eight thousand. If each copy sold for its stated price of two shillings and sixpence, then the entire production would have generated no less than £2,400, an astronomical profit to be split between publisher and author, or, in this case, the author's beneficiary. The worthy gentlemen and tradespeople who had extended credit to Sam Derrick thankfully were not acquainted with the lures of Covent Garden's ladies, nor the popularity of the *List*. Charlotte, on the other hand, who knew the price of flesh and the sums its sale commanded, would have recognized the generosity of this gesture.

As Charlotte aged, the tide of the years would have rubbed away many sharp memories of earlier lovers. This abrupt reminder of her past, and the death of a man with whom she had been intimate, would have stirred her thoughts. In her days of foolish extravagance, Sam Derrick offered her the adoration that she desired, but did not have the funds with which to support it. They had loved and assisted one another as much as was possible under the circumstances. Charlotte had always proved generous to Sam when others remained tight-fisted. She had indulged him, fed him, sheltered him and lent him money, which he had promised to repay once in receipt of his ever-elusive inheritance. In return, he could offer only affection and occasional protection from the law. After the passing of so much time, his gift would have been wholly unanticipated. It would have come as an unwarranted act of kindness, a repayment for a debt that, in the comfort of her position in St James's, she had long since forgotten.

Whether the profits of the *List* assisted Charlotte out of a tight spot in 1769 is unknown. It is likely that the bequest became simply another contribution to the maintenance of her empire. As one who expressed genuine concern for the condition of ladies of town, in the end, Sam may have gained some satisfaction by recycling the proceeds of prostitution back into the hands of those who practised the profession.

While his death and his unexpected gift would have unsettled Charlotte, the revelation that came hard on its heels overwhelmed her. She was pregnant. It was a turn of events that neither she nor Dennis could have foreseen. If she proved fertile in her early forties, then it is more than likely that this was not her first encounter with potential motherhood. In mid-eighteenth-century London, infant mortality was approaching 50 per cent: nearly half of all children born within the metropolis were dead by the age of three. Many of these deaths may have been intentional; others would have been brought about by a proliferation of diseases and untimely accidents. Many pregnancies never made it to the stage of producing a live birth, especially those conceived in a prostitute's line of work. The city was filled with surgeons, midwives and quacks willing to perform abortions or peddling potions that promised to 'remove obstructions' from the womb. Every prostitute would have learned what combination of powders and herbs was required from an apothecary's shop to bring on a miscarriage, or what solutions could be used after the sexual act to douche away 'the pernicious seed'. When these measures did not work and nine months of discomfort and fear ended with an unavoidable birth, the desperate resorted to infanticide.

There were, however, other options for those who did not want to risk their necks by committing murder, or who could not bring themselves to leave their child in the cold or smother it in its sleep. The practice of abandoning babies on the steps of parish churches was superseded, if only temporarily, by the establishment of Thomas Coram's Foundling Hospital in 1741. Within the first four years of opening its doors, fifteen thousand infants were placed into its care. Those who could manage to secure a place for their progeny in its overcrowded sanctuary were among the fortunate few. For those not so lucky, there were other options. Nursemaids, frequently described as being 'indigent, filthy and decrepit women', would take infants into their homes for small fees. Once a mother had left her swaddled child in the arms of one of these untrustworthy matrons who made their living by farming babies, she was not obliged to return. London was large enough to swallow up the anonymous. As a result, regardless of the good intentions of Captain Coram, the metropolis remained awash with begging, starving, parentless boys and girls, a fair number of whom had been the fruit of a union between a prostitute and her pleasure-seeker.

Sexually active since her early teens, for Charlotte to have remained childless after roughly thirty years of frequent intercourse, it is highly likely that she, too, would have been forced to resort to a number of these measures. In an era devoid of effective contraception and prophylactics, the menace of undesired conception, and how to rid oneself of it, would have been a constant worry for ladies of the town. A pregnant prostitute, unless guaranteed of the continuing support of a keeper, would find herself with no means of earning an income. Only fetishists sought out the services of those with swollen maternal bellies. When men paid for sex with women, they weren't interested in the consequences or in being reminded of them. Callous, wealthy keepers might even be tempted to cut their mistress loose in order to avoid complications that threatened to involve their families and inheritances; kinder ones might embrace the prospect of fatherhood, but which of these reactions a mistress might meet with was unknown. It was easier to terminate the pregnancy than to run the risk of starvation and homelessness.

Whether Charlotte brought any of her previous pregnancies to term is unknown, as are the fates of the children she may have borne. One thing, however, is certain: until 1769, there is no evidence that any of them lived with her and Dennis. It seems, though, that she had every intention of keeping this pregnancy. From the outset, plans were made for the child's birth. Charlotte announced her desire to retire towards the end of the year and made arrangements to leave 'the direction of the seminary to a trusty deputy'. Publicly, she claimed that her intention was to live quietly for a while, but those closest to her recognized the coded meaning in the phrase. Her lying-in was to take place at the couple's original residence in Great Marlborough Street. According to *Town and Country*, she and Dennis took two contiguous houses 'in order to have a door of communication to one another, and by that means, confer with greater ease'. It is more likely that one house was intended as a nursery, a place where, after the birth of their baby, the child might be reared with a degree of discretion, removed from the bustle of wanton associates and activities that were bound to take place next door.

With a child on its way, Charlotte began to take stock of her and Dennis's life together. The purchase of Clay Hill, which had been contemplated for some time, seemed most appropriate now, as the prospect before them was to shift. Just as 1769 proved to be a momentous year for Charlotte, for Dennis it would be equally so. Over the past several years, his realm of interest and revenue generation had begun to move from the gaming tables of Piccadilly to Newmarket and Epsom turf. His friendships among the noble black-leg set, men such as the Duke of Cumberland, Lord Egremont and Lord Grosvenor, had begun to solidify, helped along no doubt by the warm welcome they received as frequent patrons of Charlotte's establishment. But in order for Dennis to garner any genuine respect among these men, he had to prove that he was more than a lowly, adventuring Irishman, 'with the broadest and the most offensive brogue that his nation per-haps ever produced'. He had to become a landowner, and serious about his success on the turf. Acquiring a title of some description was easy enough. In the early 1760s, not long after his release from the Fleet, he had bought himself a commis-sion in the Westminster Regiment of the Middlesex Militia and eventually 'rose, by regular gradations . . . to the rank of Lieutenant-Colonel', but something more substantial than a military sinecure was needed in this case. In the spring,

Dennis was hatching a plan to remedy the situation: he had his eye on an impressive horse belonging to a boisterous Yorkshireman called William Wildman. The horse, known as Eclipse, outran everything on the course and succeeded in terrifying his owner. By the time Dennis O'Kelly had purchased a share of one leg, Wildman was becoming desperate to get the unpredictable beast out of his stables, and within a year Dennis had acquired the horse outright. It would be the single most profitable venture he was ever to pursue.

A new horse and a new child both required what only the open vistas of the countryside could provide, and what the estate of Clay Hill could offer. The demesne lay near Banstead Downs at Epsom, roughly fifteen miles south of London, in the heart of untouched, pastoral Surrey. While not a particularly grand estate, it had all the accoutrements required by a status-minded property owner. A recently renovated manor house, impressive expanses of land and sizeable stables demonstrated to Dennis's acquaintances that his fortune was on the increase. Most importantly, its location made it an ideal acquisition. No more than a short jaunt from the Epsom races and just under a day's ride from the capital, Clay Hill became a perfect venue for entertaining. Charlotte and Dennis (the O'Kellys, as they were now called, although there is no evidence to suggest that they ever sanctified their union) had placed themselves at the geographical heart of the racing scene. After the extension of the stables and outbuildings, Dennis was determined to fill his estate with championship winners, runners that would attract so much attention that his distinguished associates would become his constant visitors. He began with Eclipse, and after a short and highly successful season decided to retire him from racing and set him up as a stud. Horse breeders across the land transported their mares to his paddock; it has been suggested that this side of Dennis's venture alone earned him 'at least £25,000'. By the end of the 1780s, Dennis and his brother Philip, who had been invited from Ireland to manage the storehouse of thoroughbreds, had possession of some of the most heroic horses of their age.

But Clay Hill was intended for the rearing of more than just colts. Beyond the polluted air of London, the eighteenth-century English countryside offered clear water, hearty exercise and easy breathing, an ideal environment in which to raise a child. The life that Charlotte had known, born directly into the circus of carnal commerce, was not what she intended for her infant. Undoubtedly, her greatest wish would be for her baby to be born a boy. A boy, irrespective of his parentage, would be able to slide easily into his position as a landed gentleman. He would inherit Clay Hill and a prize-winning stable block. No expense would be spared on his education; he would be raised as an heir to a fortune. It was said that at the time of her 'retirement' Charlotte's business had earned her 'upwards of twenty thousand pounds', while Dennis had 'kept pace' with his own takings from the gaming tables and race courses. The couple's total worth before the purchase of Clay Hill was thought to be 'at least forty thousand pounds', a sum that by today's standards would render them millionaires. A son would reap the benefits of this in every way. All her life, Charlotte had catered to men of this class. She had placed their interests and happiness at the centre of her existence for nothing more lasting than the glint of coins. If the baby she carried proved to be a son, he would walk among them, a gentleman blessed with respectability and influence; he would take her blood into the highest circles and merit respect rather than condemnation. At Clay Hill, their child could live its life away from the evils of the city and truth of its parentage. Guarded by servants, nursemaids and tutors, its early years would be coloured by innocence rather than depravity.

The purchase of Clay Hill alone, however, did not bring about a solution to all Charlotte's problems. The life that Dennis pursued, moving within a circle of wealthy profligates, was as likely to breed trouble as it was to open doors. Although united in their own eyes and regarded as husband and wife by all who were intimate with them, Charlotte and Dennis could never lead an ordinary existence. She would always bear the stain of her profession, and he the mark of an untrustworthy Irish sharper. The conventions of society barred the O'Kellys from participating fully in public life and their background was apt to prejudice upstanding members of the community against them. Dennis may have counted among his friends some of the era's most powerful noblemen – towards the end of his life, even the Prince of Wales – but irrespective of his significant contribution to racing, he was prevented from becoming a member of the elite Jockey Club. On the track, his name, like Charlotte's, was viewed with suspicion. Shortly after the purchase of Eclipse and the O'Kellys' bid to enter the ranks of the landowning class, Dennis was to learn the limitations of his recently acquired status.

As is generally the case with stories that involve the compromise of a person's character, there are two versions of events. Dennis had been at the York races in August 1770 and, after a celebratory night spent 'with a few friends at the coffee house at that innocent and amusing diversion called hazard, which engaged him till near three in the morning', he returned to the room he had hired at a local inn. According to him, when he opened the door to his chamber, there, lying deep within the embrace of sleep, was 'a most enchanting female countenance' whom 'he conjectured and perhaps with probability that . . . being enamoured of the vast sums he was publicly known to have won at the meeting devised that method of securing by artifice and agreeable surprise what a more regular plan might have failed in effecting'. Having spent so much of his life around Charlotte and women of her caste, Dennis could only assume that any woman who had found her way into his bed was of a similar character. How mistaken he was. Miss Swinbourne was the young and chaste daughter of a local landowner with a number of particularly influential friends. In the public apology they required him to publish in the newspapers, he admitted that he 'commenced such *violent hostilities* as soon awoke the terrified, unknown object of his sensuality', and that 'In an instant she started up screaming with extreme vociferation' which 'soon alarmed the house'. But, contrary to the tattle of rumour-mongers and irrespective of his lustful attempts on her honour, he could confirm that no, he had not been successful in his approaches and that, thankfully, '. . . she remained untouched'.

Naturally, Miss Swinbourne remembered it differently. Apparently, Dennis, his brain addled by a night's worth of alcohol, forced his way into her room, mistaking it for his own. In any case, the injured party demanded that in addition to his apology he make a gift of £500 to the lady, 'to be disposed of for such charitable purposes as she shall direct'. As might be imagined, the eighteenth-century gutter press loved this scandal. One publication printed, with an artful flourish of irony, a supposed letter from an offended Charlotte, lamenting Dennis's infidelity and accusing him of 'flinging away in a drunken frolic – in the ridiculous attempt of an amour – more money, aye, far more money than I have cleared in my honest industry for a month . . .' Irrespective of their wealth or land, the O'Kellys could never make reputable society forget who they really were: a madam and a rogue.

Social stigma was easily transferable to one's offspring, especially if they were female. Even if a boy were to be compromised by the exposure to gaming, racing, bawdy houses and illicit sex, it would not hinder his progress in the world; it might even advance it. If a girl were exposed to the same, it would be her ruin. On the occasion of the birth of her daughter, Charlotte's hopes would have been dashed. She must have been reminded of her mother's situation and how she herself, fresh from Elizabeth Ward's womb, was already destined to lie under men for money. When Charlotte looked at her daughter, whom she and Dennis named Mary Charlotte O'Kelly, she herself determined that this girl should not be sacrificed as she had been. While her mother had spent Charlotte's childhood scheming how she might best utilize her daughter's virginity for her own gain, Charlotte would defend her daughter's honour with every ounce of her maternal instinct. This, however, by virtue of Charlotte's reputation, would prove to be a difficult and painful course to follow.

If Charlotte was committed to elevating Mary above the

tainted life bequeathed to her, she would have no other choice but to part with her. Respectable society would not receive into its ranks as a virtuous lady the daughter of the most notorious brothel-keeper in London. Charlotte dwelt within the shadow world of the demi-monde, a place where gentlemen might discreetly sojourn, but where their sisters, daughters, wives and mothers would never dare tread. Less than a century after Charlotte's death, Lady Augusta Fane's comments indicated that the situation had not changed, and that 'these ladies of the *half-world*' were still 'only mentioned in private and in a whisper'. Furthermore, '. . . it was unheard of for any respectable dame to acknowledge that she knew such ladies . . . existed, and even the little squares and streets where they lived were completely out-of-bounds'. In an era where virginity among unmarried women of the wealthy classes was an essential possession, a mere hint of the reprehensible about a girl's character might render her damaged goods in the eyes of companions and suitors. It was therefore crucial that Mary was seen to have been raised respectably and quietly. As an infant, she could be cared for in her mother's home, either on Great Marlborough Street or at Clay Hill, sequestered in the nursery under the auspices of the O'Kellys' staff. But as maturity came upon her she would have to be passed into the hands of another, more fitting specimen of female virtue, capable of imparting morality and an appropriate example. This role fell to Dennis's family.

Upon the purchase of Clay Hill, a number of O'Kellys made an appearance in Dennis's life. In 1769, his brother Philip, along with his wife, Elizabeth, and the youngest of their three children, Andrew, arrived at the Epsom estate. For several years, Dennis had been charitably subsidizing his brother's family, funding Andrew's education and contributing to the marriage settlements of his two nieces. His elder niece, also called Mary, described as 'a lady of great beauty and fortune', had wed an established Dublin printer, Whitfield Harvey, in 1765. Philip's younger daughter was to make an equally estimable match to Sterne Tighe, a wealthy property owner. With an air of respectability to preserve, when the Philip O'Kellys came to live on the Clay Hill estate it would have been with some reservation. It is unlikely that Elizabeth O'Kelly would have had much to do with the manor's shadowy mistress. As Clay Hill was also the venue of numerous parties frequented by Charlotte's nymphs, it is hardly surprising that the couple and their son took up residence in one of the estate's outlying houses. From the perimeters of propriety they acted as the stewards of Dennis's affairs. Philip engaged himself in the management of his brother's stables, while his wife presided over the rearing of Charlotte's child. Throughout her girlhood, Mary Charlotte was passed around quietly within the households of the O'Kelly family, frequently ferried from her Clay Hill nursery to the Dublin home of her cousin Mrs Harvey. It was only when alone, and within the private boundaries of Clay Hill, that the child would have come to know her mother. Here, removed from the critical eye of society, Charlotte would have spent some of the only meaningful hours she was to enjoy with her daughter.

As she began to blossom into womanhood, the dangers that Mary faced from any association with her mother would have increased. As Charlotte sought to raise her daughter respectably and to endow her with the hallmarks of gentility, the problem of appropriate schooling would have reared its head. Knowledge of Charlotte's name and face among the upper ranks of society would have prevented her from placing Mary at one of the more elite schools for young ladies. The only truly safe haven lay outside England, where she might enjoy the advantages of anonymity. Among wealthier parents, it was a common practice to place one's daughters in convent schools across the Channel, in France and Belgium. Ironically, it was at such an establishment that the Abbess of King's Place decided to educate her child, entrusting her virtue to the care of a bona fide sisterhood. Perhaps swayed by the sentimentality of the occasion of her daughter's departure for school, Charlotte took the risky decision of personally delivering Mary to the convent in Ostend. Believing she was unlikely to encounter any of her London acquaintances on her journey, Charlotte, with Mary and two of her King's Place nuns, set out for Margate in her carriage. Unfortunately, and much to her chagrin, she encountered William Hickey, his brother and a number of their associates, who had come to the coast for a few weeks of diversion. Hickey, when spotting her 'smart landau with four post horses' from his window at an inn, immediately set out to greet them.

The pitfalls of Mary's precarious situation became apparent during a meal they enjoyed together, after the gentlemen 'made rather too free with the champagne'. Hickey's brother, described as being 'beastly drunk', could not prevent himself from making overtures towards the twelve-year-old Miss O'Kelly, 'at which the mother was greatly enraged'. Regardless of Charlotte's anger, Joseph Hickey 'continued his nonsense, swearing the young one's bosom had already too much swell for a nun, and no canting hypocritical friar should have the fingering of those plump little globes'. Hickey's brother then lunged at the girl, 'clapping his hand upon Miss's bosom'. Much to the male guests' surprise, Charlotte was visibly horrified. Shaking with anger, she entreated that 'he would cease to use such indecent language and action before her innocent child'. 'Innocent,' echoed Joseph Hickey, 'oh very innocent to be sure; but she knows a thing or two. However I'll take her to bed with me and ascertain how matters are.' With that, a struggle ensued; Joseph Hickey attempted to pull the girl away from the table, while Charlotte, parting with her usually polite demeanour, immediately jumped from her chair and with a wrathful voice 'bestowed some tolerably vulgar abuse upon us all'. Wresting Mary from the clutches of Hickey's brother, who at that point had collapsed upon the floor, 'she seized rudely hold of [her daughter] and made her exit'. It was unlikely to have been the first of such scenes, and sadly it served as a reminder as to why they were en route to Ostend in the first place.

Although the birth of her daughter and the purchase of Clay Hill allowed Charlotte some respite from the duties of her profession, the great Abbess of King's Place was not yet in the position to which she ultimately aspired. By the 1770s, Charlotte had begun to weary of her role, particularly as the houses and streets that surrounded her were beginning to fill up with competitors. In her mid-forties by now, within her profession Charlotte was considered old and she began to speak more earnestly about severing the ties that kept her tethered to her position. Her thoughts were increasingly in

Epsom, where Clay Hill was becoming a venue for entertainment to rival her houses on King's Place.

Unfortunately, her rural residence was also causing her some anxiety. Their gatherings, although popular, were expensive, and the stabling and training of horses still too young for racing (and therefore earning) had begun to wear holes in their pockets. To complicate matters, Dennis's passion for the gaming tables continued to bring about as many losses as it did wins. Although Charlotte was growing impatient, if she were to make an exit from her lucrative career, neither she nor Dennis would be in a position to cover their outgoings. During the mid- to late 1770s, finances were stretched to their thinnest point. Every transaction that passed between a nun and her devotee helped to maintain the O'Kellys' lifestyle; every guinea earned by a 'Polly Nimblewrist' or banknote brought in for a night with 'Nell Blossom' was transubstantiated into horse feed or servants' pay. For the first time since her imprisonment at the Fleet, Charlotte found herself in debt. In what must have been a mortifying incident, she was apprehended while in the company of Dennis's nephew Andrew, then a young man in his late teens. The debt, which she had acknowledged on 1 August 1776, had been accrued as a business expense and amounted to a mere £50, not an exceptional sum for an establishment like Charlotte's, which might make that in an evening. According to the haberdasher James Spilsbury, who accused the Abbess of bankrupting him, the bill had been for 'making fitting adorning and trimming divers cloaths Garments and Masquerade dresses', in which Charlotte dressed her nymphs. By the time

Dennis, who had been at York races, learned of the situation, Charlotte had already been thrown into Marshalsea Prison. It was only upon his arrival that her bail was raised.

That Charlotte landed in debtors' prison for the trifling sum of £50 was an alarming indication of affairs. The author of O'Kelly's *Memoirs* writes that Dennis, too, notwithstanding the prodigious influx of money derived from racing and horse breeding, was yet again 'streightened in his circumstances', forced 'to borrow money on his diamond ring' simply to meet 'the enormous expenses of his stud, his house and his donations of friendship'. Charlotte would have been approaching fifty, so would have been in no state of mind to suffer the indignity of returning to the pit of poverty she had clawed her way out of nearly twenty years earlier. For all her acquired gentility, for all of what male chroniclers called her 'delicate and agreeable' conversation, 'conciliating' manners and her overall 'gentleness and modesty', Charlotte was no soft touch. Whatever horrors her return visit to a prison may have conjured in her memory, it was nothing she had not seen or contended with before. If anything, the untimely incident convinced her of the need to become more enterprising and more competitive in the face of her rivals.

By 1779, the *Nocturnal Revels* commented that every house on King's Place had been converted into a brothel, making the entire street appear as 'a constellation of nunneries'. Elizabeth Mitchell's 'bevy of beauties' next door boasted of girls just as glamorous as Charlotte's. Harriott Lewis, a former East Indian slave, specialized in exotics, while Sarah Prendergast, Sarah Dubery and Catherine Windsor were constantly vying to outdo one another, playing host to Covent

Garden's most famous actresses and staging eye-poppingly lewd events guaranteed to reel in London's lechers. One of the most memorable was conceived of by Mrs Prendergast. She entitled it her 'Grand Ball d'Amour'. Not to be outdone by Theresa Cornelys in Soho Square, who was beginning to siphon off business through her frequently held masquerades, where the demi-monde and respectable classes could scandalously meet and mingle, Sarah Prendergast offered an even more exciting entertainment. Invitations were sent to her most devoted patrons boasting that 'the finest women in all Europe would appear in *puris naturalibis*'; included was a list of those whose unclothed bodies would be on view. In addition to notable courtesans and actresses like Charlotte Spencer, Gertrude Mahon and Isabella Wilkinson, there were also aristocratic ladies of ill repute. Guests arrived by carriage and sedan chair in revealing costumes, such as those sported by Lady Henrietta Grosvenor and Lady Margaret Lucan, who both came 'disguised as Mother Eve', covering their faces with fig leaves and 'leaving their more shameful parts exposed'. After the initial excitement of ogling had worn off, the assembled naked guests danced, dined and copulated to their heart's content, leaving Mrs Prendergast at the end of the evening nearly £1,000 richer. The Grand Ball d'Amour had been a King's Place coup like none other; that is, until Charlotte decided to throw her hat into the ring.

When the worst of their financial storm had cleared, she resolved that she would bid a farewell to King's Place at the end of 1778 and turn her attention exclusively to life at Clay Hill. In a last attempt to increase business and to provide some of her most loyal clientele with an unforgettable grand finale, Charlotte planned a 'Tahitian Feast of Venus'. Captain Cook's recent voyages to the South Pacific had captured the imagination of the public, and of the many discoveries made during Cook's travels, none fascinated the male population so much as the lurid tales of sex among the 'noble savagery'. Dr Hawkesworth, who documented the experiences of those who sailed on the *Endeavour*, recorded one occasion where a young woman underwent a rite of sexual initiation. Hawkesworth was pleased to report that the ceremony, which involved a gratuitous amount of nudity and fornication, was completed without so much as a hint of embarrassment on the part of the participants. Greatly inspired by these discoveries, Santa Charlotta decided to capitalize upon them by re-creating the scene in her King's Place salon. Like Sarah Prendergast, she had formal invitations printed:

> Mrs Hayes presents her most respectful compliments to Lord – and takes liberty to acquaint him that to-morrow evening, precisely at seven, a dozen beautiful nymphs, unsullied and untainted, and who breathe health and nature will perform the celebrated rites of Venus, as practised at Otaheite, under the instruction and tuition of Queen Oberea in which character Mrs. Hayes will appear upon this occasion.

Just how 'unsullied and untainted' Charlotte's uninitiated girls were is highly suspect. She claimed to have sought out a variety of new recruits specifically for this event, but it is more likely that those already on hand 'restored' themselves with the usual *Oeconomy of Love* concoction. To enliven the show further, the Abbess spiced up the sex with some assistance from

Aretino's *Postures*, a well-thumbed sex manual which, like the Kama Sutra, explained the joys of penetration from a number of different angles. In the days leading up to the performance, suspense grew among the select group of invited guests. Charlotte put it about that she had spent the past fortnight, twice every day, putting her recruits 'through their exercises' and training them 'for a new species of amusement'. To partner her nymphs, she had also 'engaged a dozen of the most athletic and best proportioned young men that could be procured'. This included life models plundered from the studios of the newly founded Royal Academy of Art, as well as a handful of strapping lads considered 'well qualified for the sport'.

On the night of this 'salacious olympic', her efforts attracted the highest-ranking in the land. 'She had,' as the *Revels* reported, 'no less than three and twenty visitors, consisting chiefly of the first nobility,' in addition to 'some Baronets, and but five Commoners'. In the largest room of her establishment, chairs and sofas had been arranged for the audience, facing a large carpet where 'all the apparatus for the various attitudes in which the votaries of Venus were to appear, according to the Aretin system' was laid. As the clock struck eleven, the festivities began:

> The males had presented each of their mistresses with a Nail of at least twelve inches in length, in imitation of the presents received by the Ladies of Otaheite upon this occasion, giving the preference to a long nail before any other compliment, they entered upon their devotions, and went through all the various evolutions, according to the word and the command of Santa Charlotta, with the greatest dexterity, keeping the most regular

313

time, to the no small gratification of the lascivious spectators, some of whom could scarce refrain till the end of the spectacle, before they were impetuous to perform a part in this Cyprian game, which lasted near two hours and met with the highest applause from all present.

Following the main event, the male audience, now piqued to the extreme of sexual arousal, selected female devotees to repeat 'the part they had so skilfully performed'. In addition to the champagne which 'briskly circulated' in post-coital celebration, Charlotte ensured that her revellers were touched for contributions while spirits remained high. As a result of a good evening's work, 'a handsome purse was subscribed upon the occasion' for the benefit of her thaises.

In the months that followed, the author of the *Nocturnal Revels* draws the curtain on Santa Charlotta's career. As planned, by the end of the year she had begun to wind down her business, putting on the market a number of the implements of her profession, including Dennis's specially designed 'elastic beds', for which there was a great scramble among the abbesses of King's Place. Catherine Matthews, Charlotte's number two, who ran her annexe across the street, inherited the larger premises. By 1779, having sold up and moved on, Charlotte at last found herself the resident mistress of Clay Hill. However, in many respects, the fabric of her daily life was not significantly altered by her departure from King's Place. Although no longer on the front line of nunnery management, Charlotte maintained a number of smaller brothels scattered throughout St James's and Piccadilly, which she entrusted to her appointed assistants. The profits of her enterprises were then employed in funding the entertainment enjoyed by her patrons at Clay Hill. During the racing season, she and Dennis threw themselves into hosting an unrelenting round of parties, dinners and gatherings at their home. It was remarked that 'Keeping company was one of O'Kelly's chief delights, and with the help of the faithful Charlotte Hayes he made Clay Hill at Epsom renowned for its hospitality.'

Although the O'Kellys were now landowners and enjoyed the company of some of the most influential men in England, they were by no means unaware of their tenuous standing within the social hierarchy. Any influence they had managed to corner was by virtue of Dennis's success on the turf and Charlotte's precedence in King's Place, and not through noble birth or any praiseworthy activity. In order to maintain their position at the centre of the Epsom arena, they had to lay on an exceptional show. This was hard work, as the author of Dennis's *Memoirs* records. Not only did they maintain 'an open house during the time of every public meeting', but O'Kelly established himself as a mediator of disputes between those of the racing fraternity. Accordingly, he cultivated a talent in 'reconciling apparent opposites, contriving to entertain the Peer and the Black Leg at the same table'. Due to Charlotte's finesse and experience with such matters, 'The Duke of Cumberland and Dick England, the Prince of Wales and Jack Tetherington; Lord Egremont and Ned Bishop; Lord Grosvenor and Monsieur Champreaux; the Duke of Orleans and Jack Stacie' were not only able to lay aside their differences but 'were frequently seen at the same table, and circulating the same bottle with equal familiarity and merriment'.

It is unlikely such a gathering of names would have been seen at Clay Hill at all were it not for the added attraction of the nymphs that Charlotte shipped in to attend to the needs of these gentlemen. Contrary to the nature of such occasions, Dennis insisted that 'play or bets of any kind' were not 'to be made at his table or in his house'. More than likely this was to prevent the eruption of trouble between hardened gamblers. With gaming banned, the rakish gathering would have required something else equally thrilling to divert them after dinner. Sex with Santa Charlotta's beautiful nuns filled this void and helped to sustain the couple's popularity. Their reputation for 'hospitality and good living' preceded them. 'Who keeps the best house in England?' was the frequent question. – 'O! Kelly, by much – Who the best wines? O! Kelly, by many degrees. – Who the best horses? O! Kelly's beat the world. – Who the pleasantest fellow? Who? O! Kelly,' their acquaintances were said to have proclaimed.

While the racing season would have kept Charlotte occupied, the winter period, when the turf was frozen or too muddied to support contests, would have been exceptionally dull. Aside from the days that she spent alone with her daughter, she would not have acted as the hostess to any other, virtuous guest. The O'Kellys' home, which would have been recognized for its licentious activities, was hardly a suitable place for those not of the demi-monde to visit. In an era when the company of others, and particularly same-sex friendships, was the very bread and butter of landed-class life, the sudden absence of companionship would be felt most acutely. In

London, amid the bustle of King's Place, Charlotte would never have been at a loss for company, whether male or female. A constant tide of visitors would have moved in and out of her drawing rooms, bringing gossip, news and amusement. Although she would have retained a close circle of female servants and 'companions' from King's Place, in Epsom there would have been comparatively few callers. As a mistress and a procuress, she would be excluded from genteel social circles and shunned by her female neighbours. While Dennis would have been granted passage to socialize with whomever he chose, Charlotte would have spent many days and evenings with little company.

In order to alleviate lengthy periods of loneliness when Dennis travelled, as he did regularly for race meetings and as an officer in the Middlesex Militia, Charlotte and her 'female attendants' chose to accompany him. The Westminster Regiment to which Dennis belonged spent most of their time engaged in a circuit of marches, which, rather than prepare them for active service, allowed them to parade in their uniforms. As they moved 'from London to Gosport; from Gosport to Plymouth; from Plymouth to the extremities of Cornwall; from thence to Chatham, from Chatham to Lancaster, and from Lancaster to London again', Dennis could be seen 'attended by an expensive retinue', followed by Charlotte, 'who travelled in the rear of his company, with her separate suite'. She also accompanied him more frequently to various races, where, together, they became 'the life and spirit of every principle race meeting in England'. However, in spite of appearances, Charlotte was becoming increasingly unhappy.

She would not have grieved over respectable society's

refusal to admit her into its charmed circles. In fact, as one who was born into the sex trade, it is unlikely that she would have ever imagined or even desired it. Certainly, in her eyes, the debauched company she kept was far more varied and interesting. What would have plagued her, however, was the unanticipated isolation of retirement. In London, there were few public places out of bounds to her; she could enjoy the theatre, the pleasure gardens, promenades in St James's Park, assemblies and balls. The rules of rural life were different and, aside from her own lands, there were no spaces where she might comfortably roam, unscrutinized by disapproving eyes. In the country, her interactions would be limited to a male-only sphere. These would be the associates of Dennis, the boorish, drunken black legs who droned on about races and stakes and horses and stables and jockeys . . . or the officers of Dennis's band of toy soldiers, whose company might prove only marginally more interesting. In her capacity as duenna of a King's Place establishment and, even in her youth, regaled as a toast of the town, Charlotte's sphere of friends would have been broad. In the past, her confidantes had included some of the most outrageous, eccentric and brilliant men and women of her era: actors and writers, courtiers, politicians, scientists, clergymen and members of the royal family. She had no short-age of suitable female acquaintances from the demi-monde either. To then be left alone, trailing behind Dennis at race meets, following him from one encampment to the next, un-able to attend gatherings where virtuous wives and daughters might be present, and to hear little news of her friends, took an exacting toll on her spirit. After less than eighteen months, Charlotte decided to move back to London.

At some point during the late 1770s, Dennis had been advised to sink some of his winnings into Mayfair property, thereby assuring the security of his fortune. Among these purchases was the freehold of an elegant new house conspicuously situated on the corner of Half Moon Street and Piccadilly and facing on to Green Park. The strategic positioning enabled fashionable society to admire his grand townhouse while taking their constitutionals. The O'Kellys in turn enjoyed the opportunity of observing the painted faces and tailored torsos of the *bon ton* simply by looking down from their drawing-room windows. Where indications of status were concerned, there was none that announced wealth quite like this. While Dennis had intended that the Half Moon Street house should become their primary London residence, he had also made the purchase with the inheritance of his nephew Andrew Dennis O'Kelly in mind. In her late forties, it had become apparent that Charlotte would not have any more children. Since she and Dennis had never legally married, any children that Charlotte had borne were illegitimate. As it was rare for girls, and particularly those produced out of wedlock, to inherit estates, all of Dennis and Charlotte's land and possessions would one day be passed to the son of his brother. Through a series of Dennis's prudent purchases, by the early 1780s Andrew looked set to inherit a large portion of Mayfair. In addition to Clay Hill, Half Moon Street and the properties they retained on Great Marlborough Street, Dennis also accumulated numerous freeholds and leaseholds on houses in Clarges Street, Chesterfield Street, Berkeley Square, Charles Street and Manchester Square.

Upon her return to Mayfair, Charlotte chose to take up

residence at the house on Half Moon Street, where she might observe the world as it wandered by her window. Here, at the heart of the fashionable universe, so inextricable from that of the vice-ridden one, she need never feel alone or confined. Her reappearance, however, did present a problem. Although 'retired', Charlotte's return signalled an active resumption of her trade, which was something she had not desired. By basing herself in Half Moon Street, she had hoped to keep the affairs of her collection of small brothels at arm's length. Now, without her nunnery on King's Place at which to congregate, her friends and devoted clientele came calling at her home, and their visits were not exclusively of a social nature. They came as they always had, in the hope of finding a suitable keeper or a Cyprian with whom to share their bed. When they sat in her drawing room or sipped her champagne they did so in the anticipation that Santa Charlotta would provide them with access to a sexual encounter. As Charlotte would come to realize, there would be no true retirement, no escape from her role as a procuress, whether she passed her days at Clay Hill or on Half Moon Street. Wherever she went, the demi-monde dragged at her heels, pulling her relentlessly back into its embrace.

# 17

# FULL CIRCLE

JOHN HARRISON HAD BEEN anticipating trouble from the day he assumed the proprietorship of the Rose Tavern. He recognized his enemies, and knew who might attempt to fell him as his fortunes rose. Whether it was Justice Fielding or Packington Tomkins, whether the threats came from angry clients or broken women, the pimp had learned from his past experience and was ready for any sort of confrontation. What he hadn't foreseen was that the greatest challenge to his empire wouldn't emanate from any of these predictable sources. Instead it came from the Theatre Royal, just next door.

In the early 1770s his neighbour David Garrick, who was always striving to stay one step ahead of competition at the Covent Garden Theatre, had become increasingly dissatisfied with the state of the facilities at Drury Lane. The house, after years of wear by boisterous hooligans who perpetrated violence against its carved interiors, had begun to look shabby. The theatre had not seen substantial renovation in some time and, with its centenary approaching in 1774, Garrick saw this as a perfect opportunity to make necessary cosmetic improvements. However, it required more than just a simple facelift.

For years, the managers had been irked by the inaccessibility of its main entrance. It was hemmed in on all sides by the thoroughfares of Russell Street and Drury Lane and surrounded by a ring of smaller buildings, and patrons frequently complained that they were forced to navigate a series of inhospitable passages to approach the lobby. To remedy these problems Garrick was looking to substantially alter the shape and design of the theatre, and his plans spelled trouble for the Rose Tavern.

For a century, the Drury Lane theatre and the Rose had shared their prosperity, like conjoined twins. Their songs and sounds, like their clientele, passed through their shared wall, the business of one governed by the presence of the other. Those who worked in the Theatre Royal came to rely on the Rose for their refreshment and diversion, using it as an adjunct of the theatre's facilities. Although mutually dependent, there was no question as to which structure took precedence; the blossoming of the Rose's business was a credit due almost exclusively to the theatre. After years of coexistence it was suggested not that the Rose be demolished altogether, but rather that the theatre should stretch out her arms and embrace her smaller, dependent sister. To rectify the problem of accessibility, Garrick's fashionable architect, Robert Adam, suggested an extension of the theatre's façade which would in turn swallow up the tavern and incorporate it as an in-house convenience. In this decision, it seems, the Rose had little say.

Harrison could not have been pleased when the news of Garrick's renovation project reached him. Regardless of how much authority he may have been able to wield over his women, tenants and patrons, the proprietor of the Rose would be no match for 'Little Davy', one of the most powerful and well-connected men in all of Covent Garden. Adam's plans cast a long shadow across the future of John Harrison's livelihood, but it was not likely that the pimp was prepared to stand by idly while the heart of his empire was cut out before him. Harrison would have to be compensated, though how much he received from the managers of the Drury Lane theatre is unknown. In addition to taking in the edifice of the Rose, the adjoining dwelling where Harrison had been living appears to have been affected as well, and from 1775, the year the works commenced, he is no longer recorded at this address. Although disruptive, the change in circumstance did not put Harrison out of business altogether, and it is probable that Garrick may have had to indulge a number of the publican's requests in order to move forward with the redesign. Possibly the decision to integrate the tavern's signboard into the external decor was one such concession to its grumbling proprietor. Irrespective of the reduction of the Rose's scale, the tavern continued to thrive and remained a popular place of resort.

On the surface, Harrison's trade might not have diminished much, but the alterations to Drury Lane appear to have exerted a negative pull on his finances. By 1776, he had relinquished control of the other buildings he owned on Brydges Street, as well as his own home. His only dwelling space remained a set of apartments above his tavern. What caused the contraction of his trade is quite the mystery: was it an ailment or an accident, or did the law catch his collar once more? It is possible that, now in his late forties or early fifties, the ageing ruffian was having a change of heart. With a small fortune accumulated, he may have looked at himself in the mirror, felt the sagging of his jowls, straightened the stock around his neck and decided that it might better suit him to take a step back.

There is something almost disappointing in the image of a once terrible man putting himself out to pasture and ageing quietly in front of a fire in an upstairs set of rooms. Although Harrison's name remained as proprietor of the Rose, by the mid-1780s the business of tavern-keeping was conducted on his behalf by an employee, James Cresdale. Harrison, the former tiger who kept an entire street at bay, who ensured that even the night watch remained tight-lipped, was not often to be seen on the sanded floors of the Rose. In the taproom beneath his feet, the tavern's usual comedies and tragedies continued to play themselves out beside Drury Lane's stage. Above, the old pimp had probably reconciled himself to dying where he sat, in the last hold-out of his now diminished domain. Fate, however, had one card yet to play.

In the 1750s, when John Harrison was Jack Harris, one particular lady in his Covent Garden army had temporarily lost her means of making a living by becoming pregnant. One would hope that Jack Harris had it within his heart to ease her burden by offering her some money and perhaps finding her a place at one of the many privately run lying-in houses where ladies of ill repute could go to give birth. She was, after all, carrying his child. Then again, this was almost certainly not the first pregnancy to which the pimp had contributed, and it was unlikely to be the last. One of the perks of being a pimp was that he had free access to the women he controlled. He claimed that it was necessary for men of his profession to try out their 'goods' before recommending them to clients, and that they were 'not a whit worse for gentleman's use and amusement after having passed under the operation of us scurvy fellows'. While such a brash assertion may have been cooked up to inflame Dr Hill's readers, Harris's boasts reflected traditional practice. Unless plagued by bouts of infertility brought on by venereal disease, by these means John Harrison may have produced any number of illegitimate offspring, and the mothers may not have known the identity of the father, making it easy for Harrison to absolve himself of any responsibility. Although he was probably unaware of it, the pimp may have passed his sons and daughters in the streets around the piazza nearly every day of his life.

This particular woman, who bore a little boy whom she called Charles, had her own personal reasons for believing that the child was fathered by England's Pimp General. As was the convention in the eighteenth century, mothers frequently gave their babies the surname of the infant's father, whether or not the parents were married. This mother gave her boy the surname of Harris. She probably never knew that the name was not a genuine one. History has not recorded what became of Charles Harris's mother after the birth and the details of the boy's life are also lost. All that is known is that at some point he found his father.

At about the time when John Harrison had retreated into a type of retirement, the managers of the Theatre Royal were becoming restless again. Shortly after Drury Lane's previous renovation, Garrick had sold his patent to the Irish playwright-turned-politician Richard Brinsley Sheridan, who was eager to leave his mark upon the theatre through a programme of expansion. This time, the managers wanted to start entirely afresh. The old theatre and its dependent buildings had to come down, the fate that Harrison had feared most. After just over a century of service, the era of the Rose Tavern was at its end. As with its proprietor, a quiet demise for the Rose, whose interior walls had seen some of the most extravagant debauchery and could probably recount some of the most ruinous stories, did not seem a fitting conclusion to its existence. Sheridan, a newcomer to the parish of St Paul's Covent Garden and already one generation removed from the ability to recall the tavern's heyday, would not have felt so much as a pang of remorse when condemning it. The theatre's new patent holders envisioned a more modern venue for drama, something suitable for the coming nineteenth century. All around it, the area was stretching and changing. Even Brydges Street, over the years, had lengthened and almost doubled in population. London and its fickle fashions were moving forward, leaving Covent Garden like a cast-off frock coat, a remnant of elegance from a previous age. The young bucks and bloods who used to raise hell in the Rose's private rooms with posture girls and sharp-tongued harlots, with modish courtesans and flamboyant actresses, had decamped to St James's and Piccadilly, where the brothels were adorned like palaces. Defaced portraits, overturned chamber pots and the boisterousness featured in Hogarth's vision were no longer deemed acceptable in the closing decades of the eighteenth century.

For many, the demolition of the Rose would have been welcome. John Harrison had accumulated an assortment of enemies: souls whose lives he had ruined, women who had been indentured to him and his ambitions, who had sacrificed their health and any prospect of happiness so that the pimp could lead a comfortable existence. These people would have had hopes of Harrison sharing in their misery, and would have relished the imagined scenes of an old homeless wretch suffering on the streets. It would have seemed a just ending to his story. But what had possibly made John Harrison more reviled than most was the undeserving devotion shown to him by good fortune. Through a combination of luck, shrewdness and graft, Harrison always managed to come out the other end; from the position he gained at the Shakespear to his successful acquisition of the Rose, prosperity never seemed to abandon him entirely. As sure as one door closed, another swung open. It may have been the case that, until the end of his life, John Harrison had never met his son – then, one day, he simply appeared. Alternatively, he may have been at his father's side for some time, but only in 1790 did he make himself of much use to his parent.

For some time, the ageing pimp must have been sitting on a sizeable lump of money. As with his rival Packington Tomkins, it is easy to believe that the depth and breadth of his wealth had expanded and contracted at various intervals. The fullness of his purse may have been depleted by the careless living and extravagance for which men within his circle were noted. Without a wife or a legitimate family, Harrison may have seen no need to make provisions. Like Sam Derrick, his life had always been lived for the immediate pleasures it offered: riches were meant to be spent, not saved. However, it is also unlikely that a man with such a well-honed business sense would not reserve some of the fruits of his industry in case of need. In 1790, that need arose. It would be supremely naïve to suggest that, as if by magic, just at the time the Rose was slated for destruction, the lease for the Bedford Head Tavern on Maiden Lane suddenly became available. It is more likely that luck was lubricated with money, and that the two together brought about an opportunity that was more than simply financial. Harrison bought himself the comforts of a family – the one thing he had not anticipated wanting in his many years of marketing lust in place of love, and sex instead of tenderness. It may have been a sense of loneliness, or another nagging unnamed regret, that made Harrison focus his thoughts upon the Bedford Head, his father's tavern, where he had spent his boyhood and first acquired the artistry of a waiter-pimp. In some way, this place offered him a secure harbour, somewhere he could contentedly live out the last years of his life. He could have chosen to embark upon this venture with any one of those people who had served him well during his years at the Rose, but instead Harrison held out the offer to his son, Charles, and his wife. This would be a family enterprise, operated as it had been when Harrison himself was a boy. Presiding over this establishment would have allowed him a satisfaction greater than any other achievement, legitimate or ill-gotten, since the day he had left it.

Harrison provided the finances and experience necessary for the business, while Charles and his wife managed the operation. For the first year and a half, Harrison's name appeared as proprietor; his son assumed the title in late 1792. It seems that Harrison, who would have been in his mid- to late sixties, was now ailing, hindered in his movements. By the following year his condition had worsened and, as the

328

chill of winter approached, seeping through the thinly glazed windows and cold brick walls, the old man could hold out no longer. Harrison must have expired around Christmas time, when the merrymakers below were filling themselves with warm punch and proffering kisses and gropes below corners green with mistletoe. His body was taken to St Paul's, the Inigo Jones church that stood at the western end of the piazza, watching sinners indulge themselves in venal pleasures. There, in the churchyard, hardly a moment's walk from where his life had come full circle, he was laid to rest on 14 January 1794. The ground consumed his misdeeds and his secrets and left only the name John Harrison by which he could be remembered. His other identity, that of Jack Harris, would live on independently as legend.

Harrison died at around the time the penultimate *Harris's List of Covent Garden Ladies* made its annual appearance on the booksellers' stalls. It is amusing to imagine the elderly pimp still scowling at the taunts of the publication's title, and at its unwillingness after so many years to simply expire. *Harris's List* followed him remorselessly, reminding him of the folly of his youth and his inability to have foreseen the work's success. In its last incarnation, however, the book that had evolved over the decades from his prototype and Derrick's prose would be virtually unrecognizable. Not only had the publication strayed from his own bulging ledger of women to an elegant book between slim leather covers, but, according to the later version, the proclivities of the punters had changed too. The pages were filled with new names: Lydias and Sophias replaced the Molls and Nans who had since bloomed and withered. The randy roysters who had lusted after lewd women were now genteelly known as sons of Bacchus and the objects of their affection the daughters of Venus. Old man Harrison would have shaken his head ruefully. Even the delightfully base act of fornication had been ruined by these latest authors; they described the lifting of a harlot's skirts in terms of fountains and temples, conjuring all the pastoral splendour of Arcadia. The world that the former pimp had once known was evolving into something else. Society was becoming prudish.

Harrison would never know that *Harris's List of Covent Garden Ladies* outlived him by only one year. Time had run out for both of them.

# 18

# THE RESPECTABLE MRS KELLY

A<small>S BOTH</small> S<small>AM</small> D<small>ERRICK</small> and John Harrison had learned, once touched by the brush of the sex trade, one could never wholly wash its taint from one's character. Outrunning past associations was impossible. While Charlotte never attempted to hide what she was, she had hoped to place some distance between herself and the obligations of her professional life. However, if being in London meant that her friends expected her to assume her former occupation, then the retired Abbess figured she should not disappoint. She was no longer Charlotte Hayes of King's Place: her return to the flesh market warranted a new name appropriate to her status as a grande dame of property and experience. When she stepped from her front door and into the sedan chair that ferried her to one of her many discreet houses of assignation around St James's and Piccadilly, she called herself Mrs Kelly. Should she desire to retreat into respectability and shed her bawd's mantle, she might return to her elegant home on Half Moon Street and receive company as Mrs O'Kelly, the 'wife' of the landed racehorse owner Dennis O'Kelly, the 'aunt' of the fashionable gentleman Lieutenant-Colonel Andrew Dennis

O'Kelly and the mother of Mary Charlotte O'Kelly. She now took a more proactive role in maintaining the premises she had entrusted to her disciples, which included houses on Arlington Street, Duke Street and, later, in Berkeley Square. Away from the spotlight and crowded thoroughfare of King's Place, her intention was to conduct business on a much more modest scale, so that she might enjoy the freedom of turning her back on her practice whenever she desired. Such an arrangement would have permitted her at least a degree of ease and privacy behind the doors of her Half Moon Street home.

Charlotte had long since abandoned any great aspirations of Tahitian orgies or lewd masquerades. She was not in the market for new patrons, nor was she interested in competing with her rivals. She had already been to the top and had bowed out gracefully. This re-emergence was merely an encore. Neither was she especially interested in increasing her flock. Instead, she limited the number of nymphs residing in her houses to two at a time, with any additional assistance to be drafted in when needed. In the early 1780s, her Arlington Street business was home to two ladies known as the Duchess of Portland and the Duchess of Devonshire, 'from a likeness they were . . . thought to bear to those elevated personages'. Later that decade, in 1788, the *Harris's List* featured two more of her carefully selected beauties: Betsy Hudson, and another 'Betsy', known only by her first name. The author couldn't resist the temptation to fill the latter's entry with horse-racing allusions, decrying the 'often hack'd' 'Post steeds of Venus' who are 'broken winded, halt in their paces, and are well nigh founder'd', a situation which renders them 'scarce fit for anything but brood mares'. He then went on to say that, naturally, Betsy, under the expert training of Mrs Kelly, was not of this sort.

With a long-established portfolio of patrons who introduced new faces to her establishments, Mrs Kelly's businesses were entirely self-sufficient and maintained their distinctive reputation for being highly selective and discreet. William Hickey, who was among her better customers, often 'went to dine with the useful, if not respectable Madam Kelly', as she had become. In these new circumstances, Charlotte was even less willing than in the past to suffer insult. In 1781, Hickey claimed to have met 'with a volley of abuse' from Mrs Kelly for introducing one of his less salubrious friends into her house. Having trusted Hickey's judgement, she found that Captain Mackintosh, whom she referred to as a 'mean and despicable wretch' and 'a dirty dog', had bilked her and each of Charlotte's nymphs to the tune of £100. She made it clear to Hickey that at such an exclusive establishment as hers, this was not the kind of custom she had come to expect. Her base of support was such that she no longer required the patronage of any lustful gentleman with a heavy purse, and, if she felt like it, she could turn even the wealthiest from her drawing room.

In this, Charlotte's final return to business following two attempts to retire, she found herself less tied to any one of her professional premises. As she had learned upon her return to London, her 'friends' followed her regardless of where she chose to locate herself and irrespective of whether she had formally opened up shop. By the middle of the 1780s, she had relocated the focus of her trade to one of the freehold properties in Dennis's possession in Berkeley Square, conveniently near Half Moon Street. It was here in 1785 that Henry Dundas, Viscount Melville, an inveterate philanderer, escorted the Prime Minister, William Pitt, to the steps of Mrs Kelly's mansion. The sexually ambivalent Pitt, when spying Charlotte at the door, made his excuses and quickly retreated. Happily for Charlotte's enterprise, not all politicians were as reticent. Neither they nor their entirely male, landholding electorate could give a fig about the carnal exploits of political leaders. Charles James Fox, Pitt's political rival, made no bones about his relationship with the notorious houses of Mayfair or the women who found employment under their roofs. As a racing associate of Dennis and a client of Charlotte, his father's money helped to subsidize the lifestyle the O'Kellys enjoyed. As illustrated by Thomas Rowlandson's political cartoon of 1784, Fox, in the throes of campaigning for his Westminster seat, is shown in the company of his so-called 'best friends' – a handful of bawds, including one particularly ancient doyenne, who, it is suggested, may be Charlotte.

Although she was still much in demand, Mrs Kelly's public appearances became less and less frequent as the 1780s wore on. By the time she entered her sixties, an exalted age in the late eighteenth century, she became an increasingly reluctant purveyor of hospitality, choosing the quiet of her Half Moon Street residence and the company of Dennis over the loud, lewd dinners and gatherings at which she was frequently the centre. Although Charlotte had never enthusiastically embraced the prospect of returning to her old profession, her withdrawal from society was hastened by the onset of what was described as 'a lassitude and anxiety of mind and body'.

For an unspecified period between 1783 and 1785, Charlotte became a recluse in her London home and separated herself 'from a life of gay and giddy dissipation'. Through Dennis's arrangement, Dr Chidwick was engaged to attend her while she strove 'to divert the symptoms of hysteric afflicition' and convalesced undisturbed. What precisely plunged Charlotte into a sudden state of what seems to have been a clinical depression is not specified by any of the chroniclers of her or Dennis's history, although the revelation of a subsequent incident in her narrative, as told by the author of Dennis's *Memoirs*, offers a clue. Charlotte, it seems, had nearly recovered from her 'mental complaint' when news of a riding accident that had befallen her 'nephew' Andrew was delivered to her. In truth, Andrew had only been thrown from his mount, but as the *Memoirs* recount, 'by the time this accident reached the ears of Charlotte, it was magnified to dislocations, fractures, amputations and all the melancholy consequences which might possibly have attended such an event'. Andrew had been a companion, he was Dennis's designated heir and, having adopted his uncle's name as part of his own, he had stepped into the role of long-wished-for son. The rumoured news of a grievous, life-threatening injury was more than Charlotte could bear: 'at the intelligence she expressed a kind of maternal grief', from which 'it was many months before she recovered'.

Why would such an event, especially when it proved a false alarm, have had such a profound effect on Charlotte's mental state? It is most likely that the news of Andrew's accident came heavy on the heels of the death of her daughter. After Mary Charlotte was deposited at the convent in Ostend, nothing more is heard of her. Dennis, who died in 1787, does not so much as mention her in his will. A token gift of '1000 pounds', however, was granted to one of his nieces, Mary Harvey, who, along with his sister-in-law Elizabeth O'Kelly, had taken on the responsibilities of raising his daughter in Dublin when she was too old to remain at Clay Hill. Possibly through illness, the daughter whose life Charlotte had so closely guarded, the only blood relation she had fostered, was taken from her while only in her teens. The implications of this must have been too difficult for her mother to bear, perhaps causing her to throw into question the events of her own life, the babies she may have recklessly abandoned or aborted and the girls of a similar age by whom she may have done ill.

For some time, Charlotte remained inconsolable, declining invitations and refusing to interact with anyone outside her household. Cloistered in her rooms at Half Moon Street, she only gradually began to amuse herself 'with the decorations of fancy, and the ornaments of approved taste'. In order to deaden her despair, it was recommended that she fill her home with pets, so that she might 'divert her thoughts'. Soon the O'Kelly residence was filled 'by a variety of animated objects', which included 'several domestic and foreign animals', the most interesting of which was a 'wonderful parrot, whose rare and astonishing faculties, if it was not yet alive to prove their reality would scarcely be believed, even by the most credulous'. Polly, as the parrot was called, was purchased by Dennis for fifty guineas in Bristol and presented to Charlotte as a gift to raise her spirits. The ailing Mrs O'Kelly took the creature to her bosom and devoted so much time to it that she 'seemed to enjoy more satisfaction from its society than that of her own species'. The result was a pampered pet, so well trained that it 'not only repeat[ed] all things, but answer[ed] almost everything', and possessed 'so strong [a] retention, that it sings a variety of tunes, with exquisite melody!'

Throughout Charlotte's distress Dennis remained unwavering at her side, repaying her for the emotional and financial support she had given him over the years. Towards the end of his life, Dennis also succumbed to a sort of melancholia, or what his *Memoirs* describe as 'an unnatural moroseness', not unlike that suffered by Charlotte. By 1785, the normally convivial 'Count O'Kelly' was not in the best of health. Plagued by increasingly bad gout, he became irritable. He and Charlotte had come to pass most of their days in Piccadilly, sitting in their windows overlooking the park, silently observing the beribboned *bon ton* on their promenades. Since the onset of her 'affliction', Charlotte had entirely turned her back on Clay Hill. Dennis followed suit and handed the estate over to Philip. Purchased in the year of her daughter's birth as a haven in which she might raise her child, the house held far too many ghosts to entice her back. Instead, Dennis began negotiations to buy a property which he had earmarked as an ideal retreat – somewhere for himself and Charlotte to live out the last of their days in a manner befitting the station to which they had risen. An ambitious social climber to the end, 'Count O'Kelly' had his heart set on acquiring the former home of the Duke of Chandos, Canons Park.

In November 1785, an advert appeared in one of the

London newspapers for the 'Freehold estate called Cannons'. Nine miles north-west of London, it comprised:

> five hundred and forty seven acres, one rood and thirty-one perch, of remarkable rich meadow, arable and wood land. One-hundred and twelve acres of which is a fine fertile paddock, refreshed by two noble sheets of water, surrounded by a capital brick wall, a neat magnificent Portland stone dwelling house with suitable offices, pleasure grounds and gardens . . . the farms are very compact and lett to . . . good tennants; the whole annual value (exclusive of house and offices) nine hundred and fifty four pounds, fifteen shillings . . .

The estate was to be auctioned at Garraway's Coffee House on 16 November. Dennis seized the opportunity and, after many months of protracted negotiation with its owner, William Hallett, he was able to secure Canons outright in April 1787. It was a splendid purchase. Canons Park was a picture of bucolic perfection, a Georgian Arcadia where sheep and deer grazed in fertile meadowland and where one could amble contemplatively along the water's edge and through cool wooded glades. While the house at Clay Hill had been decorated fashionably and lent itself adequately to formal entertaining, the Canons Park estate was a grander address by far. Although the baroque mansion constructed under the direction of the Duke of Chandos had been demolished, a more modern, classically restrained edifice had been built in its place. Its interior was ornamented with carved marble chimney pieces and statuary, its rooms were edged with gilt mouldings and cornices, while an 'elegant stone staircase'

338

with a 'handrail inlayed with ivory and pearl' took guests to the first floor. With twelve bedchambers, a salon, breakfast room, dining room, study and several drawing rooms and dressing rooms, the O'Kellys could delight their visitors as they had at Clay Hill but in more commodious surroundings. The 'various and magnificent' items of furniture and *objets d'art* that Charlotte had purchased or been presented with, 'for meretricious services done in King's Place', were moved from Clay Hill to decorate her new rooms. Canons was described as being an hour's drive from London, closer than Clay Hill had been, which allowed visitors to come and go more freely, preventing Charlotte from succumbing to the isolation she had experienced in Epsom. Dennis had intended Canons Park to be the ideal country refuge, where neither the demands of London nor the business of horse breeding would disturb them.

For roughly eight months, Charlotte and Dennis enjoyed the tranquil pleasures of their new country abode. As his *Memoirs* state, after his establishment 'in the delightful residence of Cannons, the proprietor became more select in his company'. Dennis had begun to tire of his racing clique and the antics of some of its more blackguard members. As an older man, 'O'Kelly took many occasions to express a disapprobation of his younger days', a luxury that only those who have met with success irrespective of their youthful follies can relish. Accordingly, Dennis (but not Charlotte) was embraced 'by people of the first class of his own sex and a few female friends'. By now Charlotte was accustomed to such arrangements and would disappear back to Mayfair in order to avoid uncomfortable situations. In the end, however,

Dennis preferred the company of his lifelong companion to the ephemeral camaraderie of the local squirearchy. When his persistent gout began to 'attack him with determined violence' in early December, he chose to shut up Canons and spend his bedridden days at Half Moon Street under Charlotte's care. Shortly before Christmas, he slipped into a delirium, before expiring 'with every evidence of bodily ease', on 28 December.

Many men had claimed to love Charlotte Hayes, but those such as Dennis O'Kelly and Sam Derrick, who had seen her as more than a fashionable ornament to parade on their public excursions, did what they could in death to reward her for her devotion in life. Sam Derrick, who had praised her kindness and gentility, who had never entirely managed to remove her from his heart, bequeathed what little of value he had into Charlotte's hands. Dennis, however, was able to provide her with much more than token gestures of enduring affection. Although the years had proved that she was more than capable of looking after herself and amassing a comfortable fortune through her own efforts, Dennis recognized that as a woman who did not have the benefit of society's respect, Charlotte's position after his demise would be a vulnerable one. As many women of Charlotte's character ended their days in greatly reduced circumstances for lack of male protection, Dennis made provisions to avoid this. Of the three main beneficiaries named in his will, it was 'Charlotte Hayes, called Mrs. O'Kelly who now lives and resides with me' who stood to gain more than his legitimate blood relations. For the duration of her life, Dennis had granted his mistress the privilege of calling Canons her home. So that she might not find herself without means of getting there, he also bequeathed her 'both my chariot and coach and all such coach or carriage horses as I shall be possessed of at the time of my decease with all the harness equipage and furniture thereto belonging'. He ensured that her home continued to be well furnished, granting her 'the use and enjoyment of all the household furniture, goods and chattels', in addition to his most valuable plateware, the candlesticks, the 'silver tea urn, tea kettle, coffee pot and all ... silver whatsoever being tea equipage or property belonging to her tea table'. Into her care he placed the 'diamonds, jewels, watches, rings and other personal ornaments', in addition to the diamond ring he wore, as a token of remembrance. All further residue of his estate, all profits resulting from his stud and the sale of horses after his debts were paid, was then to be divided three ways, between Charlotte, his nephew Andrew and his brother Philip. Although the cumulative value of these possessions was substantial and would have assured a comfortable existence, Dennis promised her something that would offer her lasting peace of mind: a guaranteed income. Charlotte was to receive an annuity of £400 attached to the freehold of the property, to be paid quarterly into her hands 'during the term of her natural life without any deduction or abatement whatsoever'. At last, Charlotte Hayes was at liberty to retire.

As might have been predicted, Dennis's death had a destabilizing effect on Charlotte's mental condition. She was already susceptible to upsets following the loss of her daughter, and now her dark moods seemed to last for even longer spells, so that well into the next century O'Kelly relations were still making veiled references to 'Charlotte's state'.

Additionally, it is possible that Charlotte may have been contending with the long-term effects of syphilis as it gradually eroded her health. From January 1788, she removed herself once more from London society and from those who demanded her services. She sought refuge at Canons and leaned on Dennis's male relations for the support to which she had become accustomed. Almost everyone, from family to her established friends and business acquaintances, came to recognize this departure as being her last. The 1788 edition of *Harris's List*, compiled in the winter of 1787, just before her change of circumstances, is the last to mention her. It is certain, however, that when Charlotte took her farewell curtsey and abandoned the theatre of Venus, she did not live a solitary life. Her home was frequently the venue for Andrew's entertainments, including a revival of the great musical performances at Canons originally initiated by the Duke of Chandos. A new generation of beautiful young actresses and singers, such as Mrs Crouch and Ann Storace, was followed there by their many admirers, and the estate would have hummed with the energy of youth, love, lust and music. But what mischief may have come to pass on a warm summer's evening in the gardens or twelve bedchambers of Canons would have taken place of its own accord, without any assistance from Charlotte.

19

# THE LAST DAYS OF THE *LIST*

A T THE TIME OF her death in 1813, Charlotte had seen over eighty-five years of life. The specific circumstances of her passing are unknown, other than that she died at Half Moon Street. She had lived to witness the deaths of many of her nearest and dearest; she had survived her rivals and contemporaries in the sex trade, including John Harrison; and, remarkably, she had outlived *Harris's List*, a publication she had profited from threefold, first as a listed 'lady', then as a mentioned madam and finally as a beneficiary of its sale.

Not unlike Charlotte Hayes, née Ward, aka O'Kelly and Kelly, *Harris's List* had evolved significantly during its existence. Although it retained its original format, by the last year of its issue, 1795, it bore little resemblance to the publication that helped to spring Sam Derrick from the clutches of Ferguson's spunging house. From 1757 until his death in 1769, the *List* remained a product of Sam Derrick's invention: a witty but useful little tome which sought to document the characters who comprised Covent Garden's carnal underworld. It painted them as true flesh and blood, objectively and honestly. He had never envisioned success

343

on such a broad scale; initially, *Harris's List* was intended to appeal to the piazza's regular crowd, containing references and in-jokes familiar to the local pleasure-seeker. Sam Derrick's presence on the pages is a palpable one, as is the sense that the *List* is a community effort, coloured with wry personal observations and hearsay, relayed to the author by a variety of acquaintances.

*Harris's List* was intended to appeal to men with some education, at least a hint of discernment, and money. At two shillings and sixpence, it cost more than a day's wages for a journeyman tailor, equivalent to a week's rent for a furnished room, the price of a whole pig or a dentist's bill for a tooth extraction. The audience for *Harris's List* was not the street peddler, the soldier, or indeed the journeyman tailor; it was addressed to a readership that would have smirked at Sam Derrick's double entendres and grasped his cursory nods to the classical. In the eighteenth century this meant those of the middling classes and above. These were men who regarded themselves, by virtue of their learning (or at least their ability to read), above the poorly fed, poorly paid rabble. The retention of this readership and the *List*'s primary function as a guide were the only features to remain constant as the decades progressed. By the 1790s, the publication had strayed a considerable distance from Derrick's original prototype.

Subsequent authors of *Harris's List* remain stubbornly elusive. Although Charlotte may have reaped the profits of the 1769 edition, there is no evidence to suggest that she had any editorial control over its content, nor that she was privy to the proceeds from following years. By the 1770s, the *List* seemed to take on a life of its own, and from that point it is

reasonable to assume that its execution lay solely in the control of the publishers. *Harris's List* had become more of a
branded product than a quirky publication with literary aspirations, and it is not surprising that it begins to lose some of
its endearing flavour. With the focus of the *List* no longer on
the characters and instead more on intriguing stories of seduction, its appeal is to a broader audience, one that might not be
familiar with Covent Garden or the topography of the West
End, let alone the regulars who plied their trade there. The
author of the 1773 volume, very much against the spirit of Sam
Derrick's original, took the decision to clean up the prose, to
remove the base, grunting euphemisms and to adopt a more
genteel tone. Gone are the bawdy descriptions of 'squat,
swarthy, round-faced' wenches and breath that smells like
French cheese. Instead, classical allusions and a false flourish
of delicacy are employed to transform the prostitute into 'a
fourth Grace, or a breathing, animated Venus de Medici'. The
gentrification of the *List* is also reflected in the changes in
the illustration that appears as its frontispiece. The 1761 edition features a couple locked in an uncomfortable embrace on
a sofa: she struggles, he persists. We already know what the
outcome will be: the reluctant Miss becomes one of the obli-
ging *listees*. By the 1770s such rococo theatricality has been
abandoned in favour of a less provocative image: a gentleman
stands in conversation with a well-dressed lady. Everyone is
circumspect in this picture; manners are on display. Were it
not for the exaggerated length of the sword at the gentleman's
side, the vague, knowing smirk on the lady's face or the colonnades of Covent Garden in the backdrop, a casual browser
might miss the meaning altogether. By the 1790s, there are no

prostitutes to be found on the frontispiece, only four Arcadian nymphs frolicking nude with a garland. The image bears an unsettling resemblance to Joshua Reynolds's well-known society portrait of *The Montgomery Sisters: Three Ladies Adorning a Term of Hymen*. Surely no accident.

Alterations to the tone of the *List* pervaded every aspect of the publication in later years. As the publishers moved with the fashion for gentility, the personality of the work and its buoyant sparkle began to dim. From its outset, the *List* was about making money, but by the 1780s, as the seams of the publication start to wear through, this motivation stands out more than ever. No longer troubled by maintaining accuracy or even creative verve, those who had taken on its production had resorted to bastardizing entries from previous editions. The exploits of Miss Smith in one year were reprinted two years later as the joyous romps of Miss Jones. As long as the addresses were vaguely correct, the publishers were not concerned about names or histories. They assumed that punters weren't either. Its last extant volume, that of 1793, is but a distant cousin of the earliest work. Not much better than a cut-and-paste of previous editions, it contained very little originality and no character, the Cyprians within mere archetypes with names attached. By the time the law put its boot down on the publication in 1795, the true spirit of *Harris's List* was already dead.

Those to blame for the publication's down-slide, at least in part, are two brothers, John and James Roach, and a third conspirator, the bookseller John Aitkin of Bear Street. From the late 1780s they had been running the *List* off on their printing presses. The work's desirability, evidently on the wane, was squeezed one final time in the hope of yielding its last drops of profitability. The Roaches and Aitkin had no interest in reviving the work's content or its original concept. Even the publication's title, *Harris's List of Covent Garden Ladies*, was by this date outmoded, as almost any prostitute worth her guineas had moved west to the newer districts stretching northwards from Mayfair to Marylebone.

The Roaches and John Aitkin had become complacent and arrogant in their production of the annual register. They knew that regular buyers of the *List* would come in search of it at the time of publication each Christmas, as the poem which prefaces the 1788 edition reminds its readers:

*Again the coral berry's holly glads the eye,*
*The ivy green again each window decks,*
*And misteltoe, kind friend to Bassia's cause,*
*Under each merry roof invites the kiss,*
*Come then my friends, ye friends to Harris come,*
*And more than kisses share . . .*

However, a certain amount of advertising was still necessary to spread the word about the publication to the uninitiated. Every year the *List*'s publisher would place short promotions in popular newspapers, such as the one that appeared in the *Daily Advertiser* on 3 January: 'This Day published, priced 2 s 6d with the original Introduction, *Harris's List of Covent Garden Ladies; or a Man of Pleasure's Kalendar for the year 1775*, Containing an exact description of the most celebrated ladies of pleasure who frequent Covent Garden and other parts of the metropolis.' Unabashedly, and seemingly without fear of any repercussions, the newspaper proclaimed this across a corner of its front page, next to advertisements for products promising to cure venereal disease and 'all disorders of the genitals'. As no one had ever come after the publishers of this unlawful obscenity before, Aitkin and the Roaches probably did not feel particularly concerned about having their address appear in the newspapers. They used the sobriquet of H. Ranger on the title page, the usual veil employed to hide an otherwise reputable publisher's less respectable business.

There are a number of theories about the Roach brothers. Little exists to enlighten us about Aitkin, who, it seems, had died by the time James Roach was hauled before the King's Bench. Interestingly, the Roaches are recorded in the nineteenth-century *Dictionary of National Biography* as legitimate publishers, remembered not for stocking their shelves with smut, but rather for innocuous works such as *Roach's Beauties of the Poets of Great Britain* (1794), *Beautiful Extracts of Prosaic Writers, Carefully Selected for the Young and Rising Generation* (1795) and *Roach's New and Complete History of the Stage* (1796). There are several possible explanations for the two distinct faces of the Roach brothers' enterprise. It is possible that hard times drove them to produce and sell immoral but lucrative material. It is equally plausible that they, like the Harrisons of Covent Garden, were a family with fingers in many pies, some lawful and others not. As J. L. Wood speculates, the Roaches probably divided their publishing business among two or more addresses, with the respectable end of their trade based at Vinegar Yard, while their 'top-shelf' material was sold out of a shop on Little Bridges Street, the address printed in *Harris's List*. It is noteworthy that the name Roach, like Harrison, appears frequently during the latter half of the century in and around the piazza. A nefarious figure known as 'Tiger' Roach acted as the bully for the Bedford Arms and, later, for the Bedford Coffee House, in the 1760s and '70s. A Miss Roach is listed among Harris's ladies for the year 1773. Francis Place mentions a Mrs Roach willing to show obscene prints to young people in her shop in the 1770s and '80s. It is equally probable that there was a connection between her and the Covent Garden procuress Mrs Margaret Roach, active at the same time. In all likelihood, both women may have been the same person. As John Harrison's brief foray into the publication of obscene material proves, it was not unusual for those engaged in selling sex to seek other outlets for their enterprises.

However carefully they may have endeavoured to conduct their business, James Roach and John Aitkin were rumbled in 1795. Since 1787, a band of moral reformers headed by the Bishop of London and comprising 'A great number of Gentlemen of the Highest Rank and Estimation' had committed themselves to pursuing malefactors such as the Roaches to justice. Their primary intent had been to carry forth the wishes expressed by George III as outlined in his 'Proclamation for the Encouragement of Piety and Virtue, and for the Preventing and Punishing of Vice, Profaneness, and Immorality'. In the course of stamping out 'loose and immoral publications', they had determined on quashing the nearly forty-year-old institution of *Harris's List*. By early 1794 they had hunted down John Roach and brought him successfully to trial for libel. Undaunted by this, James rather foolishly decided to continue publishing. The 1795 edition, which had arrived on H. Ranger's shelves around December or January, inevitably led the reformers straight to his back door. In February, Roach appeared before Lord Chief Justice Kenyon and Justice Ashurst, also on charges of libel. Cowering under the prospect of incarceration, Roach repented of his folly and lied remorselessly. He claimed to be unaware of the illegality of such a publication and to hold no knowledge of anyone else being prosecuted for printing a work that 'had been published regularly every year like a Court Calendar'. On this point, Judge Kenyon reminded him that only recently 'a defendant of the name of John Roach was formerly convicted of this very offence'. Chagrined, James Roach replied simply that the said John Roach was not him.

In spite of the pleadings of Roach's legal counsel that the defendant had atoned for his sins by withdrawing the book from public sale, and that he had severed all ties with Aitkin and with their printer, Justice Ashurst was not moved. In a final bid for sympathy, Roach's lawyer begged the court to consider the defendant's wife and six children, as well as his poor state of health, worsened by the onset of asthma 'since this prosecution has been commenced against him'. Unfortunately, none of these factors assisted in mitigating his punishment. According to Ashurst, James Roach, by publishing *Harris's List of Covent Garden Ladies*, was guilty of a grave lapse in judgement: 'An offence of greater enormity could hardly have been committed.' Ashurst continued that 'A care of the growing morals of the present generation ought to be uppermost in every man's heart.' He evidently felt that this was not the case with James Roach. As a result, Roach was sentenced to a year in Newgate Prison, but to ensure that upon his release he would not be tempted to publish scurrilous filth like *Harris's List* again, he was required 'to give security for his good behaviour for three years' through the payment of £100. The severity of Roach's punishment sent a clear warning to those who lived by the proceeds of sex. On the eve of the new century, a more righteous society would have little sympathy for the purveyors of vice.

## 20

# LADIES OF THE *LIST*

THE END OF THE production of *Harris's List* is by no means the end of our story, but rather a punctuation of it. The ancient profession of prostitution was far too well established to be hindered by the passing of a mere trade publication, irrespective of how useful the *List* had proven to be in its thirty-eight-year lifespan. In truth, eighteenth-century London's thaises, nymphs, votaries of Venus, or whatever title they might have been given, required little advertising beyond the flashing of a stocking-clad lower leg or a glimpse of a silk-apparelled figure in a theatre box. Demand for their services almost always outstripped supply. Year upon year, decade upon decade, the acclaimed beauties of their day grew old and were replaced by those with fresher faces. Their experiences have been the subject of much fascination to modern authors and historians who have speculated upon their existences and sought to understand who these women were and how they came to do what they did. There are still so many untold histories of women from outside the realms of respectable society that deserve to be uncovered and recounted; Charlotte Hayes's tale is but one of them. Of all the editions of the *List* published between 1757 and 1795, only volumes from nine years (1761, 1764, 1773, 1774, 1779, 1788, 1789, 1790, 1793) have evaded the wear and the censure of time to be retained in public collections. Contained within this handful of editions, over a thousand names and short biographies of women active in the sex trade are recorded for posterity. What happened to them? What were their stories? The revelations are bittersweet; both hopeful and tragic, touching and horrifying.

For a number of women, a life of prostitution held many rewards and delivered them into an existence far more comfortable and exciting than anything they might have otherwise experienced. The thin strata of the most successful ladies of the town was made up largely of women pulled from poverty. Fanny Murray, Emily Warren, Betsy Cox and Nancy Dawson are only a few of those who came straight from the street into the company of some of the wealthiest men in the country, a feat difficult at the best of times for those in other professions. A pretty face was enough to catapult a young girl to riches and secure her future, if she played her cards correctly. *Harris's List* records numerous examples of this. Among the celebrated names that fill its pages are those of women who never quite attained the stellar heights of Kitty Fisher and Emma Hamilton but whose lives were nevertheless prosperous and comfortable. The *List* also charts the fortunes of women such as Becky LeFevre (later known as Mrs Clapereau or Clappero), a lady who made a somewhat successful debut on the stage after rising from the rank of a streetwalker. Becky's notoriety landed her a wealthy keeper who subsidized her accommodation on Frith Street. The savvy Miss LeFevre took advantage of her commodious lodgings to let unused rooms to ladies of the town and by the age of twenty-eight had established a profitable enterprise which she eventually moved to King's Place. By 1789, a Mr Clapereau, described as 'a remarkably handsome youth' and a companion of the Prince of Wales, fell under her spell and insisted that she retire from procuring to live solely as his mistress in lodgings on Gerrard Street. So exclusive in her services that she received payment only in banknotes and never took 'any messages or mandates from Bagnios', 'Mrs' Clapereau, by the age of thirty-eight, had lifted herself from the status of 'common whore' to woman of wealth. The same happy fate awaited Miss Marshall, mentioned in 1779 and 1793, and Miss Becky Child (1788, 1789 and 1793). Miss Marshall, who in later years became Mrs Marshall, is described as 'a genteel person' who was 'prudent enough to be saving so as to enable herself to appear in an elegant manner and to be provided in case of an imergecy'. Unlike many of the sisterhood, prudence had allowed the now grand 'Mrs Marshall' to remain well provided for, fashionably dressed and still in high-keeping fourteen years later, in 1793. Miss Becky Child, who also eventually changed her title to Mrs, prospered for at least ten years under the protection of a wealthy 'citizen' of London (quite probably a member of the Child family of bankers). In 1789, she was comfortable enough to 'never admit any one home with her' after visits to the playhouses and assembly rooms. By 1793, her generous lover had feathered her nest so well that she was now described as 'plump and fair' and as the keeper of her own house on Newman Street.

A large number of the names that appear in *Harris's List* are also mentioned by that inveterate womanizer William Hickey. One of these is Fanny Temple (also known as Fanny Hartford), who is featured in the 1764 edition. Like so many, Fanny began her career as an actress at Drury Lane and came to supplement her income through honouring the attentions of her admirers. At the time her entry was written, she was living in Spring Gardens and was described as having a fair complexion and 'black eyes' from which 'love shoots his golden darts'. When Hickey made her acquaintance, roughly two years later, her prospects were on the rise. She had moved to 'an excellent house in Queen Ann Street and had . . . neat lodgings in the country, pleasantly situated near the waterside just above Hammersmith, and kept her own chariot, with suitable establishment of servants'. The bill for this lavish lifestyle was not footed by Hickey, but rather by 'a gentleman of rank and fashion, possessed of a splendid fortune'. Although Hickey further supplemented her income, his relationship with Fanny was more than a simple business arrangement. He and Fanny shared a genuine affection, which caused Hickey in later years to make attempts at re-establishing contact. Unluckily for him but quite happily for her, it appeared that Fanny by the 1780s 'had married a gentleman of fortune' and now 'resided entirely in the country'.

Popular convention has led us to believe the adage that 'men never marry their mistresses', but many successful prostitutes did enjoy an existence that ended in a marriage to their keepers. Numerous women on the *List*, as well as others who shared their profession, entered into wedded unions, not only with men of aristocratic birth (who, with some leverage, could marry whomever they might be inclined to) but to those of the gentry and the wealthy middle classes. Harriet Powell, one of Charlotte Hayes's recruits, married the Earl of Seaforth; Elizabeth Armistead became the wife of the politician Charles James Fox; Kitty Fisher married John Norris, a wealthy landowner; Emma Hart became the wife of Sir William Hamilton, the envoy to Naples; Elizabeth Farren married the Earl of Derby; and Ann Day, after acting as the mistress to the 2nd Baron Edgcumbe, married Sir Peter Fenhoulet. In terms of fashion, where the aristocracy went, the rest of society followed. In an article that appeared in the January 1755 edition of *The Connoisseur*, a concerned critic claimed that keeping a mistress was becoming so much the practice that even clerks and apprentices were maintaining women in private lodgings. Worse still, many 'grow so doatingly fond of their whore that by marriage they make her an honest woman and perhaps a lady of quality'.

The reality of the situation was that not every lady of the town was rescued by a well-heeled lover, and for each penniless waif snatched from the grasp of starvation were many more who suffered brutal existences. Prostitution, as a career, made no promises to any of its recruits, and in this respect it differed little from any other course of life that a woman of the lower orders might follow. A girl born to poor parents within the confines of the rapidly expanding metropolis could expect to receive scant few of life's favours. Every day would present another hardship or struggle, whether this was the burden of harsh physical labour, the never-ending quest for food and a means of keeping oneself warm, or fighting off the ravages of disease and violence which were rampant in London's poorest corridors. For those of the lower middle classes, or what Saunders Welch termed 'the labouring classes' and the 'industrious poor', whether girls worked as laundresses, seamstresses and street sellers or managed to enter into apprenticeships or domestic service, their futures looked equally dim. Perhaps, if they were lucky, they might marry a man of the same class, a tradesman who eked out a living of twenty shillings a week as a weaver or carpenter. If they were very lucky, they might marry a slightly more prosperous shopkeeper and assist in running the family trade. Pregnancies and children would come regularly, each new arrival breeding money worries. Life was precarious and unstable. No one could guarantee that their husband would be faithful, sober or non-violent. No one could promise that a bad turn of luck wouldn't land them all on the street or in prison. It is easy to comprehend in this light how prostitution might have led the hopeful to believe that the loss of virtue was a small price to pay for the opportunity of living a life of luxury and the potential of making a match well above their station. As long as the gilded carriages of Kitty Fisher and Fanny Murray clattered over the cobblestones of Covent Garden, and actresses like Sophia Baddeley appeared dressed in her admirer's gifts of jewels and silks, a girl might reconcile herself to a life of sin.

While leading a necessitous but virtuous life offered little more guarantee of happiness than a career of prostitution, the latter held the potential for a variety of additional misfortunes. Venereal disease was primary among them, and one pitfall that a wife with a faithful husband might never have cause to experience. Both syphilis  and the clap were treated with tinctures of mercury, which if used too frequently might diminish in potency and become ineffective. If used incorrectly, such treatments might also result in a slow, agonizing death. Pregnancy, the natural by-product of a life spent selling sex, threw up a host of problems. Prostitutes often had to get rid of their offspring in order to preserve themselves. Frequent abortions and the emotional repercussions of depositing unwanted babies on doorsteps, at the Foundling Hospital or in other, more lethal locations, must have been harrowing. This situation in combination with the unpredictable violence and coercive behaviour of pimps and bawds, who regularly locked women into rooms and forced them to service customers, would have been nothing short of a living hell. Even those who had been granted some degree of success in their professional endeavours and 'traded as independent' could easily succumb to the snares of drink, especially gin, the notorious gut-churning tipple of the desperate, and later to usquebaugh (or whisky), to dull the pain of life. For someone who was constantly in taverns and plied with drink by intoxicated patrons, alcoholism became a job-related illness. In any event, performing the sexual act with a physically unappealing partner seemed less troubling when one was barely lucid. How women in these situations contended psychologically with the hazards and tragedies that life served to them so liberally can only be imagined. Not surprisingly, their patchy histories reveal that many lived only for the moment and gave virtually no thought to the management of their futures: after all, what was the point when you were the victim of circumstance and the schemes of others since the day you were born?

The stories of those who managed to retain some degree of cheerfulness in the face of such adversity are objects of wonder, particularly to modern observers. The entries for women like Sukey Baker, mentioned in the *List* in 1773 and 1779, paint touching images of the human spirit, inextinguishable even in the bleakest of times. In 1773 Miss Baker is marked out for her complete acquiescence to her customers, who 'are as capricious in their desires as a fine lady in a toy-shop'. Within six years, it seems that Sukey Baker's complete 'condescension to her admirers' has won her a 'husband' (in the loosest terms), or at least someone to defend her interests. However, by 1779, Sukey's husband has been captured by a press gang and 'is gone aboard one of his majesty's ships of war', leaving poor 'Miss' Baker to once more shift for herself as a prostitute. In truth, the author of the *List* comments, this was not such a bad turn of events, as Sukey 'was very seldom without bruises while he was with her'. Rather than dousing herself in alcohol or succumbing to the blackness of depression, Sukey remains miraculously resilient and is described as being quite chatty and 'fond of singing'. She tells humorous stories and in spite of everything 'bears a good name with respect to sobriety and dealing always with honour'.

Others did not carry the burden of prostitution so well. The sad fate of Miss Menton, who features in the *List* in 1788 and 1789, presents a picture of a lonely and injured young woman sinking into unhappiness. In 1788, we are informed, the nineteen-year-old 'independent lass' has entered into a life upon the town only in the past eight months. She sees visitors at her lodgings on Berwick Street, 'which she shares with another whore, Miss Ratcliff', but also takes 'noon and evening excursions' in search of culls. The author recommends her as 'a deserving piece', since she appears to 'enjoy the sport with unfeigned rapture' and 'seems satisfied with one guinea'. The following year, however, the situation has somewhat changed. We learn that her entry into prostitution was occasioned by a seduction which eventually resulted in abandonment by her lover, a young baronet. Miss Menton had been in keeping with him for only a short while before 'indifference took place' and 'the desire entirely vanished'. The author continues that, 'owing to the baronet's inconstancy, together with the common cares of the world, the damsel is subject to a great lowness of spirits'. Weakened by the demands of her profession, in the span of one year Miss Menton has already turned to the bottle for comfort, requiring 'three or four cheerful glasses' in order to dispel her dark mood and perform the task required of her.

Alcoholism proved to be the ruin of many otherwise successful careers. Eighteenth-century men did not like the sight of drunken ladies. Nothing was considered less genteel or feminine than a dishevelled and out-of-control woman incapacitated by drink. Kitty Euston (or Eustace), a moderately well-off thais who had been on the town at least since 1761, had by 1773 almost entirely undone herself through her love of gin. 'This lady about four or five years ago was indeed a pretty girl,' wrote the author, but 'she can now toss off a glass of gin as well as the commonest bunter in the Strand, and like them, stoop to every meanness.' At least twelve years in business had exacted a heavy toll. She had spent time in the King's Bench Prison with her keeper, a Mr Callender, and had fended off several encounters with venereal disease. Her hardships had bestowed on her a gaunt and 'masculine' look, erasing any soft traces of prior beauty. 'She has suffered much,' claimed the *List*, and like a well-used broom had been 'worn to the stump'.

For every Nancy Dawson and Charlotte Hayes who managed their careers with skilful business acumen, there was a Lucy Cooper who carelessly threw away any advantage she had gained through thoughtless behaviour and a preference for the bottle. Many more women suffered poor health and succumbed to general despair. So many names that appear on the *List* over the years are mentioned once and then never again. What became of them, the anonymous Miss Browns, Miss Joneses, Miss Williams and Miss Smiths who simply pass unidentified through the pages? We can hope for happy endings. It is not unlikely that some found long-term keepers or even married. As prostitution could serve as a stopgap between roles on the stage or positions in domestic service, it is possible that some were able to find other work. Perhaps a handful even found their way through the gates of the Magdalen Hospital, where they would be trained for positions in 'respectable life'. Regrettably, for a large number of women, this was not the way their stories ended. Those who disappeared from the *List* most likely did so for more sinister reasons. In addition to incurable syphilis and alcoholism, the march of age or the loss of beauty could bring an abrupt end to a career. Likewise, the law frequently caught up with women who coupled prostitution with pickpocketing, or those like Charlotte Hayes who found themselves unable to pay their bills. More than in any other place, death lay in prison. It is probable that many of the names on *Harris's List* ended their short and difficult days like Lucy Cooper, bereft of friends and in a pauper's grave.

It should be remembered that for the majority featured in the *List*, prostitution was never their chosen path but rather one that fate had mapped out for them. In a male-dominated society, it flattered the masculine ego to believe that once a woman had been stripped of her virginity, she became as lustful as a man. If this happened outside of marriage, quite simply she became a whore, if not in action then in thought. There were no halves in this equation. Whether a young woman willingly gave her consent to fornication or whether she was raped did not matter: the net result was the same – she was no longer pure and her carnal desires had been whetted. The world looked unforgivingly on women in this situation; they were rendered good for nothing but a life of prostitution, that necessary evil. Since the authors of *Harris's List* were male, this is the perspective that is adopted by and large in the *List*'s entries, an attitude that expresses only cursory sympathy for the woman's plight. Many of the women (who in some instances should rightly be called girls) who found themselves on the *List* arrived there as victims of rape or childhood sexual abuse. The story of Lenora Norton, who appears in the 1788 and 1789 editions, is a case of both. Her history is recorded in such a matter-of-fact tone that it is shocking to read. It is described to the reader in titillating terms how Miss Norton, the daughter of a surgeon, was 'seduced by her present keeper in a famous hotel' at a very young age. So young, in fact, that Lenora had not yet entered puberty. It seemed that nature had not 'stamped the least shadow of womanhood' on her nubile body, which as a result caused 'the naked centrical spot', 'fearful of pain, which was not accompanied by any other sensation' to 'recoil at the touch of the wicked invader . . .' The author then cheerfully concludes that, although just a girl, Lenora 'was not destitute of admirers' and soon learned to 'seize the long hated acquaintance and urge him home with the true feelings of a woman of pleasure'. Lenora then spent the next several years of her life courting the advances of other gentlemen, but eventually was seduced back into keeping with Mr Cotton, her abuser. How many other listed women suffered similarly can only be imagined.

The possibility of rape or physical assault was a spectre that always lingered in the wings of a prostitute's life. Naturally, the majority of crimes of this nature would go unreported, although women on the receiving end might find themselves scarred both emotionally and physically for life. The celebrated Betsy Weyms, mentioned in the 1761 *List*, bore a striking reminder of the risk of violence inherent in her walk of life. Called the 'wall-eyed beauty' by her admirers, at some early point in her career Betsy had been the victim of a vicious attack which resulted in the loss of an eye. A pimp or a bully could come in quite useful in preventing bloody fracases of the nature suffered by Miss Weyms. For kept mistresses in lodgings, it was always handy to have a male servant on the staff. Charlotte Barry, William Hickey's mistress, was fortunate enough to have a man who answered her door and was strong enough to repel the aggression of her former lover Henry Mordaunt. Without the presence of a male protector, many women relied on one another for security and support. One of the most common arrangements was for prostitutes to live and work in pairs or small groups, thereby ensuring that at least someone was keeping an ear and an eye attuned to the safety of the others. Only a shout from an adjoining room was required to raise the alarm and, through a collective effort, fend off any foul play.

The choice of many women to live and work together served other purposes besides that of personal safety. The need for companionship and a sense of community cannot be underestimated. Although the *List* indicates that by and large prostitutes were fully integrated into the communities they inhabited, living nestled among wigmakers, stationers and ironmongers rather than in isolated red-light districts, their relations with other women would have been somewhat strained. As prostitutes were commonly perceived as vice-spreaders – agents of disease and corruption who could insinuate themselves into a family and undermine the fabric of society – it was simpler to keep oneself to oneself and to commune only with others involved in or sympathetic to the trade. Therefore, creating and maintaining friendships and relationships with others in similar situations was crucial to avoid isolation and to sustain a sense of community. Not surprisingly, groups of siblings as well as mothers and daughters often lived together as families while practising in the sex trade. The *List* is filled with names of sisters like the Ingmires (1761) and the Bowens (1764), who entered into prostitution and created a home environment where they could continue to engage in their trade and live as a family. In a number of cases, as was the situation with the Sells sisters in 1773, three generations of women, a mother, her daughters and their female children, cohabited under the same roof.

However, such strong bonds between women did not always require shared blood. There were many who chose to live together as close friends, becoming in some cases one another's surrogate family. Polly Kennedy and Nancy Dawson, who were both considerably well off by the time they were mentioned in the 1761 and 1779 editions of the *List*, chose to live together for reasons of mutual companionship. The two were inseparable, sharing a keeper (the actor Ned Shuter) and lodgings for most of their lives. Their friendship, like that experienced between many women, was one which became as deep as a familial bond and led Dawson to will Kennedy her fully furnished house on King Street at the end of her life. While there were many who resided in 'adopted' family groups, others shared lodgings with fellow prostitutes simply in order to defray the costs of living. Much like today's single urban professionals, it was more economical if the expenses of rent, food and even transportation were shared between two or three. In 1793, Miss Townsend and Miss Charlton, both of 12 Gress Street, had thrown in their lots together and were not only splitting the rent due on their residence but the expense of keeping a carriage. They, like the noted trio of Miss Trelawney, Miss Fitzroy and Miss Wargent (all living at 9 Bateman's Buildings), were frequently seen in public together, attending the same dances and theatrical performances, laughing and gallivanting in a close-knit circle.

Ideally, a successful mistress of her enterprise would strive to eventually become the 'keeper of her house'. A wealthy enough lover would purchase the lease of a premises for his lady where she could let out the unoccupied rooms to others of her profession. By these means she could elevate herself from the rank of mistress to that of bawd, or bring friends or female relations under her roof to ward off loneliness. Many of those who 'kept the house', such as Miss Heseltine in 1779, Nancy Crosby in 1788 and Mrs Vincent in 1793, opened their doors to a mix of prostitutes, ordinary male lodgers, women who desired a place to give birth in secret (or 'lie-in'), and couples who sought a location to 'intrigue' by the hour. In fact, the letting of rooms was such a comfortable means of securing an extra income that other, more seemingly upstanding professionals saw the merit in it. The *List* is peppered with addresses of prostitutes living under the roofs of tradespeople, like Miss Seabright in 1773, who was lodging 'at a Barber's in the Haymarket', or Nancy Davenport and Sarah Cullen, who shared accommodation 'at a cabinet maker's'.

Eighteenth-century London's attitude towards the 'fair and frail' ladies who shared their pavements, parks, taverns, theatres and assembly rooms can be described as at best confused and at worst schizophrenic. A prostitute was either an object of pity or scorn, someone to be helped or avoided, a victim of society or one of society's polluters – and, at times, all of these simultaneously. She was rarely ever just a woman. A patriarchal England, where women existed to serve men, required prostitutes as much as it required faithful, fertile wives; dutiful, innocent daughters; and selfless, loving mothers. A prostitute bore the brunt of the unacceptable face of womanhood, everything that these other figures could not have or be: the sexual, the base, the greedy, the animalistic. Because the authors of *Harris's List* were men, their perceptions of the women they profiled were coloured by the preconceptions of their era. The reader receives only a one-sided view, and consequently the women of the *List* are never provided with an opportunity to tell their version of events. In many cases, it is likely that their stories would have differed quite significantly from those recounted by their customers for the benefit of the *List*'s publishers.

As might be imagined, there is much to be said in defence of Harris's ladies. The women featured in the publication were regularly maligned for the most understandable of minor offences, from apathy in bed to the display of mercenary tendencies. Dissatisfied customers were certainly not coy about coming forward with negative reports. Miss Dean, featured in the 1773 supplement, received a complaint for demonstrating 'great indifference' during the sexual act. According to her cull, she had the audacity to 'crack nuts' behind his back 'whilst he was acting his joys'. Similarly, women who didn't seem to be enjoying themselves as a whore should were described as 'lazy bedfellows' or, like Charlotte Gainsborough, scorned for being 'motionless in the very height of the sport, preferring rather a pinch of snuff to all the joys of venery'. Others failed to endear themselves by displaying qualities that their patrons found unappealing; this included the use of 'an immoderate quantity of paint' and, ironically, any honesty surrounding their true motives for prostituting themselves. Miss O'Dell was criticized for this in 1764, and was decried as being 'of a disposition a little too mercenary'. After all, who wanted to believe that prostitutes were just in it for the money? Miss O'Dell's problem was that she 'shews too plainly that the love of money is more predominant in her than the soft passion which bears the chief sway over most female breasts'. According to the beliefs of the era, prostitutes were lascivious, hot-blooded women who loved a good tumble and sold their sexual favours because they enjoyed copulation with a variety of partners. By nature, they were as lewd as any drunken libertine in Covent Garden, and any woman who betrayed evidence to the contrary was liable to be forcibly corrected. Consequently, Miss O'Dell was granted her comeuppance: 'an arch wag once put a trick upon her . . . This was no other than paying her with money of which he had picked of her pocket', a lesson which 'provoked her highly when she came to discover it'. The men who used *Harris's List* didn't want to be reminded that the women who looked so tempting and promised such a feast of delights were nothing more than accomplished mistresses of deception. They didn't want to know what happened to their little 'choice piece' once they had buttoned their breeches, or that she, like Kitty Atchison after being left alone in 1761, might have cried out, 'what a disagreeable situation is this to a generous mind! What an unhappy circle to move in, for a thinking person! – To be the sink of mankind! – To court alike the beastly drunkard and the nauseating rake – dissimulating distaste for enjoyment!' A prostitute's client wasn't interested in knowing the sad details of her life and didn't want to be reminded that, unlike him, she had little choice about with whom she would share the intimacies of her body. For those like Lenora Norton who had suffered rape as a child, and like many of Charlotte Hayes's recruits who were 'induct[ed] into the mysteries of Venus' even before the age of puberty, it is likely that sex was never anything other than a distressing experience. All things considered, who could blame these women for their sexual indifference, for behaving in ways that were deemed frigid, or for betraying their desire simply to earn money?

Complaints of infidelity and ingratitude from men who kept mistresses were frequent too. To them it seemed that gentlemen were constantly the dupes of these jades. These women were fickle in their affections, or so driven by their libidinous and material desires that they flitted thoughtlessly from the embrace of one protector to another. According to *The Connoisseur*, a kept mistress was an artful and scheming harlot who stopped at nothing to secure her own pleasure and exact precisely what she desired from her keeper. The author of an article entitled 'On Kept Mistresses and Keepers' recounted how his friend had been used by his lady:

> . . . what pains she took to bring him to the most abject compliance with all her wishes and to tame him to the patient thing he is now. A frown on his part would frequently cost him a brocade, and a tear from her was sure to extort a new handkerchief or an apron. Upon any quarrel— O! She would leave him at that moment . . . she would work upon his jealousy by continually twitting him with – she knew a gentleman, who would scorn to use her so barbarously and she would go to him, if she could be sure that she was not with child . . .

Invariably, the author concluded, men who kept whores were sure to find themselves 'deserted by their mistress, once she has effectually ruined their constitution and estate'. No one ever questioned why a lady in keeping might behave so, or why she was so keen to make the most of her situation.

Men like William Hickey scoffed at the pledges of kept ladies who claimed that they 'could never be unfaithful to any man with whom they lived'. Hickey knew these promises to be false ones and had experienced at first hand how easily such women changed their tune when better prospects appeared.

Most keepers were short-sighted enough to believe that such behaviour went hand in hand with a wanton character and chose, in the interests of their own pleasure, not to recognize the motivations of a woman who sold sex in order to survive. A kept mistress's livelihood depended upon her keeper's indulgence as well as her ability to maintain his interest. Spoilt, wealthy young men were liable to boredom, and acquiring the latest celebrated beauty contained all the transient joy of acquiring a new watch or fashionable coat. Inevitably, their interest waned; the coat was handed down to a manservant and the mistress was booted from her Queen Ann Street lodgings. With no promise of anything, no future, no security, no income, never knowing when the axe might fall and when she might find herself on the street or back in the deplorable brothel from which she came, any savvy mistress had one eye constantly towards new opportunities, scanning the horizon for anyone who might promise her something more than she currently had.

And what of love in all of this business? Where did love, if at all, figure into these dealings? Harris's ladies would not be human if they didn't dream of it or fall prey to its enticements. In a profession where the word 'love' was bandied about to describe (most of the time quite falsely) the activities that comprised their existence, did any real love exist between at least some keepers and mistresses and a handful of certain culls and their women? Of course it did. Love manifested itself in complicated ways, just as it does today. Simply because Harris's ladies were warned against forming romantic attachments did not mean they didn't, although it frequently made situations a bit more uncomfortable. An ability to shut these emotions off at will was a tool necessary for one's survival, while a harlot's greatest gift was her ability to make a man believe that she adored him. In some cases, she may have done, or if he proved to be generous, kind and affectionate, she may have grown to do so. When a genuine admirer presented himself, a certain degree of self-delusion would have paved the way for an easier life, one that opened the door at least temporarily to happiness. Without the possibility of this, a life led in such darkness would have remained intolerable.

# APPENDIX

## A LIST OF COVENT GARDEN LOVERS

Since the publication of the first *Harris's List* nearly 250 years ago, the literate public has been free to learn the names of London's fallen women. The names of their customers and keepers, however, receive an easy passage out of history's spotlight. The compilation of another equally fascinating list, one which identifies the devoted patrons of the sex trade, has been made possible through a detailed examination of *Harris's List* and related materials. The names cited below represent only a fraction of these 'Covent Garden lovers' active during the second half of the eighteenth century.

Lord Chief Justice Henry Addington, 1st Viscount
    Sidmouth
Admiral George Anson, 1st Baron Anson
Sir William Apreece
Sir Richard Atkins
Sir John Aubrey, MP
Richard Barry, 7th Earl of Barrymore

Allen Bathurst, 1st Earl of Bathurst

Sir Charles Bingham, 1st Earl of Lucan

Captain George Maurice Bissett

Admiral Edward Boscawen

Hugh Boscawen, 2nd Viscount Falmouth

James Boswell

Sir Orlando Bridgeman

Thomas Bromley, 2nd Baron Montfort

Captain John Byron

John Calcraft, MP

Archibald Campbell, 3rd Duke of Argyll

John Campbell, 5th Duke of Argyll

John Campbell, 4th Earl of Loudoun

George Capell, 5th Earl of Essex

David Carnegie, Lord Rosehill

Charles Churchill

John Cleland

Henry Fiennes Clinton, 9th Earl of Lincoln

Robert 'Cock-a-doodle-doo' Coates

Charles Cornwallis, 1st Marquess of Cornwallis

Colonel John Coxe

William Craven, 6th Baron Craven

His Royal Highness, Prince Ernest, Duke of Cumberland

His Royal Highness, Prince Henry Frederick, Duke of
    Cumberland

His Royal Highness, Prince William Augustus, Duke of
    Cumberland

The Honourable John Damer

Sir Francis Dashwood, Lord Despenser

Sir John Dashwood-King

Francis Drake Delaval

Reverend William Dodd

George Bubb Doddington, Lord Melcombe

William Douglas, 4th Duke of Queensbury

Henry Dundas, 1st Viscount Melville

George Montague Dunk, 2nd Earl of Halifax

Sir Henry Echlin

Richard Edgcumbe, Lord Mount Edgcumbe

Lord Charles Fielding (son of the Earl of Denbigh)

The Honourable John Finch

John Fitzpatrick, 1st Earl of Upper Ossory

Augustus Henry Fitzroy, 3rd Duke of Grafton

Samuel Foote

Charles James Fox

Stephen Fox, 2nd Baron Holland

George Fox-Lane, 3rd Baron Bingley

George, Prince of Wales (later George IV)

Judge Henry Gould

Sir John Graeme, Earl of Alford

James Graham, 3rd Duke of Montrose

Charles Hamilton, Lord Binning

Charles Hanbury-Williams

Colonel George Hanger

Count Franz Xavier Haszlang, Bavarian Envoy to London

Robery Henley, 1st Earl of Northington

Henry Herbert, 10th Earl of Pembroke

Joseph Hickey

William Hickey

William Holies, 2nd Viscount Vane

Rear-Admiral Charles Holmes

Admiral Samuel Hood, 1st Viscount Hood

Charles Howard, 11th Duke of Norfolk

Thomas Howard, 3rd Earl of Effingham

Admiral Lord Richard Howe, 4th Viscount Howe

Thomas Jefferson (manager of Drury Lane theatre)

John Philip Kemble

Augustus Keppel, 1st Viscount Keppel

William John Kerr, 5th Marquess of Lothian

Sir John Lade

Penistone Lamb, 1st Viscount Melbourne

William Langhorne (poet laureate)

Lord Edward Ligonier

Field Marshall John Ligonier, 1st Earl of Ligonier

Simon Lutrell, 1st Baron Carhampton

Thomas Lyttelton, 2nd Baron Lyttelton

Kenneth Francis Mackenzie, 4th Earl of Seaforth

Charles Macklin

The Honourable Captain John Manners

John Manners, 3rd Duke of Rutland

Captain Anthony George Martin

Charles Maynard, 1st Viscount Maynard

James McDuff, 2nd Earl of Fife

Captain Thomas Medlycott

Isaac Mendez

Major Thomas Metcalfe

Sir George Montgomerie Metham

John Montague, 4th Earl of Sandwich

Alexander Montgomerie, 10th Earl of Eglinton

Arthur Murphy

Richard 'Beau' Nash

Francis John Needham, MP

Henry Nevill, 2nd Earl of Abergavenny

John Palmer (actor)

Thomas Panton

William Petty, 1st Marquess of Lansdowne

Evelyn Meadows Pierrepont, 2nd Duke of Kingston

Thomas Potter

John Poulett, 4th Earl of Poulett

William Powell (manager of Drury Lane)

Charles 'Chace' Price

William Pulteney, 1st Earl of Bath

Richard 'Bloomsbury Dick' Rigby

Admiral George Brydges Rodney, 1st Baron Rodney

David Ross (actor)

Francis Russell, 5th Duke of Bedford

John Frederick Sackville, 3rd Duke of Dorset

Sir George Saville

George Selwyn

Ned Shuter

John George Spencer, 1st Earl Spencer

The Honourable John 'Jack' Spencer

Charles Stanhope, 3rd Earl of Harrington

Philip Dormer Stanhope, 4th Earl Chesterfield

Sir William Stanhope, MP

Edward Stanley, 12th Earl of Derby

Sir Thomas Stapleton

George Alexander Stephens

John Stewart, 3rd Earl of Bute

Frederick St John, 2nd Viscount Bolingbroke

Colonel Sir Banastre Tarleton

Commodore Edward Thompson

Lord Chief Justice Sir Edward Thurlow

Robert 'Beau' Tracy

John Tucker, MP

Arthur Vansittart, MP

Sir Henry Vansittart, MP

Robert Vansittart

Sir Edward Walpole

Sir Robert Walpole

John Wilkes

William, Duke of Clarence (later William IV)

Charles Wyndham, 2nd Earl of Egremont

Henry Woodward (actor)

His Royal Highness, Edward, Duke of York

His Royal Highness, Frederick, Duke of York

Lieutenant Colonel John Yorke

Joseph Yorke, 1st Baron Dove

# GLOSSARY OF
# EIGHTEENTH-CENTURY TERMS

**Abbess:** female keeper of a high-class brothel

**Adventurer:** con man, usually well dressed and seemingly genteel

**Aretino's *Postures*:** popular series of engravings illustrating the sexual positions featured in Pietro Aretino's 1534 work, *Sonetti Lussuriosi*

**Bagnio:** bath house, usually a location where sexual favours could be received

**Bawd:** woman who procures prostitutes

**Bawdy house:** brothel

**Bilk:** to cheat someone out of their pay

**Black legs:** gambler who bets on horse races and other outdoor sports. 'Black legs' refer to the tall black boots generally worn by such men

**Blood:** 'riotous and disorderly fellow'

**Bow Street:** headquarters of the magistrate John Fielding and his flying squad, the Bow Street Runners

**Bridewell:** Clerkenwell-based prison for prostitutes

**Buck:** 'man of spirit' or a debauchee

**Bulk-monger:** homeless prostitute who lives and plies her trade from the benches below shopfronts

**Bully:** man who acts as a protector to a prostitute, also the eighteenth-century equivalent of a bouncer

**Bunter:** destitute prostitute

**Cantharides:** aphrodisiacs

**Chair/sedan chair:** chair enclosed within a small cabin and carried on two poles by two bearers, usually used for covering short distances

**Chariot:** phaeton or two-wheeled carriage (could also be a reference to a coach)

**Clap:** 'venereal taint', usually gonorrhoea

**Compter/round house:** local lock-up or gaol

**Cull/cully:** prostitute's customer

**Cundum:** condom. In the eighteenth century these were generally made of animal intestine and fixed in place with a ribbon and were used as a prophylactic rather than a contraceptive device

**Disorderly house:** legal term used to describe a brothel

**The Fleet:** London's main debtors' prison

**Gin:** a cheap, frequently adulterated alcoholic drink favoured by the London poor

**Higgler:** a peddler

**High-keeping:** the extravagant maintenance of a prostitute in expensive lodgings

**'In keeping':** state of being financially supported by one man as his mistress

**Jellies/jelly houses:** gelatine dessert favoured by both high and low society. Jelly houses, which were a mid-eighteenth-century fad, were outlets that specifically sold moulded jellies and tended to be patronized by prostitutes

**King's Bench Prison:** Southwark-based prison generally used for holding debtors and those guilty of libel

**Lock Hospital:** hospital for the cure of venereal diseases, founded in 1746

**Magdalen Hospital:** reformatory for repentant prostitutes

**The Marshalsea:** Southwark-based prison mainly used to house debtors in the eighteenth century

**Mercury:** primary ingredient in treatments for venereal diseases

**Newgate:** London's chief prison, where its most dangerous felons were held

**Night constable:** parish constable on duty in the evenings

**Night watch:** lowest-ranking law-enforcers notorious for their dishonesty and their susceptibility to bribes

**Nunnery:** high-class brothel, usually based on or around King's Place

**Panderer:** slightly higher-ranking pimp who worked indoors

**Pimp:** man who seeks 'to bring in customers and to procure . . . wenches'

**'Plead her belly':** when a woman claims she is pregnant in order to save herself from execution

**Pox:** syphilis

**Rake:** 'lewd debauched man'; other terms include ranger or roué

**Register office:** employment office where jobs were advertised

**Sal/salivation/'down in a sal':** someone in the midst of a mercury treatment for venereal diseases, so-called because, among other side effects, the ingestion of mercury brought on profuse salivation

**Sérail**: high-class, French-style brothel

**Sharper**: cheat, 'one who lives by his wits'

**Spunging house**: bailiff's lock-up 'to which persons arrested are taken till they find bail, or have spent all of their money'

**Tyburn**: location where public hangings were conducted during the eighteenth century

# NOTES

## CHAPTER 5: THE RISE OF PIMP GENERAL JACK

1. Brown-haired girl.
2. In other words, a prostitute one might find sitting in the side boxes of either of the two theatres.
3. It will be easy to trick punters into thinking that she's a virgin.
4. Just moved into the West End six months ago.
5. Here Harris has supposedly written a note to remind himself that Jewish merchants are willing to pay over the odds for prostitutes like Fanny.
6. The Lock Hospital was devoted to the cure of venereal disease.

## CHAPTER 9: AN INTRODUCTION TO HARRIS'S LADIES

1. Members of high society such as Lady Seymour Dorothy Worsley and Lady Sarah Bunbury, who indulged in scandalous affairs, would be considered whores by society.
2. In the mid-eighteenth century these were generally high-born or seemingly respectable women who conducted extra-marital sexual relations with whomever they desired.

3. Generally an unmarried woman who allowed her admirers sexual favours.

4. Those who might at this period be defined as courtesans, or any woman supported by a man in lodgings in exchange for rights to sole sexual access.

5. Generally, polite, attractive and accomplished prostitutes who worked in high-class brothels such as Charlotte Hayes's, or who saw men in their own lodgings without being under the care of a specific keeper.

6. Those women who belonged to lower-ranking brothels and who plied their trade openly in taverns, coffee houses and at the theatre.

7. Similar to their streetwalking sisters, but generally plying their trade with a semblance of modesty in the parks.

8. Those openly (and aggressively) plying their trade on the streets. These women offered a cheap but medically risky sexual experience that might be had in a dark alley or in their filthy lodgings.

9. The lowest, rudest and lewdest of the streetwalking class – frequently diseased and often described as 'half-starved wretches'.

10. Generally, homeless beggars who make their beds on the bulks below shop windows. Considered the lowest of the low, riddled with disease and ravaged by drink, these women occupy the place closest to death.

## CHAPTER 10: THE *LIST*

1. Sir Orlando Bridgeman.
2. Gertrude Mahon, a fashionable courtesan.
3. A term for a public dance or assembly.

4. Mary Young (alias Jenny Diver) was one of the most notorious pickpockets of her generation. She was hanged in 1740.
5. With furious passion.
6. Quite possibly a licentious gentlemen's society known as 'The Choice of Paris'.
7. A type of carriage.
8. A slang term for tea.
9. Soled or sold – a play on words.
10. Noble was a publisher who ran a lending library.
11. A term used to describe locations of 'infamy and debauchery'.
12. Ranelagh pleasure garden, a popular evening venue for entertainment.
13. John Cleland, *Fanny Hill; or Memoirs of a Woman of Pleasure.*
14. To be salivated, or 'in a sal', refers to the effects of undergoing a mercury treatment for venereal disease. Taking small doses of mercury led, among other things, to the patient producing vast quantities of saliva.
15. A slang term for guineas.
16. Going out on the street.
17. 'Uncle' was slang for pawnbroker.
18. A fashionable lady's hairdresser.
19. Cull or cully: a man, or in the case of prostitutes, the term used for clients.
20. 'Son of Esculapius': a physician.
21. Sea-holly.
22. A drug mixed with honey or syrup.
23. The Magdalen Hospital for repentant prostitutes was founded in 1758 and offered a place of refuge and reform for women who wished to renounce their former trade.
24. To cheat someone of their pay.

# CHAPTER 15: 'THE LITTLE KING OF BATH'

1. Quin's nickname.
2. David Garrick rose to fame as 'Bayes' in the Duke of Buckingham's play *The Rehearsal*.
3. In this poem Derrick refers to how truly passé Quin's style of acting had become. He recounts how the cowardly Quin, outdone by David Garrick and his natural style of dramatics, retired to Bath. Quin's performance of Falstaff was legendarily bad, but Derrick claims it was actually the most convincingly played role of his career, due to his belief that Quin was typecast.

# SELECT BIBLIOGRAPHY

## JACK HARRIS/JOHN HARRISON

Anon., *The Characters of the Most Celebrated Courtezans* (London, 1780)

—, *A Congratulatory Epistle from a Reformed Rake to John Fielding Esq. Upon the New Scheme of Reclaiming Prostitutes* (London, 1758)

—, The *Fruit-Shop, a Tale; or a Companion to St. James's Street* (London, 1766)

— (Samuel Derrick), *The Ghost of Moll King; or A Night at Derry's* (London, 1761)

—, *Kitty's Attalantis for the year 1766* (London, 1766)

—, *Memoirs of the Bedford Coffee House, by A. Genius* (London, 1751)

—, *The Memoirs of the Celebrated Miss Fanny Murray* (London, 1759)

—, *Nocturnal Revels or the History of King's Place and Other Modern Nunneries, by a Monk of the Order of St. Francis of Medmenham*, 2 vols. (London, 1779)

Brown, Thomas, *The Midnight Spy* (London, 1766)

Burford, E. J., *Wantons, Wits and Wenchers* (London, 1986)

— and Wotton, Joy, *Private Vices, Public Virtues* (London, 1988)

Cobbett, William, *Cobbett's Complete Collection of State Trials* (London, 1928), 'The Trial of John Clarke, Robert Knell and Joseph Carter, Printers of *Mist's Weekly Journal*, 1729' (vol. 17), pp. 666–8

Derrick, Samuel, *Memoirs of the Shakespear's Head* (London, 1755)

Foster, D. (compiler), 'Inns, Taverns, Alehouses, Coffee Houses, etc. in and around London' *c*.1900, Cuttings Book in the Westminster City Archives

Hill, John, *The Remonstrance of Harris, Pimp-General to the People of England* (London, 1758)

Thompson, Edward, *The Courtesan* (London, 1765)


## Articles and Periodicals

*Connoisseur* (11 April 1754)

*Monthly Review*, vol. xix (London, 1758)


## Archival Material

WESTMINSTER CITY ARCHIVES:

St Paul Covent Garden:

Rate Books and Receipts (1730–95)

Records for Births, Baptisms and Marriages

LONDON METROPOLITAN ARCHIVES:

Middlesex sessions papers

Victualling Licenses and Recognizances (St Paul, Covent Garden)

# SAMUEL DERRICK

Anon., *The Bath Contest; Being a Collection of all the Papers, Advertisements, etc. published before and since the death of Mr. Derrick by the Candidates of the Office of Master of Ceremonies* (Bath, 1769)

—, *Derrick's Jests; or the Wit's Chronicle* (London, 1767)

—, (Samuel Derrick), *The Ghost of Moll King; or A Night at Derry's* (London, 1761)

—, *The Life of Mr. James Quin, Comedian* (London, 1766)

—, *Memoirs of the Bedford Coffee House by A. Genius* (London, 1751)

—, *The New Bath Guide* (Bath, 1798)

—, *Nocturnal Revels or the History of King's Place and Other Modern Nunneries, by a Monk of the Order of St. Francis of Medmenham*, 2 vols. (London, 1779)

—, *Quin's Jests, or the Facetious Man's Pocket Companion* (London, 1766)

—, *The Thespian Dictionary, or Dramatic Biography of the Present Age* (London, 1805)

Aikins, Janet E. (ed.), *The Dramatic Censor; Remarks Upon the Tragedy of Venice Preserv'd by Samuel Derrick* (Los Angeles, 1985)

Baker, David Erskine, *Biographia Dramatica, 1764–1782*, 2 vols. (London, 1782)

Bleackley, Horace, *Ladies Fair and Frail, Sketches of the Demi-Monde of the Eighteenth Century* (London, 1925)

Burford, E. J., *Wits and Wenchers* (London, 1986)

— and Wotton, Joy, *Private Vices, Public Virtues* (London, 1988)

Chalmers, Alexander, *The General Biographical Dictionary* (London, 1812)

Craig, Maurice, *Dublin 1660–1860* (London, 1992)

Derrick, Samuel, *The Battle of Lora* (London, 1762)

—, *A Collection of Original Poems* (London, 1755)

— (ed.), *A Collection of Travels thro' Various Parts of the World; but more particularly thro' Tartary, China, Turkey, Persia and the East Indies* (London, 1762)

—, *Fortune, A Rhapsody* (London, 1751)

—, *Letters Written from Leverpoole, Chester, Corke, the Lake of Killarney, Dublin, Tunbridge-Wells, and Bath*, 2 vols. (London, 1767)

—, *Memoirs of the Count du Beauval* (London, 1754)

—, *The Memoirs of the Shakespear's Head* (London, 1755)

—, *The Miscellaneous Works of John Dryden, containing all His Original Poems, Tales and Translations* (London, 1760)

—, *A Poetical Dictionary, or the Beauties of the English Poets Alphabetically Display'd* (London, 1761)

—, *Sylla; a Dramatic Entertainment* (London, 1753)

—, *The Third Satire of Juvenal* (London, 1755)

—, *A Voyage to the Moon, with Some Account of the Solar World* (London, 1753)

Dickson, David (ed.), *The Gorgeous Mask, Dublin 1700–1850* (London, 1987)

Dublin Corporation Libraries, *A Directory for Dublin for the Year 1738* (Dublin, 2000)

Fagan, Patrick, *The Second City; a Portrait of Dublin 1700–1760* (Dublin, 1986)

Genest, John (ed.), *Some Account of the English Stage*, 10 vols. (Bristol, 1997)

Gentleman, Francis, *The Theatres: A Poetical Dissection* (London, 1772)

Highfill, Burnim and Langhans, *Trials for Adultery, or the History of Divorces* (Stott Trial, 1765; London, 1780)

Hinde, Thomas, *Tales from the Pump Room* (London, 1988)

Melville, Lewis, *Bath under Beau Nash and After* (London, 1926)

Morash, Christopher, *A History of Irish Theatre, 1601–2000* (Cambridge, 2002)

Napier, Alexander (ed.), *The Life of Samuel Johnson by James Boswell*, 5 vols. (London, 1884)

Patrick, John, and Rogers, William, *Grub Street, a Study in Subculture* (London, 1972)

Pottle, Frederick (ed.), *Boswell's London Journal; 1762–63* (London, 1950)

Price, Cecil, *Theatre in the Age of Garrick* (Oxford, 1973)

Rider, William, *An Historical and Critical Account of the Lives and Writings of the Living Authors of Great Britain* (London, 1762)

Smollett, Tobias, *The Expedition of Humphry Clinker* (London, 1771)

Stone, G. W. (ed.), *The London Stage, 1660–1800*, vol. 4: 1747–76 (London, 1962)

Taylor, John, *Records of My Life*, 2 vols. (London, 1832)

Troyer, Howard, *Ned Ward of Grub Street: A Study of Sub-literary London in the Eighteenth century* (London, 1946)

Ward, Robert E. (ed.), *Prince of Dublin Printers; The Letters of George Faulkner* (Lexington, Kentucky, 1972)

Watkins, John, *The Universal Biographical Dictionary*, 8 vols. (London, 1821)

Watt, Robert, *Bibliotheca Britannia; or a General Index to British Literature*, 4 vols. (London, 1824)

Wilkes, Thomas (and Derrick, Samuel), *A General View of the Stage* (London, 1759)

## Articles and Periodicals

*Baldwin's London Weekly Journal* (22 March 1769)

*Connoisseur* (16 January 1755 & 6 June 1754)

*Gentleman's Magazine*, 1st Series, 39 (1769), p. 215

*St. James's Chronicle* (28 March 1769 & 1 April 1769)

*Town and Country Magazine, or Universal Repository of Knowledge, Instruction and Entertainment* (April & June 1769), (vol. 1), pp. 177–80

## Archival Material

National Art Library (Victoria and Albert Museum): Forster Collection 48. G3 – 30: *Correspondence and Miscellaneous Papers of Samuel Derrick*

## CHARLOTTE HAYES

Anon., *The Genuine Memoirs of Dennis O'Kelly Esq., Commonly Called Count O'Kelly* (London, 1788)

—, *The New Foundling Hospital for Wit*, 'OMIAH, an Ode Addressed to Charlotte Hayes' (London, 1784)

—, *Nocturnal Revels or the History of King's Place and Other Modern Nunneries, by a Monk of the Order of St. Francis of Medmenham*, 2 vols. (London, 1779)

Black, Robert, *The Jockey Club and Its Founders* (London, 1891)

Blyth, Henry, *The High Tide of Pleasure; Seven English Rakes* (London, 1970)

Brown, Roger Lee, *A History of the Fleet Prison* (Lewiston, 1996)

Burford, E. J., *Wantons, Wits and Wenchers* (London, 1986)

— and Wotton, Joy, *Private Vices, Public Virtues* (London, 1988)

Cleland, John, *Fanny Hill; or the Memoirs of a Woman of Pleasure* (London, 1749)

Cook, Andrea Theodore, *Eclipse and O'Kelly* (London, 1907)

Fillinham Collection, vol. 2: *Carlisle House and White Conduit House*, 'Masquerade Intelligence', 5 May 1772

Home, Gordon, *Epsom, Its History and Surroundings* (London, 1971)

Quennell, Peter (ed.), *The Memoirs of William Hickey* (London, 1960)

von Archenholz, W., *A Picture of England; Containing a Description of the Laws, Customs and Manners of England* (Dublin, 1790)

## Articles and Periodicals

*Gentleman's Magazine*, 1st Series, 57 (1787), pp. 1196–7

*Town and Country Magazine, or Universal Repository of Knowledge, Instruction and Entertainment*, 1769 (vol. 1), pp. 65–7, 1770 (vol. 2) pp. 474–7

*Universal Magazine*, 'An Account of the parish of Whitchurch, or Little Stanmore in Middlesex: With a Perspective View of Canons; the Elegant Villa of Patrick (Andrew) O'Kelly' (October 1794)

## Archival Material

UNIVERSITY OF HULL BRYNMOR JONES LIBRARY:
O'Kelly family papers:
DDLA 40/1, 40/3, 40/10, 40/13, 40/44, 40/53, 40/55, 40/56, 40/64, 40/66, 40/70

ARCHIVES OF THE NORTH LONDON COLLEGIATE SCHOOL, CANONS PARK:
Cuttings on History of Canons Park, Eclipse, Dennis O'Kelly

**SURREY HISTORY CENTRE:**
Clay Hill Estate Papers: 6632/2/ 1–9

**WESTMINSTER CITY ARCHIVES:**
St James's, Piccadilly, St George, Westminster and St Anne, Soho:
Rate Books and Receipts (1730–95)
Parish records for Births, Baptisms and Marriages

**LONDON METROPOLITAN ARCHIVES:**
Burial Records for St Lawrence, Stanmore

**PUBLIC RECORDS OFFICE:**
PCC Wills for:
Andrew Dennis O'Kelly
Dennis O'Kelly
Robert Tracy

## HARRIS'S LIST

Turner, E. S., *The Shocking History of Advertising* (London, 1952)

### Articles and Periodicals

Atkins, P. J., 'The Covent Garden Ladies', *Factotum*, no. 30 (December 1989), p. 13

Denlinger, Elizabeth Campbell, 'The Garment and the Man: Masculine Desire in *Harris's List of Covent Garden Ladies*, 1764–1793', *Journal of the History of Sexuality*, vol. 11, no. 3, July 2002

Wood, J. L., 'Meaner Beauties of the Night', *Factotum*, no. 30 (December 1989), p. 13

*Centinel* (2 June 1757)

*Ranger's Magazine; or The Man of Fashion's Companion* (London, 1794)

*The Times* (10 February 1795)

## Archival Material

BRITISH LIBRARY:

*Harris's List of Covent Garden Ladies; or a Man of Pleasure's Kalendar* (1788, 1789, 1790, 1793)

Spedding, Patrick (ed.), *Eighteenth Century British Erotica*, vol. 4, *Harris's List for 1773*

LEWIS WALPOLE LIBRARY, FARMINGTON, CONNECTICUT:

*Harris's List of Covent Garden Ladies; or a Man of Pleasure's Kalendar for the year 1779* (annotated by Horace Bleackley)

LONDON GUILDHALL LIBRARY:

*Harris's List for the Year 1764* (London, 1764) (photocopy including Horace Bleackley and E. J. Burford's notations and *Harris's List Supplement for 1773*)

Typescript of E. J. Burford's notes *Harris's Lists*

NATIONAL LIBRARY OF SCOTLAND:

*Harris's List of Covent Garden Ladies or New Atalantis for the Year 1761* (London, 1761)

## GENERAL

Anon., *A New Atlantis for the Year 1758* (London, 1758)

—, *Intrigue-à-la-mode, or, The Covent Garden Atalantis* (London, 1767)

—, *The Histories of Some of the Penitents at the Magdalen House, as supposed to be related by themselves* (London, 1760)

—, *The Life and Character of Moll King late Mistress of King's Coffee-House in Covent Garden* (London, 1747)

—, *Nancy Dawson's Jests* (London, 1761)

Ackroyd, Peter, *London, the Biography* (London, 2000)

Appleton, William, *Charles Macklin, an Actor's Life* (London, 1960)

Bindman, David, *Hogarth* (London, 1997)

Bleackley, Horace, *Ladies Fair and Frail, Sketches of the Demi-Monde of the Eighteenth Century* (London, 1925)

Brewer, John, *The Pleasures of the Imagination: English Culture in the Eighteenth Century* (London, 1997)

Brown of Yarmouth, Richard, *The Description of a Bawdy House* (London, 1776)

Burney, Fanny, *Evelina, or the History of a Young Lady's Entrance into the World* (London, 1779)

Clayton, Antony, *London's Coffee Houses* (London, 2003)

Davidoff, Lenore, *Family Fortunes; Men and Women of the English Middle Class, 1780–1850* (London, 1987)

Fielding, John, *A Plan for the Preservatory and Reformatory for the Benefit of Deserted Girls and Penitent Prostitutes* (London, 1758)

Green, John (George Henry Townsend), *Evans's Music and Supper Rooms: Odds and Ends about Covent Garden and Its Vicinity* (London, 1866)

Hanway, Jonas, *Thoughts on the Plan for a Magdalen House* (London, 1758)

Harvey, A. D., *Sex in Georgian England* (London, 2001)

Henderson, Tony, *Disorderly Women in Eighteenth Century London* (London, 1999)

Hickman, Katie, *Courtesans* (London, 2003)

Hitchcock, Tim, *English Sexualities, 1700–1800* (London, 1997)

Johnston, Edith Mary, *Ireland in the Eighteenth Century* (Dublin, 1974)

Kahrl, George, and Stone, George Winchester, *David Garrick, a Critical Biography* (London, 1979)

Kendall, Alan, *David Garrick, a Biography* (London, 1985)

Lecky, W. E. H., *A History of Ireland in the Eighteenth Century* (London, 2000)

Linebaugh, Peter, *The London Hanged; Crime and Civil Society in the Eighteenth Century* (London, 1991)

Ludovicus, M., *A Particular but Melancholy Account of the Great Hardships, Difficulties and Miseries that those Unhappy and much to be Pitied Creatures, the Common Women of the Town, Are Plung'd into at this Juncture* (London, 1752)

Mannix, D. P., *The Hell-Fire Club* (New York, 1959)

Moody, T. W., and Vaughan, W. E. (eds.), *A New History of Ireland, Eighteenth Century Ireland, 1691–1800*, vol. 4 (Oxford, 1986)

Mountaigue, James, 'The Old Bailey Chronicle' in *The Newgate Calendar* (London, 1783)

O'Connell, Sheila, *London, 1753* (London, 2003)

O'Keefe, John, *Recollections of the Life of John O'Keefe, Written by Himself* (London, 1836)

Ogle, Luke, *The Natural Secret History of Both Sexes or, a Modest Defense of Public Stews* (London, 1740)

Oliver, Francis, *The Memoirs of Lady Hamilton* (London, 1815)

Peakman, Julie, *Mighty Lewd Books* (London, 2003)

Phillips, Richard, *The Memoirs of Samuel Foote*, 3 vols. (London, 1805)

Picard, Liza, *Dr Johnson's London: Life in London, 1710–1770* (London, 2000)

Porter, Roy, *English Society in the Eighteenth Century* (London, 1990)

Stone, Lawrence, *The Family, Sex and Marriage in England 1500–1800* (London, 1979)

Thompson, Edward, *The Meretriciad* (London, 1765)

Thrale, Mary (ed.), *The Autobiography of Francis Place* (London, 1972)

Timbs, John, *A History of Clubs and Club Life in London* (London, 1886)

Trumbach, Randolph, *Sex and the Gender Revolution; Heterosexuality and the Third Gender in Enlightenment London*, vol. 1 (London, 1998)

Valentine, Edwin (ed.), *The Newgate Calendar, Comprising Interesting Memoirs of the Most Notorious Characters that have been convicted of outrages on the laws of England* (London, 1928)

Welch, Saunders, *A Proposal to Render Effectual a Plan to Remove the Nuisance of Common Prostitutes from the Streets of the Metropolis* (1758)

Williams, Clare, *Sophie in London, 1786* (London, 1933)

Wilson, Frances, *The Courtesan's Revenge: The Life of Harriet Wilson* (London, 2003)

## Articles and Periodicals

Nelson, T. G. A., 'Women of Pleasure', *Eighteenth Century Life*, XI, n.s., 1 (1987), pp. 181–98

Rogers, N., 'Carnal Knowledge: Illegitimacy in Eighteenth Century Westminster', *Journal of Social History*, XXIII, 2 (1989), pp. 355–75

Simpson, Antony E., ' "The Mouth of Strange Women is a Deep Pit": Male Guilt and Legal Attitudes towards Prostitution in Georgian London', *Journal of Criminal Justice and Popular Culture*, vol. 4 (3) (1996), pp. 50–79

*Annual Register*
*Busy Body*
*Covent Garden Chronicle*
*Critical Review*
*Faulkner's Dublin Journal*
*Gentleman's Magazine*
*Lloyd's Evening Post*
*London Chronicle*
*London Gazette*
*Monitor*
*Monthly Review*
*Owen's Weekly Chronicle*
*Public Advertiser*
*Rambler*
*Read's Weekly Journal*
*St. James Chronicle*
*Theatrical Monitor*
*Town and Country Magazine, or Universal Repository of Knowledge, Instruction and Entertainment*
*Universal Magazine*

## Online Sources

*Old Bailey Sessions Papers*: Old Bailey Proceedings online (www. oldbaileyonline.org)

# PICTURE CREDITS

*Page 5, top*
Portrait of Charlotte Spencer © The Trustees of the British Museum.

*Page 5, middle*
Portrait of Fanny Murray © The Trustees of the British Museum.

*Page 5, bottom*
Portrait of Betsy Coxe (or Cox) © The Trustees of the British Museum.

*Page 6, top*
*The Rake's Progress*: 'The Rose Tavern' by Hogarth: Archivart/ Alamy stock photo.

*Page 7, top*
*A Late Unfortunate Adventure at York*: Illinois Library: https:// digital.library.illinois.edu/items/b79db2e0-4e7d-0134-1db1-005 0569601ca-f

*Page 7, bottom*
*Miss S–t–n, the beauty of Arlington Street*: The National Libraries of Scotland, under a Creative Commons Attribution (CC BY) 4.0 International Licence: https://creativecommons.org/licenses/ by/4.0/

*Page 8, top*
Canons Park, 1782: Archivist/Alamy stock photo

*Page 8, bottom*
Covent Garden (eastward view), 1786 © Look and Learn/ Bridgeman Images.

# ACKNOWLEDGEMENTS

Researching and writing this work has been a fascinating voyage of discovery, not only for me but for a number of others involved. First and foremost, I would like to express my gratitude to Jonathan Reeve at Tempus for his insight, his assistance and for his unwavering faith in this book. An expression of thanks is also due to Frances Wilson for taking the time to read the manuscript in its early incarnation.

Similarly, the completion of my research would not have been possible without the contributions of several individuals. Elizabeth Denlinger's generosity in sharing her unpublished research and engaging with me in lengthy 'e-conversations' about *Harris's List* has not gone unappreciated. Neither has the interest demonstrated and assistance given by Susan Walker at the Lewis Walpole Library. Kieran Burns, Helen Roberts, Sarah Peacock, Paul Tankard, Robin Eagles, Matthew Symonds, James Mitchell, Declan Barriskill and Elen Curran have all been instrumental in helping to pull together the various strands of this history. I would also like to extend my gratitude to the staff at the British Library, the National Art Library, the London Metropolitan Archives and the Westminster City Archives, where the majority of my research was conducted.

Finally, but certainly not least on my roll of honours, my husband, Frank, deserves a special commendation for agreeing to share his home and his life with Jack Harris, Samuel Derrick and the O'Kelly family for two long years. Without his support and that of my parents, it is unlikely that their stories would have been given the airing they deserve.

# INDEX

# THE FIVE

## The Untold Lives of the Women Killed by Jack the Ripper

### HALLIE RUBENHOLD

---

**Polly, Annie, Elizabeth, Catherine and Mary-Jane** are famous for the same thing, though they never met. They came from Fleet Street, Knightsbridge, Wolverhampton, Sweden and Wales. They wrote ballads, ran coffee houses, lived on country estates, they breathed ink-dust from printing presses and escaped people-traffickers.

What they had in common was the year of their murders: 1888.

Their murderer was never identified, but the name created for him by the press has become more famous than any of these women.

**In this devastating narrative of five lives, historian Hallie Rubenhold finally gives these women back their stories.**

---